PRAISE FOR
EMPOWERING UNDERREPRESENTED GIFTED STUDENTS

"As a child, I was told and understood that there was something different about me. I was a little Black girl growing up in a military town in North Carolina with a vocal presence who asked tons of questions about almost everything. Once I was identified as gifted at a young age with a number of my Black friends, I gained more confidence in expressing my academic talents. Little did I know that I was much more fortunate than most Black and Brown children who demonstrate their advanced academic abilities, but never receive the support they need to flourish. Now, as the parent to a beautiful, Black, gifted daughter, thirty years since my time participating in gifted programs, we are still fighting the same social justice battles in gifted education. Not much has changed and we have to do better! *Empowering Underrepresented Gifted Students* was written to change the tide and help educators support children who are historically underidentified for gifted programs reach their full academic potential."

—Shawna L. Young, former executive director of Duke Talent Identification
Program (TIP) and executive director of Scratch Foundation

"The diversity of our gifted population cannot and must not continue to be ignored. Our gifted students come from a variety of backgrounds and social identities that make who they are, and as such they have unique needs. Advocating for these students and helping them grow into their own powers of self-advocacy is the goal of *Empowering Underrepresented Gifted Students*. This book is a must-have for families, educators, and counselors who fight daily to ensure that these students are recognized for who they are and for the value of the stories that they bring to our classrooms. We can no longer sit on the sidelines as these students go unrecognized for their academic and social-emotional needs. We must do better; we can do better. This book is an important step on that journey."

—C. Matthew Fugate, Ph. D., assistant chair, urban education, and assistant professor,
educational psychology at University of Houston Downtown,
and coeditor of *Culturally Responsive Teaching in Gifted Education*

"Editors Dr. Joy Lawson Davis and Deb Douglas have brought together some of the greatest minds in the field of gifted education to help us empower underrepresented gifted students to advocate for educational justice. Each chapter is rich with the voices of students in their quest toward self-advocacy for equity, access, and excellence. The authors present the most current research and share strategies and techniques educators can use to make their gifted programs more inclusive and diverse. This text is a must-read for every educator!"

—Richard M. Cash, Ed.D., educator, author, and consultant, nRich Educational Consulting, Inc.

"In *Empowering Underrepresented Gifted Students*, Davis and Douglas have assembled an impressive array of diverse voices to discuss the urgent issue of representation and equity in gifted education. These expert contributors explore the change still needed, consider the challenges and opportunities ahead, and share their own stories of bright students whose talents went unrecognized for too long—and ultimately offer educators the tools and inspiration for empowering historically marginalized students to speak up for themselves and attain the visibility, respect, and education they deserve. I love their emphasis on the importance of self-advocacy. This is a truly timely and important book."

—Scott Barry Kaufman, Ph.D., cognitive scientist, author, podcaster, editor of *Twice Exceptional*

"This book highlights the importance of empowering minoritized students to use the skills of self-advocacy while also pointing out the systemic and structuralized racism that oppresses students into needing these skills in the first place, just to obtain their very basic rights to an education. The layout of the chapters is ideal for professional learning, whether self-directed or in group settings. Of note, the vignettes help the reader to learn from multiple perspectives, and each chapter has questions that can serve as personal reflection questions or guided group discussion. Teachers, counselors, and administrators seeking to be change agents will find this text illuminating."

—Angela M. Novak, Ph.D., Diversity and Equity Committee co-chair and Rural SIG founding coordinator, NAGC; Board of Directors, membership coordinator, CEC-TAG; and co-editor, Best Practices in Professional Learning Series

"Every so often, a book comes along that presents fresh perspectives and understandings, reveals hard truths and facts, and offers clear and direct guidance for a wide audience seeking to enact change. *Empowering Underrepresented Gifted Students* is that book, taking the reader on a journey of the lived experiences of underrepresented and underserved gifted and talented students while simultaneously recommending tools, strategies, and ideas for educators. An absolute must for any personal or professional library!"

—Jeff Danielian, teacher resource specialist, NAGC, and editor-in-chief, *Teaching for High Potential*

EMPOWERING
UNDERREPRESENTED
GIFTED STUDENTS

Perspectives from the Field

Edited by Joy Lawson Davis, Ed.D., and Deb Douglas, M.S.

free spirit
PUBLISHING®

Library of Congress Cataloging-in-Publication Data
Names: Davis, Joy Lawson, 1953– editor. | Douglas, Deb, 1950– editor.
Title: Empowering underrepresented gifted students : perspectives from the field / edited by Joy Lawson Davis, Ed.D., and Deb Douglas, M.S.
Description: Minneapolis, MN : Free Spirit Publishing Inc., 2021. | Includes bibliographical references and index.
Identifiers: LCCN 2021002651 (print) | LCCN 2021002652 (ebook) | ISBN 9781631984884 (paperback) | ISBN 9781631984891 (pdf) | ISBN 9781631984907 (epub)
Subjects: LCSH: Gifted children—Education. | Gifted teenagers—Education. | Social advocacy.
Classification: LCC LC3993 .E47 2021 (print) | LCC LC3993 (ebook) | DDC 371.95—dc23
LC record available at https://lccn.loc.gov/2021002651
LC ebook record available at https://lccn.loc.gov/2021002652

Free Spirit Publishing does not have control over or assume responsibility for author or third-party websites and their content. At the time of this book's publication, all facts and figures cited within are the most current available. All telephone numbers, addresses, and website URLs are accurate and active; all publications, organizations, websites, and other resources exist as described in this book; and all have been verified as of March 2021. If you find an error or believe that a resource listed here is not as described, please contact Free Spirit Publishing. Parents, teachers, and other adults: We strongly urge you to monitor children's use of the internet.

Edited by Cassandra Sitzman and Alison Behnke
Cover and interior design by Shannon Pourciau

10 9 8 7 6 5 4 3 2 1
Printed in the United States of America

Free Spirit Publishing Inc.
Minneapolis, MN
(612) 338-2068
help4kids@freespirit.com
freespirit.com

FSC
www.fsc.org
MIX
Paper from
responsible sources
FSC® C005010

Free Spirit offers competitive pricing.
Contact edsales@freespirit.com for pricing information on multiple quantity purchases.

Dedication

This book is dedicated to the countless numbers of gifted students from communities across America who go unnoticed and underestimated each day. Our hope is that this book will give them an opportunity to have a voice in their education and the resources needed so that their dreams are no longer deferred.

—Joy & Deb

Acknowledgments

As co-editors, we acknowledge the contributions of Dr. Tarek Grantham, whose foreword aptly captures the themes in this important book; all expert contributors; and our Free Spirit editors—Meg, Cassie, and Alison. We will forever be grateful for your dedication to our vision.

—Joy & Deb

Contents

List of Figures

List of Tables

Foreword Tarek C. Grantham, Ph.D.

Too often, parents, teachers, counselors, administrators, and other education professionals have limited authentic and useful tools to understand and support the needs of gifted and advanced students from underrepresented and underserved populations who are trying to identify and access resources and opportunities to achieve their dreams. I appreciate the opportunity to share this foreword with you because I know your reading this book will be time well spent. I applaud and celebrate the editors and authors of *Empowering Underrepresented Gifted Students* for answering the call to increase the body of literature on and advocacy for special populations of underrepresented and underserved students. My hope is that your engagement with the content and recommendations in this book will decrease inequities and barriers in gifted and talented education (GATE) and inspire greater levels of advocacy, self-advocacy, and success for all students with gifts and talents, regardless of their cultures, languages, backgrounds, or experiences that may differ from those of the majority of students enrolled in gifted and advanced programs.

Two important perspectives guided my reading and thinking about this book and its contribution. First, as a professor at the University of Georgia in the Department of Educational Psychology, Gifted and Creative Education Program, I reflected on educator preparation programming and professional development in schools. Second, as a father of children identified for gifted education services, I considered ways in which parents and caregivers may connect with self-advocacy and the book's content. Through these perspectives, I aim to offer a view of how the book is organized and to identify some of the highlights you can expect from it. The organization of this book offers an essential framework and guide for you to:

> empathize with the lived experiences of students with gifts and talents whose accomplishments and goals are often thwarted by institutional and systemic barriers that keep them trapped in patterns of underachievement and in debilitating feelings of inferiority, disengagement, and hopelessness

> understand self-advocacy and why it is important for underrepresented and underserved students to develop self-advocacy knowledge and skills

> navigate a GATE system not historically designed for culturally, linguistically, or economically disadvantaged students to fully know about or benefit from their rights to an appropriate, challenging, and meaningful education that empowers them to reach their full potential (Ford et al. 2018)

> evaluate and apply gifted education models, culturally responsive strategies, and equity-oriented tools to empower students to be proactive in their advocacy efforts with their caregivers or allies and to pursue pathways in the direction of their dreams

As a university professor with over twenty years of experience in higher education, teaching courses in educational psychology focused on preparing researchers, teachers, counselors, administrators, and other professionals in gifted and creative education, I am always searching for high-quality resources to support my instruction and work on equity and excellence in gifted education. It is important to identify resources that are grounded by equity-oriented scholars and professionals who have authentic experiences and success with the groups they advocate for or represent. Often, research reports, books, and literature professing to support the needs of underrepresented populations and groups are produced by well-intentioned but noncredible individuals. This is not the case with the chapters in this volume. *Empowering Underrepresented Gifted Students* is an important resource that can be used in the instruction of undergraduate and graduate students and in professional development associated with GATE programs. In addition, it can be a useful supplemental text in teacher/educator preparation programs and in professional learning communities, where case studies of and strategies for gifted and talented learners from underrepresented groups can be examined and applied to school- and community-based field experiences and training.

All university and college professionals in educator preparation programs and all professional development specialists in state and local agencies are governed by national standards and professional principles. For example, the National Association for Gifted Children (NAGC) and the Council for Exceptional Children (CEC) are leading associations that provide guidance for gifted and talented education. A recent standard-bearer for the design of gifted education services is NAGC's *Pre-K to Grade 12 Gifted Programming Standards* (NAGC 2019). The self-advocacy focus of *Empowering Underrepresented Gifted Students* directly aligns with many of the NAGC standards for student outcomes shown in **figure 0.1**. Instructors and professional development specialists for GATE preparation programs build their instruction using the NAGC standards and can use this book as part of the foundation of their programs.

FIGURE 0.1 Sample of Student Outcomes from NAGC Standards Embedded in *Empowering Underrepresented Gifted Students*

NAGC STUDENT OUTCOMES	DESCRIPTION
Personal competence	Students with gifts and talents demonstrate growth in personal competence and dispositions for exceptional academic and creative productivity. These include self-awareness, self-advocacy, self-efficacy, confidence, motivation, resilience, independence, curiosity, and risk-taking.
Responsibility and leadership	Students with gifts and talents demonstrate personal and social responsibility.
Self-understanding	Students with gifts and talents recognize their interests, strengths, and needs in cognitive, creative, social, emotional, and psychological areas.
	Students with gifts and talents demonstrate understanding of how they learn and recognize the influences of their identities, cultures, beliefs, traditions, and values on their learning and behavior.
Awareness of needs	Students identify and access supplemental, out-of-school resources that support the development of their gifts and talents (families, mentors, experts, or programs).
Cognitive growth and career development	Students with gifts and talents identify future career goals that match their interests and strengths. Students determine resources needed to meet those goals (supplemental educational opportunities, mentors, financial support).
Equity and inclusion	All students with gifts and talents are able to develop their abilities as a result of educators who are committed to removing barriers to access and creating inclusive gifted education communities.
Ethics	All students with gifts and talents, including those who may be twice-exceptional, who are English language learners, or who come from underrepresented populations, receive equal opportunities to be identified and served in high-quality gifted programming as a result of educators who are guided by ethical practices.

continued >

FIGURE 0.1 Sample of Student Outcomes from NAGC Standards Embedded in *Empowering Underrepresented Gifted Students* (continued)

NAGC STUDENT OUTCOMES	DESCRIPTION
Cultural competence	Students with gifts and talents value their own and others' languages, heritages, and circumstances. They possess skills in communicating, teaming, and collaborating with diverse individuals and across diverse groups. They use positive strategies to address social issues including discrimination and stereotyping.
Communication competence	Students with gifts and talents develop competence in interpersonal and technical communication skills. They demonstrate advanced oral and written skills and creative expression. They display fluency with technologies that support effective communication and are competent consumers of media and technology.

Used with permission. National Association for Gifted Children. 2019. *Pre-K to Grade 12 Gifted Programming Standards.* nagc.org/resources-publications/resources/national-standards-gifted-and-talented-education/pre-k-grade-12.

As a father of children who are identified for gifted education services and as a member of several formal and informal parent and family networks for gifted and advanced students from underrepresented groups, I find *Empowering Underrepresented Gifted Students* to be a great tool for network or advocacy group leaders to engage parents and families of culturally diverse students. Davis and Douglas's well-selected contributors speak to issues faced by parents and families in some of the most adversely impacted special populations of students in GATE. The student stories in each chapter are engaging and poignantly unpacked by leading scholars and professionals who have consistently done the work for equity in gifted and advanced programs. I applaud the authors for their careful and intentional analysis of the experiences of some remarkable students and of the barriers these young people have had to confront.

Parents and caregivers of gifted children or GATE advocates who represent young people with gifts and talents will find the stories of Black, Hispanic, American Indians and Alaska Natives, LGBTQ+, low-income, and other special populations of students and their parents compelling. They will also ponder important questions and recommendations posed by chapter authors and be invited to empathize and take action. Regardless of their own background or connection to the special populations featured, parents, caregivers, and GATE advocates who strive for equity will have an opportunity to connect with the contexts and experiences of students within and outside their own group. For example, as an underachieving creatively gifted Black male, I identified with the disciplinary concerns raised by Lucas's teachers and parents that are presented by the authors in chapter 6. I also recalled how my experiences and some of my friends' backgrounds were connected to Sam, his single mom, and their grandparenting challenges in chapter 7. Written with credibility and passion, *Empowering Underrepresented Gifted Students* will guide and ground you and other educators in your individual and collective efforts to empower gifted and advanced students to self-advocate.

> Written with credibility and passion, *Empowering Underrepresented Gifted Students* will guide and ground you and other educators in your individual and collective efforts to empower gifted and advanced students to self-advocate.

I commend the editors and authors of *Empowering Underrepresented Gifted Students,* and I would like readers to know how grateful I am for the invitation to contribute a foreword to this important book. It is an honor to offer a preview and perspective to help guide you on your journey into a work that has been crafted to support the personal and professional trek toward equity for advanced students in gifted and talented education. This unique volume will surely become an important resource to help prepare advanced learners from underrepresented and underserved groups and their families to effectively self-advocate with confidence and intentionality.

References

Ford, Donna Y., Kenneth T. Dickson, Joy Lawson Davis, Michelle Trotman Scott, and Tarek C. Grantham. 2018. "A Culturally Responsive Equity-Based Bill of Rights for Gifted Students of Color." *Gifted Child Today* 41 (3): 125–129.

National Association for Gifted Children. 2019. *Pre-K to Grade 12 Gifted Programming Standards.* nagc.org/ resources-publications/resources/national-standards-gifted-and-talented-education/pre-k-grade-12.

Harlem
by Langston Hughes

What happens to a dream deferred?

Does it dry up
like a raisin in the sun?
Or fester like a sore—
And then run?
Does it stink like rotten meat?
Or crust and sugar over—
like a syrupy sweet?

Maybe it just sags
like a heavy load.

Or does it explode?

Langston Hughes, one of America's greatest bards, shared his poem "Harlem" at a time when the United States was recovering from its participation in World War II, a battle in which it was seen as one of the victors. But although the war was over, the nation was in turmoil regarding the equal rights of all its citizens. "Harlem" was Hughes's examination of the conditions of his life as an African American in a racially unjust society, with the American dream out of reach for so many. It was 1951, and for most African Americans, the dream of prosperity, fair housing, access to healthcare, and equal education was unfulfilled. "Harlem" was considered one of the most influential poems of its time. It was a call for a better understanding of the barriers, inequities, and challenges faced by so many Americans who deserved conditions that would allow them to accomplish their dreams. It shares what potential outcomes may result when others don't believe in those dreams or fail to help in accomplishing them.

Here we are so many decades later, and conditions are much the same. This poem was selected as a foundation for *Empowering Underrepresented Gifted Students* to help readers understand the critical importance of the role of all stakeholders providing support for gifted learners from underserved groups to help them in the fulfillment of their dreams. It is our belief that with the consistent and steady support of parents and educators, and through the self-advocacy of students themselves, more of them will be able to accomplish the goals they set to achieve their dreams.

Current research and practice have demonstrated that gifted learners come from a variety of racial, cultural, income, gender, and geographic backgrounds and may also be neurodivergent. However, the US federal definition of giftedness does not specifically address the unique psychosocial needs of gifted students from these diverse backgrounds. This definition, which appears on the next page, focuses heavily on the academic needs of the majority of identified gifted students, who are typically White and affluent:

Students, children, or youth who give evidence of high achievement capability in areas such as intellectual, creative, artistic, or leadership capacity, or in specific academic fields, and who need services or activities not ordinarily provided by the school in order to fully develop those capabilities. (US Department of Education 2004)

For over half a century, the field of gifted education has worked to develop, research, and advocate for appropriate instruction and support systems for our nation's students with high performance and ability across multiple domains. Sometimes these students have been labeled as genius, profoundly gifted, exceptional learners, or high-ability learners as compared to their same-age peers. Regardless of the label used, one very contentious issue has yet to be sufficiently addressed: the systemic underrepresentation of gifted students from racially diverse groups, of those who originate from low-income environments, and of those who may differ from the majority in gender identity, sexual orientation, other exceptional conditions, and language. Collectively, the aforementioned groups are known as "special populations." As underserved gifted learners, they struggle daily to have their exemplary strengths valued and developed in school settings that are often ill-equipped to support their unique needs and where, sadly, they sometimes even seem to be invisible. As school programs for gifted students continuously overlook these populations, these students' gifts and talents continue to be underdeveloped and their future potential to become productive and innovative members of society continues to be destroyed, their dreams deferred.

> As school programs for gifted students continuously overlook these populations, these students' gifts and talents continue to be underdeveloped and their future potential to become productive and innovative members of society continues to be destroyed, their dreams deferred.

Attempts to address the needs of underserved gifted students have typically been focused on how students are identified for programs and how educators are trained to work with gifted learners (Davis 2019; Ford 2014; Grissom and Redding 2016). Seldom has the conversation about improving education and support services for underserved gifted learners turned to asking students themselves what they believe they need. The importance of listening to the voices of students has historically been understated. Only recently have scholars begun to focus attention on the power of student voice (Douglas 2018; Simmons 2020). In the past several years, more attention and conversation have focused on the need to teach gifted students to self-advocate, to tell us what their own needs are (Douglas 2018).

Student self-advocacy has the potential to bring the needs of underserved gifted students to the attention of advocates, administrators, policymakers, and practitioners. Hearing about students' lived experiences being gifted, underserved, and overlooked can have a more powerful effect on educators than hearing only from researchers and other adult advocates. Teaching students to self-advocate enables them not only to be a voice for themselves, but also to empower other students to speak up and ask for what they need from education to be able to realize their dreams.

About This Book and Its Definition of Self-Advocacy

To frame our conversations in this book around the self-advocacy of underserved and underrepresented gifted students, we developed a new and expanded definition of self-advocacy specifically for the gifted students who are also part of one or more special populations:

Self-advocacy is the dynamic process that enables high-potential students to claim their right to an education that addresses their unique intellectual, academic, psychosocial, and cultural needs without endangering their self-esteem or that of others. It is a compilation of culturally responsive and inclusive empowerment strategies that open opportunities for positive academic and life outcomes previously precluded for some students due to stereotyping, systemic biases, and limited access to resources.

This definition urges all stakeholders to action, prompting them to engage in creating and supporting dynamic and inclusive strategies that can lead to typically underserved students having their dreams fulfilled rather than nullified or deferred. It sets educators on a new course of action that centers equity-based conversations and program development in student voice. Gifted students are typically the most socially cognizant and sensitive of our student populations. It is our expectation that among this group are those who will, with some guidance, share with educators, parents, and policymakers their specific intellectual, academic, and social and emotional needs.

This book contains chapters that describe our expanded view of self-advocacy and has chapters written by students and expert scholars who specialize in addressing equity in our nation's gifted and advanced learner programs. Chapter one shares the stories of a group of secondary-level students from a specialized school for gifted students in Florida. These students formed an organization to advocate for the need to increase the number of culturally and racially diverse students at their school. Their self-advocacy convinced the school administration to host a forum to discuss the issue of equity so that they could share their stories and discuss why they believed more students like themselves should be able to attend a school like theirs. Other chapters in this book provide descriptions of specific groups of underserved gifted students whose academic and social and emotional needs have not been met in their schools. The expert authors share student vignettes, rooting each chapter in the voices of those we're serving.* At the close of each chapter, authors present key concepts and questions that readers can use to guide their own reading or discussion of the book (whether independently or with a PLC or book study group) and their pursuit of increased equity in their school gifted and talented program. One chapter is devoted to the voices of parents of diverse learners and provides advice to strengthen their advocacy skills.

Intersectionality: Navigating Multiple Worlds

The special populations of gifted students included in this book are also those students whose lived experiences are very often characterized by challenges with converging identities and multiple worlds. These challenges can be framed by the concept of intersectionality. The term *intersectionality* was coined in 1989 by legal scholar Kimberlé Crenshaw to describe the overlap of social identities that contribute to the complexity of oppression and discrimination individuals face based on their gender identity, sexual orientation, race, socioeconomic status, or other social constructs. Crenshaw suggests that these unique social identities cannot be examined separately from each other, but only when consideration is given to the impact of the lived condition in each. Earlier, in 1903, Dr. W.E.B. Du Bois articulated his converging experience as a highly gifted Black man in a segregated society as "double-consciousness." Du Bois described navigating between these two worlds as his constant state of "two-ness":

---

*Throughout the book, the authors have used the terms *African American* and *Black* as well as *Latina*, *Latino*, and *Hispanic*. These terms are used interchangeably and varied authors have taken the liberty of using the terminology best suited to their work.

It is a peculiar sensation, this double-consciousness, this sense of always looking at one's self through the eyes of others, of measuring one's soul by the tape of a world that looks on in amused contempt and pity. One ever feels his two-ness, an American, a Negro; two souls, two thoughts, two unreconciled strivings; two warring ideals in one dark body, whose dogged strength alone keeps it from being torn asunder. (Du Bois 1903, 3)

Crenshaw's description of intersectionality is an even broader view of Du Bois's double-consciousness. She posits that multiple identities create a more complex sense of self that is constantly impacted by social oppression.

Although the chapters in this book are separated by specific identities, readers must understand the complexity of the intersectional status of gifted special population groups. For example, consider the gifted low-income Black teen who lives in a rural community where many students may not be encouraged to pursue education beyond high school. His intersectional status impacts his life daily and should be considered as resources are made available to increase his self-advocacy. Or consider the twice-exceptional learner whose gender identity poses challenges in the social atmosphere of their school and community. Being twice-exceptional has its own unique traits and must be clearly understood for the student to become a strong self-advocate. Thus, educators and parents who are teaching this student self-advocacy need background knowledge of her disability, giftedness, and gender identity. Native American students with high potential who attend underresourced schools are at a particular disadvantage, as are gifted STEM students from culturally diverse backgrounds who typically have less access to high-level science, technology, engineering, and math courses than students from affluent White backgrounds do. It is recommended that readers, as they review each chapter, keep in mind the intersectional status of the students discussed, as well as that of students at their own school.

For too long, stereotypical beliefs have led many educators to presume that special populations lack the intellectual strengths that White and affluent students possess. Underserved gifted students have very likely encountered bias and even neglect in their education; and beyond missed opportunities, real harm has been experienced. The impact and oppression of racism and discrimination in school and community settings need to be considered when seeking to understand who students are and how they respond to schooling. Listed below are some of the realities and identities experienced by students discussed in this book:

> Socioeconomic status

> Language

> Race and/or culture

> Twice-exceptionality

> LGBTQ+

> Gifted/talented

How to Use This Book

We have intentionally organized the book to provide, up front, a foreword and introduction to help readers understand why self-advocacy for underrepresented student populations is important. We highly recommend that readers begin with those two sections and then read how diverse students respond to the need for self-advocacy in chapter one. After that, we welcome you to read the book in any order that works for you.

Each chapter presents one or more student stories that portray the lived experiences of particular gifted students and their experiences with self-advocacy. Also included in each chapter are recommended strategies and key questions educators may use to target the needs of their students. We urge readers to review and utilize strategies that reflect all of the potentially intersecting identities of their particular student groups.

It is our belief that students' multiple, intersecting voices are the key to securing the attention they so desperately need and deserve in school programs for gifted learners. We believe that arming special populations of gifted students with self-advocacy strategies will move all of us closer to ensuring equity, access, and excellence in GATE and AP programs and empowering these remarkable students to fulfill their dreams.

References

Crenshaw, Kimberlé. 1989. "Demarginalizing the Intersection of Race and Sex: A Black Feminist Critique of Antidiscrimination Doctrine, Feminist Theory and Antiracist Politics." *University of Chicago Legal Forum* Vol. 1989: Issue 1, Article 8. chicagounbound.uchicago.edu/uclf/vol1989/iss1/8.

Davis, Joy Lawson. 2019. "Reframing Professional Learning to Meet the Needs of Teachers Working with Culturally Diverse Gifted Learners." In *Best Practices in Professional Learning and Teacher Preparation: Special Topics for Gifted Professional Development, Vol. 2*, edited by Angela M. Novak and Christine L. Weber. Waco, TX: Prufrock Press.

Douglas, Deb. 2018. *The Power of Self-Advocacy for Gifted Learners: Teaching the 4 Essential Steps to Success.* Minneapolis, MN: Free Spirit Publishing.

Du Bois, William Edward Burghardt. 1903. *The Souls of Black Folk.* Chicago: A.C. McClurg & Co.

Ford, Donna Y. 2014. "Segregation and the Underrepresentation of Blacks and Hispanics in Gifted Education: Social Inequality and Deficit Paradigms." *Roeper Review* 36 (3): 143–154. doi.org/10.1080/02783193.2014.919563.

Grissom, Jason A., and Christopher Redding. 2016. "Discretion and Disproportionality: Explaining the Underrepresentation of High-Achieving Students of Color in Gifted Programs." *AERA Open.* doi:10.1177/2332858415622175.

National Association for Gifted Children. n.d. "Frequently Asked Questions About Gifted Education." nagc.org/resources-publications/resources/frequently-asked-questions-about-gifted-education.

Simmons, Dena. 2020. "Confronting Inequity/Who Has the Privilege to Be Empowered?" *Educational Leadership* 77 (6): 88–89. Washington, DC: ASCD.

US Department of Education. 2004. "Title IX—General Provisions." ed.gov/policy/elsec/leg/esea02/pg107.html.

1

Student Voices: The Power of Self-Advocacy

Vinay Konuru, President of the DIGS Taskforce, Pine View School for the Gifted and Talented, and Members of DIGS

In early 2019, I received an email invitation to speak at a town hall hosted by the Pine View School for the Gifted in Osprey, Florida. The Pine View School is one of the nation's premier secondary schools for gifted learners. The invitation was initiated by student Vinay Konuru, the leader of a diverse group of Pine View students who were actively working with the school on issues of diversity. The group, named Diversifying and Integrating Gifted Schools (DIGS), was created to draw attention to the need for Pine View to recruit and retain more students from culturally diverse backgrounds. The topic of the town hall was "How can we increase minority representation in gifted programs?"

Vinay also shared with me that he was reading my book *Bright, Talented, & Black: A Guide for Families of African American Gifted Learners* and believed that my message aligned well with the group's purpose. Within a few months, the school's principal, Dr. Stephen Covert, reached out to me with a formal invitation to serve as a keynote speaker at the Pine View School Town Hall/Equity Symposium. At the symposium, I met Vinay and the other members of DIGS and listened as they shared their stories. I was so moved by their testimonies that I believed we should share them in our book as an example of students self-advocating to address an issue of concern to them. I believe, too, that educators will benefit from hearing these students' views, as they represent some of the populations addressed in this book. In this chapter, members of DIGS share the story of their group and their own journeys toward self-advocacy.

—Dr. Joy Lawson Davis

Diversifying and Integrating Gifted Schools: A Student-Led Initiative

Diversifying and Integrating Gifted Schools (DIGS) is a student-led initiative from Pine View School, a second- through twelfth-grade gifted magnet school in Osprey, Florida. For the last several years, our members have aimed to bring attention to—and resolve—the lack of diversity on our campus. Through numerous trials and errors, we have learned lessons about how to effectively voice our beliefs as students. Though we are still learning every day, we hope that sharing our stories and advice will help other students in their journeys to self-advocate and become leaders.

Our Stories
Vinay Konuru, Grade 12

I started DIGS in my freshman year with the strong support of our principal, Dr. Covert, who is passionate and dedicated to eventually fixing the issue of underrepresentation of minority students at our school. I began working on this project in eighth grade. Of the two thousand students at Pine View, fewer than 1 percent are Black, even though our surrounding community has a student population that is nearly 20 percent Black. This has been a problem at my school since it was founded fifty years ago, and a similar divide exists in nearly every gifted program in our community. However, the underrepresentation of Black students in gifted education is so deeply rooted in our culture that it is simply accepted as a fact. The opportunity gap is detrimental to every group: the students who do not receive the education they deserve, the White students in schools for the gifted who lose out on the opportunity to learn in a more diverse community, and our communities that lose potential transformational leaders, inspiring authors, and game-changing scientists. As members of DIGS share their stories, I hope you find a story you can relate to and recognize that advocacy does not belong to any one race, group, or culture. Successful advocacy requires the combined voices of everyone. It has been difficult, but I truly believe that the work my friends and I initiated at DIGS has set the stage for real change in our community.

Kaila S., Grade 12

Ever since kindergarten, I've been the only Black student in my grade. I took advanced classes at a predominantly White school, and after being tested and identified as gifted, I began to attend an International Baccalaureate (IB) school. Shortly after, I moved to Sarasota, Florida, and attended an elementary school known for its diversity. However, I was put into the gifted SPARK class and, once again, I was the only Black student.

When I came to Pine View in the third grade, it did not take long to notice that I was the only Black student in my grade, again. While this was not new to me, I realized that, unlike in my previous schools, there were no other Black students for many grades above me at Pine View.

I'm now in twelfth grade, and I remain the only Black student in my class. Even with this prominent lack of diversity, Pine View does not show much discrimination toward its people of color. However, I am still faced with identity issues that no one around me can relate to. Honestly, before two summers ago, I barely had any close Black friends. I felt as if no one could understand my love for R&B and old-school hip hop or the many troubles I had with my hair, my body, and family traditions. Until I went to a historically Black summer camp in Massachusetts, I had no idea that there were other people who shared my experiences. I finally felt like I belonged.

I thought, *I don't ever want any other Black girl to have to go through the same thing I did just to feel whole.*

Over the years, I have noticed a steady increase in Black and Hispanic students at Pine View in the grades below me. Although I believe our school could be more diverse, I also believe it is taking the right steps toward improving its acceptance of diversity.

Diego P., Grade 12

When I was nine years old, my parents felt that it was in our family's best interest to leave our native country of Mexico. I was forced to leave behind everything I knew to seek a better future in an alien territory by the name of "Texas." A few years later, I was moving again. This time, it was from Dallas, Texas, to

Sarasota, Florida. As a new sixth-grade student with significantly better English than when I first entered the country, I did not struggle as much as I had in Texas to make new friends at my new middle school. Still, my parents suggested the unthinkable: moving schools.

I had heard of Pine View School from friends, and the stories that I heard terrified me. They had impossible tests, scary teachers, snobby kids filled with self-interest, and endless amounts of homework. My parents scheduled an appointment to have my IQ tested, and it put me into a serious internal conflict. I could either take the IQ test and probably pass (I had previously been identified as gifted), or I could purposefully fail and not have to worry about the stories I had heard. Why would I intentionally make my life more difficult if I simply did not have to?

Then it hit me. I realized that maximizing my academic opportunities was unarguably in my best interest. High school is supposed to be a time of growth and maturity, and holding myself back from opportunities to grow and mature seemed irresponsible. I made the decision to try the hardest I possibly could on that IQ test and, thankfully, I met the admission criteria for Pine View. Although it was tough to adjust to a new school, a new level of rigor, and a brand-new set of people, things eventually fell into place.

Making the decision to push myself to my academic limits has not been easy, but I do not recall ever being told that life is supposed to be easy. Gifted education has benefited me in ways I never thought possible and has provided me an environment in which students grow, learn, and mature together.

Andrea C., Grade 12

I was born in a city called Barranquilla on the Atlantic coast of Colombia. When I was twelve, my parents told me that we were making a very big move—to the United States. Despite it being sudden, I accepted the move pretty quickly. I had always dreamed of traveling to America. And since I had spent a lot of time on the internet, I spoke English fluently. When we got to Florida, I was enrolled in a public school in Nokomis. I had little difficulty adjusting academically and was weirdly automatically enrolled in an ELS (English Language School) class despite not needing it.

Academically, it was not challenging for me to receive perfect grades in classes. My history teacher recognized that I would do better in a more advanced curriculum and recommended me for gifted testing. Initially, I did not score high enough, but later, once my success in school continued, I got tested again and met the criteria for admission. So, by the end of my first year in the United States, I had been admitted to Pine View School. I am thankful to the teacher who recognized my capabilities because I know many other gifted students are not as fortunate. If there was anything that made my transition possible, I think it was the devotion I had to my classes and to learning. It might have been what made me stand out.

Cara K., Grade 12

I was fifteen when I moved to Sarasota, Florida, and began attending Pine View. Not only did I struggle with a new experience of gifted education, but I was also dealing with being diagnosed with dyscalculia, a math disorder similar in effect to dyslexia. I frequently mixed up numbers, struggled to count change, and took longer to process mathematical information. Consequently, my sophomore year, and my first year at Pine View School, consisted of late-night math practice and homework that took me far longer to complete than it took any of my peers. And frankly, I had moments when I thought that there was no place for somebody like me in gifted education. Thankfully, I had teachers, friends, parents, and a school system that cared.

At past schools, I struggled to find ways I could learn outside of the classroom. Gifted education has given me the opportunity to find those unique, unconventional ways to process information. My grades in math improved, and I now take accelerated math courses. I have learned that being gifted does not mean that you do not struggle in language arts, math, science, or another subject. However, it does mean understanding that you struggle, and tackling your problems head-on.

I believe that it is vital that the teaching staff at a school know the backgrounds of gifted students such as myself. It is vital to have teachers invested in students' upbringings, their stories, and their struggles.

Christiana G., Grade 12

I've been a student at Pine View since second grade, which means I've been here for most of my life. I've always been cognizant of the lack of diversity in the school. But what I did not realize until recently was the impact this lack of diversity had on Pine View itself. This summer I had the chance to attend a summer program focused on diversity and inclusion, and the culture there starkly contrasted with what I had experienced at Pine View. It was an overall refreshing experience. Many of the students there also attended predominantly White schools, and my experience in the program made me realize how much diverse students miss out on.

The lack of diversity at Pine View is reflected in various ways, both obvious and more subtle. There's the obvious lack of physical diversity, which is evident upon entering campus or in viewing photos, but there are also the more out-of-sight effects. For instance, even though Pine View is generally inclusive, there's still a level of ignorance in the culture that is reflected in cultural appropriation and the stigmatization of diverse students. Creating a more understanding student body is so important in improving diversity, and diversity is vital to any student's experience.

Aidan C., Grade 11

After I completed eighth grade, my parents enrolled me at Pine View School in Sarasota. I was eligible to go since I had met the requirement with an IQ test when I was in sixth grade. Initially, the only people I met at Pine View were the people I talked to in my classes. The only time I got to meet students outside of my grade level was at soccer club. Yet soccer club had a large base of members, and I struggled to know people beyond their first names.

In my sophomore year, I was sitting in class when my teacher, Mr. Schweig, said that a club named DIGS was going to present to our class. The presentation was about the imbalance in racial demographics at Pine View and the importance of solving this issue. Though I had never been negatively impacted by this issue, I realized that the imbalance largely impacts underrepresented demographics of students through their opportunities and interactions within gifted education. After the presentation, the leader of the club, Vinay Konuru, asked those who were interested in joining the club to write down their email addresses. I was the first sophomore in the club. Vinay gave me more information at the end of the meeting about the club's plans to set up a town hall meeting to share ideas for fixing the racial imbalance at Pine View.

This year, I got to be a part of the presentation process in Mr. Schweig's room. This time, I was the older student presenting information about DIGS to incoming sophomores. Overall, DIGS has been an awesome experience. I have met new friends who are passionate about making a necessary but difficult change that, if done, will leave a legacy on both Pine View School and gifted education for many years to come.

Gabe M., Grade 12

I was born in the heart of New York to parents who never went to college. Statistics would tell you that I would not go to college either. A Hispanic born in that area? Statistics would tell you that I would live my whole life in Brooklyn too. But many times, statistics are wrong. I now live in Sarasota, Florida, and attend Pine View School, the greatest opportunity I have ever received. Hear me out and you'll begin to understand why there is a need for gifted education in my life and in the lives of all gifted students.

The reason gifted education is so important in my life is very simple. I was too smart to stay at the level I was being taught at. Now I don't say that to brag; it's simply true. In the fourth grade, I would get a perfect score on the pretest before we even started learning the subject. It was obvious that I needed more. When I came to Pine View, I finally gained the right amount of rigor and competition I needed to succeed. But that's not all I got at Pine View. I also found a community, a family. I found other people who were in the same boat I was in. They may not have looked like me or acted like me, but they thought like me. This is what I needed, and it has led me to achieve a higher degree of success in academics than anywhere else I've been.

My life has completely been turned for the better. I am no longer simply a Dominican boy from New York. I am a committed, challenged, hardworking student ready to make the world a better place. I hope all the gifted students in my area and in the world can have the same opportunity regardless of their background or color so that together we can change the course of history.

Steps for Advocacy

Through our experience in this work, the DIGS team formulated four steps that we feel can encourage any student to begin advocating for their beliefs. It is important to note that these steps should be regarded as general guidelines. Every situation is unique. Even so, with this plan we hope to give student leaders a base from which to build their own projects and initiatives.

1. Research
2. Find and build a team
3. Build a base of awareness
4. Implement practical ideas

Step 1. Research

Learn the facts and history behind the problem that you hope to tackle.

Before DIGS was created, a serious amount of work was put into learning the facts and history behind the lack of diversity in our district's gifted programs. This began with finding and comparing accurate data on the demographics of both our school and the surrounding district. We then dug deeper by researching the underlying causes that contributed to this problem in the first place.

When we first began this work, there was no clear path to address the issue. The prominent lack of African American students at Pine View was already well known, but there was no obvious place on campus where we could openly address the topic.

It started as a debate in speech class about the critical importance of this issue. But without any research to back up our claims that Black and Hispanic students are underrepresented at Pine View, our points were based on nothing more than feelings and impressions. This experience affirmed our conviction of the importance of building a solid base of evidence to effectively back up claims in any advocacy work.

The next several months were some of the most critical. We spent this time gathering demographic data, interviewing retired and active administrators, and reading reports from other school districts that faced similar issues. Our conversations and research debunked many of the beliefs and assumptions we'd held regarding this topic. We didn't yet have answers to solve the problem at hand, but our eyes were opened to an entirely new perspective on it. We began to understand the sheer complexity of the opportunity gap and the intricate-yet-delicate system surrounding it. This process of reshaping ideas on an issue is where the power of thorough research lies.

> One cannot consider how to bring more diversity to gifted education without first exploring what economic, cultural, geographical, and historical issues restrict certain groups from accessing these resources.

We initially only saw the diversity problem at Pine View in a very two-dimensional sense. We thought that the source of the problem was purely the demographic numbers on a page. It was not until we spoke with our assistant superintendent, Dr. Kingsley, that we realized how many layers there really are to the issue. One cannot consider how to bring more diversity to gifted education without first exploring what economic, cultural, geographical, and historical issues restrict certain groups from accessing these resources.

By gaining a wider understanding of the problem, we could now provide more compelling reasons for its importance and have a focused direction to channel our efforts. We realized that our district's lack of representation could be simplified into two core problems.

First, to be identified as gifted in the state of Florida requires a student to score 130 or above on an IQ test. Initially, in recognition of a divide in scores between low-income and high-income students, there was a policy created to lower the cutoff score to 120 points for low-income students. However, this did not grossly change the lack of representation in gifted programs like Pine View. We learned that the fundamental issue lay in the requirement of a teacher recommendation for a student to even take an IQ test. With fewer students of color being offered the opportunity to take IQ tests, coupled with a lack of access to private psychologists (who often administer the tests and are paid for independently by parents), the number of identified students from these groups is bound to be significantly lower.

Second, the snowballing nature of this issue only makes the situation worse. For example, with so few African Americans on our campus, new African American students often feel out of place. With not many people to relate to and not many who look like them, these students tend to leave for an environment where they feel more comfortable. With growing cultural divides between already separated communities, the lack of integration within our gifted schools and programs only deepens.

Identifying and recognizing these two major contributors to the issue has allowed DIGS to push for change that we believe will make a real impact. Our research, however, has never really stopped, and it never should. The body of information on which we base our work is constantly evolving, and, therefore, so should our understanding of it. We continue to learn about new developments in this field, which lead to fresh ideas that we could bring to light and advocate for. Keeping ourselves informed and up-to-date with relevant discussions has been vital to having our own voices be heard and taken seriously.

We cannot stress enough the importance of research being a key element of advocacy. To have your efforts be a powerful contributor to change, it is essential that your words be informed and your ideas be relevant. By thoroughly researching a topic and continuing to expand and reshape your understanding of it, the message you send will ring much louder and the effects will be much greater.

Step 2. Find and Build a Team

The force of a team is exponentially more powerful than a single voice.

One of the most challenging aspects of student advocacy can be finding someone who is willing to listen. Although having the necessary research and evidence to back your points can help, support may still be an uphill battle. By gathering a group of voices, both student and adult, with an equal commitment to the same idea, your message will strike with greater force. It may take time and persistence, but finding a committed team will be invaluable to your journey of advocacy. This is exactly how we started DIGS.

When DIGS began, the first thing we had to do was find teachers who were willing to sponsor our work. This took several months, but the long wait would prove to be worth it. Up to that point, we had already spoken with many faculty members about this issue to learn more about its history. We wanted to learn if there was a group already working on a similar project within the school because we recognized that joining an existing effort would be more productive than creating a new one. In this search, we were able to learn more about past attempts to target this issue at our school, one of which had occurred only eight years earlier. Although this initiative had not lasted, we reached out to the faculty that had spear-headed it: Mrs. Steele and Mr. Schweig. Both of them were extremely receptive to our goals and ideas and, ever since the day we came to them with this project, they have been extremely generous with their time, knowledge, and advice. We cannot thank them enough for all the help they have given us.

The next step we took was building a stronger student membership. We knew that keeping the group small in its early stages would be necessary because of the sensitive nature of the work, but we also needed a dedicated team that would be large enough to make an impact. By presenting to several students in classrooms, clubs, and around campus, we found a group of members who were excited about the work and passionate about making a change.

Our principal, Dr. Covert, recognized the potential of our team early on and offered to work with us in targeting the issue. Over the last three years, he has encouraged our drive and has been highly supportive of our ideas. Mr. James, a local activist and Pine View alumnus who was introduced to us by Mr. Schweig, has also been a strong supporter of our work. He has given us advice and guidance amid difficult decisions. These adults, along with the core student members, have been essential to the success of DIGS.

By building a team of passionate student advocates and utilizing the guidance and knowledge of adult supporters, your group will be equipped for success. However, patience and persistence are necessary in this process. Seek out others who care as much as you do about whatever you are advocating for. Look for ongoing projects at your school and join them. Approach everyone you can and learn what has been done before and who did it. All of this may take months of hard work, but by bringing together group members that all stand behind the same idea, you amplify the voice of each person involved.

Step 3. Build a Base of Awareness

Awareness is not change in itself, but rather is the prerequisite to change.

When DIGS first began, one of the biggest hurdles we faced was getting the necessary support for the initiatives we attempted to introduce. Although we had support from the adults who sponsored our effort, the majority of people we met had never even recognized this issue. Almost every discussion we had began at square one: attempting to illustrate the importance and urgency of fixing the underrep-resentation of diverse students at our school. Many times, if we were not able to secure a meeting with some important official, it would mean that a project we had planned would not happen. The whole process often felt like pushing a boulder up a steep hill. We realized that if this pattern continued, we would be left with burnt-out spirits and wasted efforts—the exact thing that ended every other initiative on this topic before ours.

In time, we began to recognize the importance of momentum in any type of advocacy. We needed people to know what the problem was and why a solution was so critical. We needed to start a conversation about why there was a lack of low-income students of color in our gifted programs and what we could do to fix it. We needed more people to be aware and to care about the situation. With that, the issue itself would become the fuel necessary for people to find and drive its solution.

In order to build this base of awareness, we began to organize a town hall workshop and discussion. We invited alumni of Pine View, local principals of other gifted programs, current Pine View students, and district administrators to speak about this issue, with a keynote address given by Dr. Joy Lawson Davis. We invited teachers and community members from across our county to attend. Organizing this event was a huge logistical challenge, but the effects it had were powerful. The stories our speakers shared made the audience emotional. They illustrated how this issue has split our school district across racial and socioeconomic lines and the difficult experiences many students have faced as a consequence.

Although this town hall did not directly solve the issue of underrepresentation, it made a difference by increasing the relevance of the issue to more people's lives. Most issues that advocacy targets cannot be solved overnight, but by giving people a reason to care and talk about it, you can keep the conversation alive. When working on your own student advocacy efforts, keep in mind the importance of building and maintaining a strong base of awareness, because when the conversation ends, so does the solution.

Step 4. Implement Practical Ideas

Use the resources you've gathered to implement developed ideas.

This final step is the culmination of all the hard work that took place in the previous three steps. Based on the research you've gathered, with the guidance from your supporters and the momentum you've built, you can effectively implement ideas that have real impact. Of course, this is not an exact formula. Many times, you may start advocating for ideas much earlier on, but following the previous steps will help your team implement projects or programs with fewer obstacles.

Currently, DIGS is working on a few different avenues for tackling the opportunity gap in gifted education in our area. One of these avenues has been advocating for the implementation of a universal screening program to replace teacher recommendations in the gifted identification process. There has been a pilot program for second graders in Title I schools for the last two years, and it has proven to significantly increase the number of identified low-income students of color. The solutions your team will come up with will be a result of the work you've done up to this point. But each idea you intend to implement must still be thoroughly planned, discussed, and thought out.

We hope these steps can be helpful in guiding your students on their journeys of self-advocacy. Because they are largely based on our own experiences, the challenges you face may be different. Nevertheless, these steps can give you a solid base from which you can launch your work.

Educators Listening to Gifted Student Voices

It is extremely important for educators to listen to the voices of gifted learners. Oftentimes, we feel a strong sense of purpose in improving situations for the benefit of those around us. However, it can be difficult to pursue our passions in the face of adversity, or even worse, apathy, from those whom we learn from and respect. When educators discount the thoughts and opinions of students, it not only discourages our involvement in advocacy efforts in the future, but it also may be a lost opportunity for the school. As students, we understand the problems we deal with on a daily basis. By listening and taking student voices into account, educators gain an invaluable perspective that allows them to make better and more informed decisions.

Key Concepts

> It is critical that programs and schools for gifted learners recruit and retain more students and staff from culturally diverse backgrounds.

> Diversity is vital to every student's experience.

> Creating a student body that is more knowledgeable about gifted programming is important to improving diversity.

> By sharing their personal stories, students play an important role in increasing awareness of the problems caused by lack of diversity.

> Successful advocacy on issues of diversity requires the combined voices of everyone.

> Four steps can help increase the effectiveness of student advocacy:

1. Research

2. Find and build a team

3. Build a base of awareness

4. Implement practical ideas

Discussion Questions

1. Does the diversity in your gifted program accurately reflect the diversity in your community?

2. Which populations in your community might be underserved and/or underrepresented by your gifted program?

3. Which students in your program might have feelings similar to those of the Pine View students?

4. How can you encourage students from underserved populations to share their stories with you and other decision-makers?

2

Self-Advocacy: An Essential Tool for Breaking Through Barriers

Deb Douglas, M.S.

With the words of those wise students from Pine View School fresh in our minds, let's examine the concept of self-advocacy and its possible impact on the lives of our brightest—and frequently most underserved—young people.

What Is Self-Advocacy?

In simplest terms, self-advocacy is "the action of representing oneself or one's views or interests." It is essential that each of us feels comfortable representing ourselves in situations throughout our lives: in personal relationships, in family life, in school, and in the workplace. Within the K–12 educational system, it is especially important that students whose abilities lie outside grade-level norms—both struggling and advanced learners—find their voices. And for underserved gifted learners from special populations, it is critical. As the enhanced definition of self-advocacy in the introduction makes clear, self-advocacy is not a one-and-done event. It is a *dynamic process* that enables high-potential students to break through barriers and claim their right to an education that addresses their needs.

Why Is Self-Advocacy Critical for Gifted Students?

Unfortunately, we have no assurance that gifted children in the United States will be well-served throughout their school years. With neither a national mandate on gifted education nor federal funding for it beyond research grants, it is up to each state to decide if it will support the needs of gifted learners.

Of the forty states that responded to the NAGC 2014–2015 "State of the States in Gifted Education" report (NAGC 2015), thirty-two had some form of legislative mandate related to gifted and talented education. Of the states with mandates, only four fully funded the mandate at the state level. Twenty partially funded the mandate. Twelve of the forty reporting states provided no state funding. Additionally, only twenty-one of the responding states monitored and/or audited local programs.

Obviously, if gifted learners must rely on federal, state, or local agencies to recognize and address their needs, some will receive the education they require; many will not. Some will have families that are comfortable accessing the system and advocating for their needs; many will not. Some will have teachers who recognize their gifts and provide for their acceleration and enrichment; many will not. And thus, gifted education in the United States is often, correctly, charged with being inequitable. I have joined advocacy groups at the local, regional, state, and federal levels, hoping to increase funding, accountability, and fairness. But support for gifted education rises and falls with the economy, political interests, and assessment data. Despite years and years of effort, we have seen very little long-term change.

> Self-advocacy is not a one-and-done event. It is a *dynamic process* that enables high-potential students to break through barriers and claim their right to an education that addresses their needs.

This is why empowering students to self-advocate is key to ensuring that they find the educational challenges and social and emotional support they need to succeed. Nobody knows better than students themselves what they are thinking and feeling when they sit in classes, relate to teachers, interact with peers, take tests, and complete homework assignments. When given the requisite information, insights, and strategies, nobody is in a better position than they are to craft their route to graduation and beyond. Our role as adult advocates must be to provide students with that knowledge and support their plans for change.

Who Needs to Self-Advocate?

Students who are outliers by virtue of their exceptional abilities, and outliers times two or three or more because of their special population status, must learn self-advocacy. They are underrepresented in schools that identify gifted students, or they live in areas where there is insufficient programming to address their needs. Too often their schools spend more time focusing on what makes them "different" and celebrating the moments when they "fit in" than on identifying their exceptional abilities and providing opportunities for their growth. Imagine, for instance, how educators in an overcrowded, underfunded urban school would address the needs of a mathematically gifted Hispanic English language learner with dyslexia from a low-income household. This student's multiple identities position her as an outlier times five or six. Sadly, my guess is that providing appropriately challenging math experiences for her is a low priority for the school. So, while it is important for all students to self-advocate, it is essential for special populations of gifted learners.

Although there are calls for greater equity in providing access to enriching and accelerated coursework for all, too often they are met with plans to eliminate gifted programming altogether. The message seems to be, "If only the affluent, education-savvy population is getting the 'good' stuff, then the simple solution is to deny it to everyone." We know that isn't the answer. All learners deserve "good stuff"—high-quality curriculum and instruction that is matched to their needs. But high-potential students often need greater academic challenges (beyond grade-level benchmarks), encouragement to seek out and accept those challenges, and social and emotional support as they tackle them.

Kou's Story

Like many Southeast Asian immigrants in the United States who settle near relatives and friends, Kou, her parents, and younger siblings lived in a close-knit, insular community of Hmong families in our small Midwestern city. Her father had a factory job and her mother cared for their children and maintained the home. Neither had a formal education, having grown up in the refugee camps of Thailand.

Kou was quiet, compliant, and seemingly happy to just blend in. She did fine academically and was recognized for her artistic talent, but her teachers and counselors primarily focused on getting her to "come out of her shell." It was her fifth-grade teacher who recognized Kou's attributes of giftedness and brought them to my attention: excellent memory, great numbers sense, quick language acquisition, keen sense of humor, and fascination with puzzles of all kinds. But she also said Kou seemed content doing grade-level work in their heterogeneous classroom and was disinterested in enrichment activities or accelerated academic opportunities. As gifted education coordinator, I set out to see if that was true. I got to know Kou better when we began having weekly lunch dates, and I expressed interest in her culture and heritage. She opened up to me about the frustrations she was experiencing, the conflicts between traditional Hmong culture and her life as an American preteen. We talked about the concept of giftedness, her specific gifts, her rights and responsibilities, and possible programming opportunities. Together we found ways for her to bridge her two worlds, and over time she was able to break through the cultural barriers, stereotypes, and systemic biases at home and at school that had kept her from speaking up and taking charge of her own education.

> The benefits of self-advocacy are immense for gifted learners whom educators welcome as partners in their education.

Who Benefits When Students Self-Advocate?

The benefits of self-advocacy are immense for gifted learners whom educators welcome as partners in their education. In general, when students sense that school is being done *with* them and not *to* them, they feel less frustration and greater equanimity. When they are supported in taking the lead in their educational decision-making, most grow toward greater independence and self-efficacy. Many feel more intrinsically motivated when they experience appropriately challenging curriculum and succeed at it. Academic performance may improve for those who were previously underachieving due to slow-paced and undemanding schoolwork. **Figure 2.1** shows how self-advocacy helps students increase their awareness of an issue, put into motion the process of self-advocacy, and effect changes that address the issue.

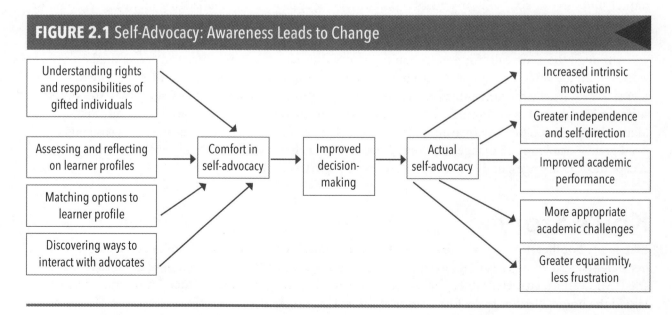

FIGURE 2.1 Self-Advocacy: Awareness Leads to Change

Understanding rights and responsibilities of gifted individuals →

Assessing and reflecting on learner profiles →

Matching options to learner profile →

Discovering ways to interact with advocates →

Comfort in self-advocacy → Improved decision-making → Actual self-advocacy →

Increased intrinsic motivation

Greater independence and self-direction

Improved academic performance

More appropriate academic challenges

Greater equanimity, less frustration

As a bonus, the gifted learner who self-advocates often finds that others also benefit from their actions, including:

> **Other gifted students:** What begins as a successful experience for one learner may allow other students with similar needs to follow the same path.

> **Other students of varying abilities:** Classroom accommodations for the gifted learner may lead to more differentiated instruction and curriculum with options to match student abilities across the spectrum.

> **Parents and families:** Empowering students to speak up can help reassure parents that their children will receive what they need when they need it.

> **Classroom instructors:** Teachers want all their students to learn, and less is left to chance in the traditional classroom when learners know they can talk with teachers about their needs.

> **Gifted education directors and coordinators:** Self-advocacy gives gifted education coordinators another strategy for their toolbox, allowing them to develop partnerships with their students.

> **Counselors:** When high-potential learners better understand their own academic, social, and emotional concerns, they can more clearly and effectively present those issues to their school counselors and work together on a solution before a crisis arises.

> **School districts:** Districts that effectively partner with students through self-advocacy are more likely to challenge *all* learners to grow, to stretch their minds. Ultimately there are fewer student complaints and less pressure from parents who can see firsthand that their children's needs are being addressed. Self-advocacy has even been known to reduce school dropout rates: at-risk gifted learners, who often fail to adapt to the seemingly rigid educational system, may discover that they *can* adapt the system to better meet their needs.

When Kou was given the keys to self-advocacy—the requisite information, insights, and strategies—she was better able to explain her academic needs and desires to her family. Through careful and considerate negotiations, she received their permission to participate in gifted programming. Additionally, her self-advocacy led to better communication between teachers and other Hmong families in her community, which led to the identification of more gifted Hmong children, which led to programming changes that better accommodated their needs. By the time she was a freshman, Kou chose her own appropriate challenge in our International Baccalaureate Diploma program, paving the way for others in her community to do likewise.

Do Students Self-Advocate? If Not, Why Not?

During my first five years as a district coordinator of gifted education, not one student asked me for help in improving their education. Oh, I did hear a lot of parents complaining that we weren't meeting their children's needs, that their kids were bored, or that the teachers just gave advanced learners more work than the other students. And educators, too, complained that some of the identified students in their classrooms weren't working hard or were whining or turning in poor work. I did my best to respond to the adult concerns, but to be honest, I hadn't done very much to solicit input from the students themselves. I don't believe my students felt they had either the right or the responsibility to change the system.

My "aha" moment came during a conference with Selena, a gifted eighth grader, and her parents. We adults were doing all the talking and Selena was looking back-and-forth between us, not saying a word. I caught her eye, and at that moment it dawned on me: one of the greatest skills I could instill in my students would be the ability and confidence to speak for themselves. I quickly redirected the conversation toward Selena while her parents took a secondary role as occasional contributors on the sideline. Given the opportunity and encouragement to contribute to the conversation, Selena willingly began to take charge of her own education. And so, for nearly thirty years, I've worked to introduce thousands of students to the concept of self-advocacy, providing them with the initial information, insights, and skills they need to successfully self-advocate.

Student Perspectives on Self-Advocacy

One of my main forums for this work has been my GT Carpe Diem self-advocacy workshop, which I've presented in many settings: at the SENG (Supporting the Emotional Needs of the Gifted) conference, during family day at the NAGC conference, at regional and state conferences, during a summer camp program, and within individual districts and regional school consortiums.

The only criterion for workshop participation is to have been identified as gifted. Generally, students are invited to attend by the gifted education personnel in their school district. The students complete surveys at the beginning and end of our six hours together. Their responses allow me to continually improve workshop activities based on their input, but also to gather insights into their past experiences self-advocating and their current needs. A selection of the questions asked and summaries of student responses follow.

Using the US federal definition of giftedness that gifted students "need services or activities not ordinarily provided by the school in order to fully develop [their] capabilities" (US Department of Education 2004; US House of Representatives 2015), I asked 642 students at my workshops for their perspectives on how well we are doing in that regard. Then I asked if, in fact, they have self-advocated for those services or activities. The tables below share students' responses.

TABLE 2.1

How often have you wished a teacher would modify something to better meet your needs?

ANSWER	PERCENTAGE OF STUDENTS
Never/Almost never	14%
Occasionally	38%
Frequently/Always	48%

TABLE 2.2

How often have you asked a teacher to modify something for you?

ANSWER	PERCENTAGE OF STUDENTS
Never/Almost never	58%
Occasionally	33%
Frequently/Always	9%

If nearly half of the learners who have been identified by their districts as needing special services say they frequently or always wish for more, we are not doing a very good job. And yet over 50 percent of students surveyed say they never or almost never talk to their teachers about it.

I initially thought gifted learners' silence was due to discomfort. But by their own admission, just 18 percent are *very comfortable* asking for modifications (see **table 2.3**). Why, then, don't more students ask for the challenges they want?

TABLE 2.3

How comfortable are you asking a teacher to modify something for you to make your work more challenging or more interesting?

ANSWER	PERCENTAGE OF STUDENTS
Very uncomfortable	18%
Somewhat uncomfortable	52%
Very comfortable	30%

In further discussions with students, I hear the same comments over and over again:

"I tried once and nothing happened, so I just gave up."

"People tell me to just be glad I don't have to struggle to get good grades."

"I'm afraid I'll just get more work, not different work."

"I didn't know I could ask."

"I didn't know who to ask."

"I didn't know what to ask for."

"I didn't know how to ask."

These comments indicate a lack of information and support. Further analysis of student perspectives in the workshop surveys showed that:

> 32 percent of participants said *no one* has told them what it means to be gifted.

> 44 percent said *no one* has told them about programming in their school that would address their needs.

> 58 percent said *no one* has encouraged them to self-advocate.

If this is the perception of students who are recognized as gifted in their school districts and who have adults who are willing to encourage their self-advocacy by bringing them to the workshop, it begs the questions: What about those students who are not at the workshop? Who are unidentified? Who are underserved?

Special populations of gifted learners are underrepresented in my workshops for many of the same reasons they are underrepresented in gifted programs: their gifts and talents and their need for differentiated educational experiences are not recognized within their schools. It's probable, however, that they would have the same responses as workshop participants: no one has talked to them about giftedness, programming options, or speaking up for themselves.

My efforts to facilitate workshops in two urban school districts with potentially large numbers of students from special populations fell on deaf ears. When I met with the directors of gifted education for each of these districts, we discussed the unique needs of gifted outliers and I offered pro bono workshops. I sensed that these directors were interested, but both turned me down, contending that there were greater issues that took precedence over self-advocacy. Unfortunately, that meant the students who *were* ready to self-advocate wouldn't have the encouragement and support to do so. Of course, self-advocacy is not the only answer to solving the underrepresentation problem, but it must be one of the strategies in every educators' toolkit.

Barriers to Self-Advocacy

Throughout my years working with gifted learners, I've discovered five primary barriers to their self-advocacy:

1. Lack of knowledge regarding their right to an appropriate education and their responsibility to claim that education

2. General misunderstandings about giftedness

3. Limited personal assessment of and reflection on their own gifts

4. Insufficient information regarding options that could address their learning needs

5. Failure to connect with the adults around them who could support their desire for change

Each gifted individual from special populations may face additional barriers including but not limited to the following:

> stereotypes and myths regarding giftedness

> stereotypes and myths regarding specific populations

> faulty identification processes

> lack of options, especially in rural and urban schools

> inequitable instructional and support services

> limited gifted education personnel

> lack of educator training in addressing the needs of gifted learners

> lack of educator training in culturally responsive practices

> limited student and family familiarity with navigating the gifted education system

> limited connections between family, community, and school

An example of those multiple barriers can be found by returning to Kou's story. As we worked together, the obstacles she faced became clearer to both of us. Contrary to her teacher's assessment, Kou wasn't disinterested in school. Rather, she had realized early on in her education that, as a first-generation immigrant, her cultural and familial milieu was at odds with the system, creating hurdles to self-advocacy. Within traditional Hmong society, cultural norms meant that intellectual and academic pursuits for girls were of low priority. Outside of school, Kou had multiple family responsibilities: watching her three younger siblings, helping with housework, and, as she grew older, finding gainful employment to supplement family income and preparing for her own marriage and motherhood. Since her parents had limited English language skills, throughout her teen years she also served as family translator for assistance programs, school district communiques, and all medical and legal concerns. In order to focus on the educational experience she wanted, Kou and her teacher needed to work through her family dynamics to help her parents and other elders understand the importance of her education.

Eliminating Barriers

As elaborated in the following chapters, those of us who work with underserved gifted students have three major roles in minimizing the obstacles they face:

1. We must advocate for them by identifying their gifts and offering appropriate services.

2. We must help them recognize their personal barriers.

3. We must provide them with insights and strategies that allow them to break the barriers and chart their own course.

Of course, self-advocacy is not necessarily that simple or easy. As the new definition offered in the introduction states, it is a "compilation of culturally responsive and inclusive empowerment strategies that open opportunities for positive academic and life outcomes previously precluded for some students due to stereotyping, systemic biases, and limited access to resources." Still, setting students on the road to self-advocacy can be fairly straightforward:

> We must help students recognize their gifts and understand their status as outliers. What do they know about themselves as learners? In what ways are they outside the norm? What are their strengths?

1. First, we must help students recognize their gifts and understand their status as outliers. What do they know about themselves as learners? In what ways are they outside the norm? What are their strengths? Limitations? Interests? Preferences?

2. Second, we must foster their belief in their right to an appropriately challenging education and their responsibility to seek and find success within it. What are their legal rights? What are the district's goals for all students? For those with exceptionalities? What help do they need in order to succeed?

3. Third, we must direct them to options and opportunities that match their needs. What already exists? What could be created? What could be adapted? How could we increase awareness within their communities?

4. Finally, we must connect them with those who will support them and their plans. How do we bring families and teachers on board? Who sees the big picture? Who can provide day-to-day encouragement? Who needs to give approval? Who are the "yes" people? The "no" people? The counselors? The culture brokers? The role models?

I have found that direct instruction in these steps is an effective way to increase students' understanding and can jump-start their willingness and ability to self-advocate. By the end of my workshops, students have created a plan, large or small, for change. Typical goals include finding more challenging work, exploring a special interest, increasing time with intellectual peers, and making accommodations at home or school that address their personal "outlier" needs. These goals are a great beginning, but it is the effort expended (and the support provided) during the following days and weeks and years that builds comfort and success in self-advocating.

Based on student survey responses, instruction in self-advocacy does improve the likelihood that they will speak up for themselves.

TABLE 2.4

How likely are you to talk with someone at your school in the near future about better meeting your needs?

ANSWER	PERCENTAGE OF STUDENTS PRE-WORKSHOP	PERCENTAGE OF STUDENTS POST-WORKSHOP
Not likely	39%	10%
Likely	39%	30%
Very likely	22%	60%

For Kou to eliminate her major barrier to self-advocacy, she needed a culture broker, someone who could bridge the gap between her, her family, her community, and her school. That person turned out to be Bao, a social worker in a nearby city and herself the mother of a gifted Hmong child. What began as mentoring Kou led to greater understanding of gifted programming within the Hmong community. As Bao's guest, I attended several meetings at the Hmong Community Center where I got to know families, described our district gifted plan, answered their many questions (thanks to Bao's interpreting skills!), and outlined the ways we could work together.

> Rather than waiting for systemic change to occur, these students can use self-advocacy to adapt the system from within, creating their own paths to individualized educational programs that match their unique strengths and propel them forward.

There is much that individual educators can do to increase the likelihood that gifted learners in their classrooms develop self-advocacy skills. But in order for our efforts to be continuous and systematic, it is also helpful to have district-wide support. The District Assessment of Support for Self-Advocacy of Gifted Students form on page 27 (and available for download at freespirit.com/eugs) can help you and your colleagues determine what your district is already doing regarding student self-advocacy and where there is room for improvement. It will also help you prioritize your next steps and create your own action plan for change. If you check IDK (I don't know) for any item, be sure to find the person who can provide you with the answer.

Conclusion

Each special population of students faces obstacles. Each has struggles. Each has reasons for not engaging. But the barriers students face can be minimized or eradicated when educators empower these students and help them recognize their rights, assess and reflect on their unique learner profiles, and discover ways to interact effectively with advocates. Rather than waiting for systemic change to occur, these students can use self-advocacy to adapt the system from within, creating their own paths to individualized educational programs that match their unique strengths and propel them forward. We must do our part to assure there are no more dreams deferred.

Key Concepts

> While self-advocacy benefits everyone, it is critical for underrepresented gifted students if they are to find the challenge and encouragement they require.

> The first step in breaking the barriers for special populations of gifted learners is to recognize their needs and identify them for appropriate programming.

> The second step is to ensure they have the information, insights, and skills needed to effectively self-advocate.

> The third step is to support their efforts and help them connect with other advocates.

Discussion Questions

1. How would you summarize your responses to the District Assessment of Support for Self-Advocacy of Gifted Students form?

2. In what ways does your district already encourage and support the self-advocacy of gifted learners?

3. What barriers exist that might keep students from self-advocating?

4. What can you do, personally and as a district, to increase the chances that your students will self-advocate?

Recommended Resources

Douglas, Deb. 2017. "Changing Blah to Ahhhhh!: Student Guide to Being a Self-Advocate" and "Letting Go While Holding On: Parent Guide to Teaching Self-Advocacy." *Parenting for High Potential* 6 (4). nagc.org/parenting-high -potential-1. An article written directly to students, accompanied by a brief explanation for parents.

Douglas, Deb. 2018. *The Power of Self-Advocacy for Gifted Learners: Teaching the 4 Essential Steps to Success*. Minneapolis: Free Spirit Publishing. For educators, an in-depth look at the why, when, and how of teaching gifted students to self-advocate. Includes a facilitator guide for a student workshop.

National Association for Gifted Children and Deb Douglas. 2018. "Self-Advocacy." nagc.org/sites/default/files/ Publication%20PHP/NAGC-TIP%20SHEET-Self%20Advocacy.pdf. This "Timely Information for Parents" is a two-page hand-out that summarizes the role parents can play in supporting their children's self-advocacy.

References

Douglas, Deb. 2004. "Self-Advocacy: Encouraging Students to Become Partners in Differentiation." *Roeper Review* 26 (4): 223–228. doi.org/10.1080/02783190409554273.

National Association for Gifted Children and the Council of State Directors of Programs for the Gifted. 2015. "State of The States in Gifted Education: Policy and Practice Data." nagc.org/resources-publications/gifted-state /2014-2015-state-states-gifted-education.

US Department of Education. 2004. "Title IX—General Provisions." ed.gov/policy/elsec/leg/esea02/pg107.html.

US House of Representatives. 2015. "Title 20, Chapter 70, Subchapter IV, Part F, Subpart 4: USC 7294: Supporting High-Ability Learners and Learning." uscode.house.gov.

District Assessment of Support for Self-Advocacy of Gifted Students

		Yes	No	IDK
Student Rights	Do students receive direct instruction on their specific rights as gifted individuals?			
	Are there state laws or statutes regarding gifted students?			
	Are gifted students included in the district mission/vision statement, either specifically or implicitly?			
	Are there district policies regarding gifted students, e.g., acceleration, early entrance, dual enrollment, or early graduation?			
	Does the district have a mission statement regarding gifted students and/or gifted education?			
	Does the district have a gifted education programming plan?			
	If yes, does the district publish the plan and related materials on its website and communicate about it to all parents and students?			
	Does the district clearly communicate the concept of giftedness to identified students and their parents?			
	Does the district clearly communicate students' specific learner needs to them and their parents?			
	Does the district share resources with students and their parents regarding giftedness?			
	Does the district develop Differentiated Education Plans (DEPs) for gifted students?			
	If yes, do educators collaborate with students and their parents to develop the DEPs?			
Student Responsibilities	Do students receive direct instruction on their specific responsibilities as gifted individuals?			
	Are gifted students given opportunities to assess and reflect on their academic progress?			
	Are students encouraged to speak with educational staff when they experience frustration?			
	Are gifted students encouraged to acquire the attributes of good character expected of all?			
Learner Profiles	Do gifted students receive direct instruction on creating their unique learner profiles?			
	Are gifted students encouraged to assess and reflect on their learner profiles?			

continued >

Adapted from *The Power of Self-Advocacy for Gifted Learners: Teaching the 4 Essential Steps to Success* by Deb Douglas, copyright © 2018. Free Spirit Publishing Inc. From *Empowering Underrepresented Gifted Students: Perspectives from the Field*, edited by Joy Lawson Davis, Ph.D., and Deb Douglas, M.S., copyright © 2021. Free Spirit Publishing, Inc., Minneapolis, Mn; 800-735-7323; freespirit.com. This page may be reproduced for use within an individual school or district. For all other uses, visit freespirit.com/permissions.

		Yes	No	IDK
	Are gifted students allowed access to records that indicate their academic and intellectual ability?			
	Are gifted students provided materials to assess their learning preferences and interests?			
	Are gifted students provided materials that assess their personality traits associated with giftedness?			
	Are gifted students guided in assessing and recognizing areas for improvement?			
Options and Opportunities	Are gifted students guided in matching educational options and alternatives to their learner profiles?			
	Do gifted students receive information about available options that address their learner profiles?			
	Are gifted students informed of new alternatives that may address their learner profiles?			
	Are gifted students informed of opportunities outside the school/district that may better address their learner profiles?			
Advocates	Are gifted students introduced to the various adult advocates in the district who can support their needs?			
	Are gifted students given the opportunity to meet one-on-one with the gifted coordinator?			
	Are classroom teachers informed about self-advocacy and their role in supporting it?			
	Are school counselors informed about self-advocacy and their role in supporting it?			
	Are school principals/administrators informed about self-advocacy and their role in supporting it?			
Goal-Setting	Are gifted students encouraged to set short- and long-term personal educational goals?			
	Are gifted students guided in making sure their goals match their learner profiles?			
Action Plans	Are gifted students supported in writing action plans for change?			
	If yes, does the plan list specific steps and deadlines?			
	If yes, are adult advocates given roles in supporting the plan?			
	If yes, does the plan list dates for feedback, review, and revision?			
General Assessment	Do you feel your district is doing a good job encouraging and supporting the self-advocacy of gifted students?			

3 I Got This: Helping Gifted and Talented Black Students Advocate for Themselves in the Face of Educational Injustices

Donna Y. Ford, Ph.D., Gilman W. Whiting, Ph.D.,
Edward C. Fletcher Jr., Ph.D., James L. Moore III, Ph.D.,
Brian L. Wright, Ph.D.

Arie's Story: Interest Ignored

Arie, a third-grade gifted Black girl, enjoys school. She is one of two Black children in her school's gifted education program of fifty-two students. Arie's school is in an affluent neighborhood and community. She is the top reader in her advanced reading group, reading on a seventh-grade level, and is often asked by her teacher, Ms. C. (a White woman), to assist peers who struggle with reading and other subjects.

Arie takes great pride in helping others become better readers and in being a leader. She is also advanced in her other subjects and is very talented in music—playing piano and violin. Despite Arie's numerous gifts and talents, her academic and social awareness needs go unsupported by her teachers and gifted coordinator; she feels isolated and unchallenged.

Arie's mother and father are well-educated and employed as doctors. They are social justice–minded and have exposed their daughter to African American and Black diasporic history and community activism. As a result, Arie is conscious about topics like race and racism. This led to a desire to call attention to the problem in a schoolwide essay contest about how to make her school and community better. The first prize was recognition in the community's local newspaper, a writing kit, and $2,000. Topics chosen by Arie's classmates included adding a swimming pool to the nearby park, longer recess, better lunch options, and more field trips. Ms. C. asked Arie what she planned to write about. In a matter-of-fact tone, Arie boldly said, "Racism and inequality."

Surprised, Ms. C. asked, "Do you think racism is a problem in this school and community?"

Arie answered yes and explained how she often wonders why there are not a lot of kids who look like her in her gifted classes and her school.

To distance herself from Arie's poignant topic and question, Ms. C. responded quickly, "Well, there are not a lot of kids who are smart like you."

Arie did not accept this "compliment," and said, "But there are. My parents told me and they showed me! I know a few in my neighborhood."

Ms. C. then requested that Arie choose a different topic. "Maybe you should write about something else because this topic makes people feel uncomfortable."

Arie retorted, "No! I want to write about this topic and show others that there are a lot of smart Black kids like me. Look at the books we read, and those in the school library. There are not a lot of books about Black people.* This is one of the reasons I don't like school. My interests don't matter but a swimming pool does. My mom and dad are happy I chose this topic. I want them to talk to you."

Dwight's Story: Presumed Incompetence

Dwight, a ninth grader, is one of three Black students enrolled in AP English and math at his predominantly White high school. Many of his peers are from affluent and privileged backgrounds. Dwight, on the other hand, lives across town in one of the city's three housing projects with his parents and two younger siblings.

Dwight's parents are high school graduates, and both work two jobs. Their struggle to make ends meet to provide for their three children leaves very little time for them to be attentive to Dwight's and his siblings' educational needs. Although aware that their son is smart and has excelled in school since Head Start, they know very little about gifted education and AP courses. As a result, Dwight is left to negotiate and navigate the politics of his majority White high school alone and is subject to isolation, bullying, and victimization as a gifted Black student, and a lack of support from school personnel, much of the time.

His overwhelmingly White teachers often do not know how to engage in and support Dwight's cultural and personal identities, and the one Black counselor at Dwight's school is swamped with class enrollments, room assignments, and college admissions applications, which leaves little to no time to provide social, emotional, and cultural guidance.

Whenever Dwight reaches out for academic support, his teachers are quick to recommend that he request to be removed from his AP courses and take general courses instead. One White teacher, Mr. A., told Dwight, "It's no big deal, you can still graduate high school and get a good-paying job."

Annoyed, Dwight said, "But I want more than a good-paying job; I want to go to college like everybody else in this school." Mr. A. responded that college is not for everyone, which prompted Dwight to say, "Well, it's for me, and it's what my parents have encouraged me to do for a long time."

Mr. A. followed Dwight's self-advocacy with, "Hmm, I don't think I have ever met your parents. Do they come to parent-teacher conferences?"

Annoyed and frustrated, Dwight responded, "They work two jobs and can't come here in the middle of the day or the evening. And I work part-time. I want to better myself for me and my family. That's why I gotta keep my grades up and need you, other teachers, and counselors to help me when I ask for help."

Feeling "attacked," Mr. A. asked, "Are you saying we don't support you at this school?"

Dwight responded, "I just feel like when I ask for help, I am ignored and y'all be acting like I can't do the work. It's wrong and unfair. I need help. I would do better *with* your help. Work with me, not against me."

Hopes and Dreams Denied and Deferred

Missing from the discourse and dialogue on advocacy regarding the recruitment and retention of Black students in gifted and talented education (GATE) and Advanced Placement (AP) are the voices of students themselves. Like Arie and Dwight, Black students are often astute in discerning inequalities in

---

*Arie is correct. Too few children's books are multicultural. And their authenticity must be evaluated. For one of the many discussions on this topic, see blog.leeandlow.com/2017/03/30/the-diversity-gap-in-childrens-book-publishing-2017 and readingrockets.org/blogs/page-page/books-are-key-future-interview-wade-hudson-and-cheryl-willis-hudson.

education and using self-advocacy skills to ask for what they want and need to not simply survive, but thrive, in school overall, which includes having access to GATE and AP courses.

Students advocating for themselves with the support of culturally competent teachers and guidance counselors goes a long way in disrupting the all-too-familiar racial imbalances in GATE and AP programs in the United States (Ford 2013). Culturally competent teachers and counselors are able to develop trusting relationships with students, integrate culture into curricular materials, utilize representative teaching materials that strengthen students' self-esteem, and express respect for students' community members by engaging them as mentors to support students' social and emotional needs (Gay 2002; Ladson-Billings 1995).

> Black students are often astute in discerning inequalities in education and using self-advocacy skills to ask for what they want and need to not simply survive, but thrive, in school.

Too few teachers have formal preparation to understand the gravity of the intended and unintended consequences of ignoring and discounting how racism and sexism circumscribe the academic and social experiences of Black students. For more on this topic, see Ford (2013) for a comprehensive treatise on what is needed to maximize the gifts and talents of Black students, and Wright with Counsell (2018) for a focus on young brilliant Black boys. Later in this chapter, we share Whiting's (2014) Scholar Identity Model as a well-developed and implemented framework grounded in theories and research to equip Black students to be self-advocates in academic and other settings.

Attitudes Toward and Misperceptions of Black Gifted and Talented Students

Although many people want to believe that, as a nation, the United States has moved beyond racism, classism, and other discriminatory practices, it has not. The attitudes and beliefs of some (and, dare we say, many) school officials regarding the intellectual and academic prowess of Black students continue to impede students' opportunities to fully access and thrive in advanced programs.

Many contemporary Black scholars of gifted and talented education (Joy Lawson Davis, Donna Y. Ford, Tarek Grantham, Michelle Frazier Trotman Scott, James Moore, Malik Henfield, Ken Dickson, Gloria Taradash) and legendary Black scholars who laid the foundation for it (Mary Frasier and Alexinia Baldwin) have challenged popular definitions and theories of giftedness and the unfair tests, checklists, policies, procedures, and practices that contribute to the persistent and reprehensible underrepresentation of Black students in GATE and AP. For example, current definitions of giftedness continue to place major emphasis on standardized intelligence tests reflective of White middle-class values and, therefore, discriminate against students of color. These tests do not embrace students' languages, literacies, and cultural practices, norms, and values. (For an excellent example of test bias in popular culture, see the "IQ Test" episode of the TV sitcom *Good Times*, in which the youngest son, Michael, who was very bright, did not do well on an IQ test. He decided to walk out on the test because he believed it was unfair. He scored low because he chose not to finish the test. "I didn't like the questions, so I walked out," he told his parents. His rationale was that the exam was "nothing but a White racist test . . . given by the White people, made up by White people, and even graded by White people.")

Furthermore, cultural and economic class differences cause gifted and talented behaviors to manifest differently across racial and ethnic groups. Thus, as Robert Sternberg and Howard Gardner have asserted and theorized, gifted and talented behaviors defined and performed by White middle-class students are not necessarily the same as those displayed by students of color (Wright and Ford 2017). Identification measures based on narrow standards that reflect, represent, and enforce the languages, literacies, and cultural practices of the dominant culture are bound to ignore and marginalize much of what Black students learn in their homes and communities, and to treat that as irrelevant for school, substandard, and inferior.

This practice of ranking and sorting students based on their intellectual capacity to think, speak, and act in ways that represent White students undermines the cultural strengths and assets of Black students. Adding socioeconomic status to the injustice equation greatly compounds the problem of underrepresentation. Dwight and other students living in generational poverty and those among the working poor do not, unfortunately and wrongfully, have comparable experiences with students from more affluent homes. When financial resources are lacking, children may not have access to developmental and cognitively stimulating toys and materials, nor to culturally relevant books and literature.

> We refute and debunk the myth that Black families do not place a high value and priority on education.

This is not a matter of families not recognizing the importance of having their children engaged in a variety of experiences, such as trips to the local museum, zoological park, library, and so on, but a matter of financial limitations, transportation, and availability of these resources in neighborhoods like Dwight's.

We refute and debunk the myth that Black families do not place a high value and priority on education when consideration is given to longstanding structural inequalities that have prevented and limited their access and opportunities. To put those remarks in context, recall that Arie does not live in poverty and has highly educated and involved parents, yet she still faced racial injustices. Both families have instilled dreams in their gifted and talented children that educators must not diminish or defer.

The education of Black students is often compromised, which gives little opportunity for their gifts and talents to be recognized and cultivated at school. GATE and AP teacher preparation programs must critically educate their teacher and school administrator candidates. Likewise, Black families and caregivers must equip their very capable sons and daughters with self-advocacy knowledge and skills to request and demand an education that affirms and supports their interests, dreams, and career aspirations.

Affirming the Gifts and Talents of Black Students

Too few teachers are formally and adequately trained in teacher preparation programs to work with and understand the experiences and needs of gifted and talented students, and even fewer are trained to recruit and retain culturally diverse students in GATE and AP (Ford 2013). We must develop and cultivate self-advocacy skills in all underrepresented and underserved students so they can take their rightful seats at the GATE and AP tables.

For decades after *Brown v. the Board of Education* in 1954, general education, GATE, and AP have made insufficient progress—segregation is extensive and increasing (Ford et al. 2018). Relatedly, we find it beyond a coincidence that the National Association for Gifted Children (NAGC) was founded the same year (1954) that Black students were finally legally entitled to attend schools with White students. The quest and challenge to integrate GATE for many Black students feels, in an analogous way, like the hostile experiences felt by the Little Rock Nine as they sought to be educated safely, rigorously, and equitably. Black students' belonging, being, and becoming full participants in GATE and AP classes (in public, private, and charter schools) where they are viewed as intellectually and academically capable is long overdue.

Some of our Black students who agree to accept placement in GATE and AP still face hostility from classmates and educators, which is sad and egregious. This is a source of anxiety for their families (Davis 2010) and requires students and their families to cope with stress that over time is exhausting. This further justifies the dire need for culturally competent counselors, teachers, and school administrators who can positively influence Black students' preK–12 experiences as advanced learners.

Schooling and Inequality Impact Self-Advocacy

Decisions made about who has access to a rigorous education (GATE and AP) are often viewed as if they are politically neutral. We argue that such decisions are never neutral, but instead are operated with political clarity by those in positions of power and influence. In other words, by those who serve as gatekeepers to advanced educational opportunities. Moreover, such decisions are tied to social, political, and economic structures that are framed, defined, and enacted by society, resulting in differences in the way Black students are treated by teachers and school administrators who are not culturally competent and who lack knowledge and understanding regarding the languages, literacies, and cultural practices of Black students in general, and those in gifted education in particular. For example, research shows that compared with White students, Black students are more likely to be suspended or expelled, less likely to be placed in gifted programs, and subjected to lowered academic and social expectations from their teachers (Wood, Harris, and Howard 2018; Wright and Counsell 2018).

In discussions with teachers and administrators of gifted programs, many contend that such differential treatment by individual teachers and school administrators is not malicious or intentional. However, the perpetuation of racism, discrimination, and gatekeeping to keep advanced programs overwhelmingly White and middle class *is* intentional. It is important to note that public schools have been a central location for reproducing inequalities, particularly for students of color. Hence, it is critical that Black students develop self-advocacy skills in the early grades (recall Arie) to speak up and act on their own behalf to challenge institutional practices that are oppressive and discriminatory.

Self-Advocacy Skills and Strategies for Gifted and Talented Black Students

Data from the National Center for Educational Statistics' *Early Childhood Longitudinal Study* (2002) found that Black students were 54 percent less likely than White students to be recommended for GATE programs, even after adjusting for factors such as students' standardized test scores. Notably, Black students were three times more likely to be referred for GATE programs if their teacher was Black rather than White (Grissom and Redding 2016). These findings suggest that when White teachers' implicit biases, stereotypes, and just plain racism are in operation, it makes them less effective at teaching Black students and less likely to refer Black students for inclusion in GATE and AP. For these and other reasons, it is critical that Black students learn self-advocacy skills to disrupt and dismantle these practices. Learning and developing self-advocacy skills increases the potential for to Black students to survive and thrive even in hostile and discriminatory environments.

As high-achieving Black scholars, we have faced our share of challenges and setbacks in academic settings. We identify with the countless Black students who endeavor to achieve—in spite of income level, insufficient or limited resources, parental education levels, peer pressures, culturally insensitive or assaultive teachers, inadequate guidance and counseling, and more. Following are a few recommendations for promoting Black students' self-advocacy skills. Instilling such skills in Black students will take assistance from families, teachers, counselors, administrators, and mentors. In other words, such skills need to be taught formally (in classes and conversations) and via exposure (through observation and experience).

> **Encourage students to seek help.** An important message that must be communicated by families, educators, and mentors is that asking for help is a sign of strength and self-advocacy—not a weakness. All Black students must understand this and develop this skill, but especially boys and advanced students. We are pleased that Dwight exercised his right to seek help, in spite of the negative responses from his teachers. Black students must be encouraged to persist.

> **Provide ethnic matching.** Schools need more Black counselors and gifted Black teachers. Donald Easton-Brooks's 2019 book on ethnic matching speaks to the myriad benefits for students when their educators are from their same cultural background. A central finding is that Black students perform higher academically with the support of Black teachers and counselors.

> **Give students access to mentoring and tutoring.** Many mentoring organizations exist in all types of communities. Help students connect with mentors and tutors in community and civic organizations to provide support for future planning and success in higher education.

> **Use bibliotherapy.** Bibliotherapy can be an effective means of self-advocacy. Students can read books about the lived experiences of other gifted and talented Black students who are now successful adults. (See, for instance, *Gumbo for the Soul* by Donna Y. Ford et al. 2017.) They can read about children and young adults in books with gifted and talented Black protagonists. For Arie, we recommend *Maizon at Blue Hill* by Jacqueline Woodson (1992, 2002), and for Dwight we recommend *Fast Talk on a Slow Track* by Rita Williams-Garcia (1998). We also highly recommend nonfiction for Dwight, such as Ron Suskind's *A Hope in the Unseen: An American Odyssey from the Inner City to the Ivy League* (1998). Also recommended for both students is The Cruisers series by Walter Dean Myers.

> **Share about role models.** Relatedly, we suggest sharing with students real-life role models of gifted and talented Black students in their age group. Some include the Javits-Frasier Scholars.[*] Joy Lawson Davis (one of the co-editors of this book) and Donna Y. Ford (a coauthor of this chapter) are two of the founders of this unique and needed scholarship designed for highly gifted and talented Black students.

> **Teach about racial discrimination.** Older students like Dwight can be introduced to one or all components of microaggressions (Sue et al. 2008; Ford et al. 2013). Most relevant for Dwight is "ascription of intelligence," given that his teachers encouraged him to drop AP classes when he asked for additional support. Since Arie's parents are social justice advocates, we feel comfortable introducing her to the concept of colorblindness, which is considered by many to be a form of racism (Scruggs 2009).[+] You will recall that Arie's teacher did not want Arie to focus on racism as her essay topic.

> **Build college and career readiness.** This can be invaluable for students who live in poverty or whose parents did not attend college, both of which apply to Dwight. Such exposure can disrupt the cycle of generational poverty, which is often perpetuated by too little information about how higher

---

[*]See nagc.org/about-nagc/nagc-awards-scholarships/javits-frasier-scholars-program for more information.

[+]Using an ideology of colorblindness allows those with privilege the option of dismissing the importance of the race, which is why the adoption of colorblindness is viewed as a type of racism.

education can improve fiscal and occupational outcomes. Additionally, a robust definition of college and career readiness should reflect the knowledge, skills, and dispositions students need to be prepared academically as well as the necessity for students to acquire employability and technical skills (Fletcher, Warren, and Hernández-Gantes 2018; Stone and Lewis 2012; Symonds, Schwartz, and Ferguson 2011). While academic preparation is needed with basic skills such as language arts, mathematics, and science, that type of education speaks only to the college readiness aspect of high school students' education. Students also need employability skills by the time they exit high school. These include the skills needed to compete in today's knowledge-based and technologically rich economy—what are often referred to as twenty-first-century skills—like collaborative, technological, critical-thinking, problem-solving, and strong work-ethic competencies. Similarly, technical skills are also needed by exiting high school students to make them more competitive in the workforce. Technical skills are related to specialized knowledge and skill bases required by specific occupational areas.

> **Share other accelerated college credit options and benefits with students.** Accelerated college credit initiatives include Advanced Placement (AP), International Baccalaureate (IB), dual credit (high school students earn college credit), and dual enrollment coursework (students earn both college and high school credit from a course taken at a college). Dual enrollment has increasingly become popular in the United States as an initiative that enables high school students access to postsecondary education, increases the rigor of the high school curriculum, strengthens the links between high school and college, and reduces college debt (Bailey and Karp 2003; Thomas et al. 2013). Where students take such courses varies. Students might take a course on a college campus, at the local high school (taught by a high school teacher who also serves as a college adjunct), or online. Funding and requirements for dual enrollment vary across each state. For example, Florida (with over 60,000 dual enrollment participants) requires students to achieve a minimum score on a common placement test and have a 3.0 GPA to enroll. Dual enrollment students benefit from free tuition, books, and fees. Because all levels of postsecondary education increase future earning potential, underrepresented students who participate in dual enrollment could have better opportunities to overcome their socioeconomic origins and move up the social ladder.

> **Teach a pedagogy of Black brilliance** (coined by Brian L. Wright). The practice of intentionally teaching Black students in early childhood (recall Arie) that they are equal to anyone and everyone in any context is fundamental to self-advocacy. This means standing up in their Black brilliance, which is linked and tied to the legacy of educational excellence as valued by the Black community.

Scholar Identity and Self-Advocacy

Arie's and Dwight's stories are just two examples of what happens daily inside classrooms in America to our students who are gifted, talented, and Black. Unfortunately, the reality is that students of color who are intellectually capable, like Arie and Dwight, experience schooling that is fraught with missing opportunities and limited access, and their gifts and talents go unnoticed and uncultivated. Students' self-advocacy can only be successful if they, with the assistance of support systems (family, school, community, and mentors), develop a scholar identity. What follows is a brief overview of the constructs of the Scholar Identity Model™, a framework that was originally designed to give educators guidance to empower Black male students and which is equally impactful for all Black students (Whiting 2014). Listed below are the constructs of the Scholar Identity Model.

Self-Efficacy

A crucial component of self-advocacy is the belief in one's ability to accomplish what one is advocating for (self-efficacy). In Arie's case, her strong family ties and her experiences in a home with family members who themselves had to negotiate an educational system where self-advocacy was required helped Arie advocate for what she felt strongly about.

Future Orientation

Students who utilize self-advocacy demonstrate a high level of future orientation. They are motivated and have thought through short-term and long-term (depending on the age of the student) outcomes of being denied an opportunity. In Dwight's case, he is forced to self-advocate, speak up for himself, and even make demands that will impact his future.

Teachers, administrators, and guidance counselors must support students' future orientation by:

> Understanding each student's life circumstances. When educators build good relationships with students, most students will share their concerns, thoughts, and rationales for their visions of the future.

> Thinking about how intellectually and culturally brave students are and must be, given the many social and educational injustices they face.

> Recognizing and appreciating how students will be contributing members of society, especially when they have the advocacy of culturally competent educators. Black students with gifts and talents who are forced to make high-stakes decisions that impact their futures and peer relationships are not only bright, but often resilient.

Willing to Make Sacrifices

This construct is difficult for many adults and even more difficult for children and adolescents. Educators frequently expect GATE students to be more mature than other students. But when a Black student has made this sacrifice to self-advocate, the student's self-advocacy is often viewed by those same teachers, counselors, administrators, and GATE program coordinators as unruly, disrespectful, and adult-like and as a reason to not accept the student into or to remove them from GATE programming.

Accordingly, all educators must:

> Recognize and understand that most students who are not the numerical or racial majority in GATE programs and services have made sacrifices to take the road less traveled.

> Encourage and support students to be children as long as possible—deserving of protection and nurturing. Childhood is fleeting and unequal; imagine that this student is your child.

Internal Locus of Control

In most high-stakes academic situations, children very early on internalize the praise that comes from being considered "good" different. Being selected for a GATE program can be a source of honor and pride, partly for being included in such a group. However, these same praises can bring about fears of being found to be unworthy of the honor (i.e., presumed incompetent). When the expected outcomes don't occur, who or what does the student blame for the shortfall? A student who has learned to self-advocate is more likely to have an internal locus of control—to be more willing to take responsibility for shortfalls and, most importantly, address and correct them.

To help students develop and strengthen this internal locus of control, teachers, administrators, and guidance counselors need to:

> Understand that the pressures for Black students in GATE programs are different from those for other students. Black students are constantly being reminded of how "fortunate" they are to be given GATE services.

> Recognize that Black students' self-advocacy when they believe they have been wronged may be misinterpreted negatively (for example, as an argument).

Self-Awareness

Self-awareness (Who am I? What are my strengths? What are my needs? What do I like?) is pivotal to self-advocacy. A sense of identity is crucial to identifying one's strengths, as well as areas that need work or change. Before students can self-advocate, they must first know themselves.

Teachers, administrators, and guidance counselors can and should:

> Have and share an honest, fair assessment of Black students via a culturally responsive framework and lens.

> Give students constructive feedback—be specific, direct, and encouraging, keeping in mind cultural mismatches and inequities.

Achievement Greater Than Affiliation

For children and adolescents like Arie and Dwight, the decision to self-advocate is a crucial one. Peers and peer pressure are real, and students who self-advocate in the face of having chosen their academics over peers—in other words, having chosen achievement over affiliation—should be given empathy (not pity) and should receive support and advocacy from their educators. The draw of friendships is constant. Because of this, it is important that students' self-advocacy not go unheard. When students' attempts to self-advocate are not recognized or are ignored, this can cause the student to revert to affiliation with friends over achievement (i.e., underachievement).

To support students in this construct, teachers, administrators, and guidance counselors need to:

> Consider the ever-present pressure of peers and friends.

> Understand the loneliness and isolation Black students in GATE programs experience.

Academic Self-Confidence

We have found that many Black students in GATE programs and services have high levels of academic self-confidence. Because of Black students' frequent "only one" status, it is important that teachers, administrators, and counselors:

> Do not put Black students in a position where they need to prove that they belong or that they are good enough.

> Provide opportunities for student success and encourage them to continue being confident in academic settings.

Race Consciousness

As the student stories in this chapter illustrate, both Arie and Dwight appear to recognize their ever-present racialized status in their GATE programs. No matter what teachers, administrators, and guidance counselors believe, race consciousness permeates Black students' lives in general and is intensified in GATE events, programs, and services in particular. For example, being the only Black member on an otherwise all-White science team requires a student to try to ignore feelings of separateness.

Teachers, administrators, and guidance counselors should:

> Imagine that same team with several Black students and only one White student.

> Consider how, after years of being the lone one, that isolated student might view themself.

> Continually work toward becoming more culturally aware and sensitive by participating in ongoing and culturally relevant GATE professional development.

In Dwight's situation, he had a guidance counselor and a teacher who both clearly needed to attend ongoing professional development and very possibly needed to be monitored until they became aware that students' self-advocacy is a call for help.

Gender-Related Issues

Far too many African American students have had no option but to self-advocate for GATE services. This oppressive climate is mainly generated by racism, discrimination, ignorance, mass media, and historical events that cause teachers, administrators, and guidance counselors to view underrepresented minority students as somehow less qualified. This and other stereotypes often encourage practitioners to view Black boys and girls of all ages as difficult, defiant, deficient, and dangerous. Stereotypes encourage the primarily White and female education profession to view Black boys and girls as ill-mannered, loud, and bad. For example, some scholars have examined the impact on the adultification of Black girls as a form of discrimination that impacts their entry and retention in gifted education programs (Cotton, Davis, and Collins 2021). Educators with a negative view of Black girls' self-confidence are unlikely to develop strong relationships with these girls and thus influence whether they will have access to gifted programs where they have the potential to flourish as strong, outspoken students. Race consciousness is the understanding that self-advocacy is an effective way to address these stereotypes (including stereotypes that apply to both race and gender) and that race is not just a four-letter word.

Teachers, administrators, and guidance counselors can teach race consciousness by having students:

> Critically examine their beliefs, feelings, and actions regarding matters of race, including where these overlap with matters of gender.

> Strengthen their race identity through exploration of the lives and experiences of Black scholars, inventors, and others who exemplify a strong race consciousness.

We all must not only try to recruit for statistics, but to retain students in gifted programming because it is the right thing to do. We are obligated, in the name of equity and professionalism, to be equitable, culturally responsive, and responsible to all students. Until teachers, administrators, guidance counselors, and school counselors do this, students must, unfortunately, take charge and be their own sole or primary advocates. This is an enormous and unnecessary responsibility to place on children.

Conclusion

Arie and Dwight represent thousands of Black students of all ages and income levels who are in GATE and AP (or should be) and who face challenges and injustices due to racism and other discriminatory practices. We share their two stories to illustrate how growing up young, gifted, and Black in very different contexts often still results in the same problematic outcomes—dreams deferred and denied—when the mainly White teachers, counselors, administrators, and other school personnel do not get to know Black students and do not honor these students' gifts, talents, and passions.

As Black scholars who grew up in different backgrounds—single-parent and two-parent, high-income and low-income, urban and rural settings—we have experienced and witnessed educators who discount and/or deny how racism and classism can and do hinder the dreams, interests, and goals of students in general, and young, gifted, and Black students in particular. Arie's and Dwight's stories are reflective of our lived experiences in so many ways. We achieved *in spite of*, which led to our passion to become scholars who advocate for highly capable students of color from all backgrounds.

We hope Arie's and Dwight's stories will resonate with you and all who care deeply about advancing equity in GATE and AP programs and services. We hope you will recall and reflect on former Black students, and widely implement the recommendations provided in this chapter to help your current and future Black students proudly proclaim and demonstrate "I got this!"

Key Concepts

> Families and educators must advocate for students, and students can be and must be taught to advocate for themselves.

> Students of all ages can become self-advocates when encouraged and taught to do so.

> Self-advocacy skills are especially important for students who face social and educational injustices and inequities. Black students, in particular, must be taught to self-advocate to experience more success and deal with racial inequities.

> A scholar identity is important to success in school and life, especially for Black students. Educators and families must understand and promote the constructs of this identity.

> Educators must commit to becoming culturally competent professionals as a fundamental way to recognize and nurture the potential, gifts, and talents of Black students.

Discussion Questions

1. To what degree are Black students underrepresented in gifted and talented education and other classes for advanced learners?

2. To what extent does underrepresentation exist in your school and district? What are the causes?

3. What role do educators play in Black students' having too little access to gifted and talented education and AP?

4. Why do the authors maintain that income is not always a barrier to Black students getting identified as gifted and talented? How does Dwight's story highlight their point?

5. What role does multicultural and anti-racist education play in students of color being engaged in school? How does Arie's story illustrate this need?

6. How can educators empower gifted and talented Black students to be self-advocates? What role does a scholar identity play in doing so?

Recommended Resources

Allport, Gordon W. 1954. *The Nature of Prejudice.* Cambridge, MA: Addison-Wesley.

Delpit, Lisa. 2006. *Other People's Children: Cultural Conflict in the Classroom.* New York: W.W. Norton.

Kendi, Ibram X. 2019. *How to Be an Anti-Racist.* New York: Random House.

Kozol, Jonathan. 1991. *Savage Inequalities: Children in America's Schools.* New York: Crown.

Love, Bettina. 2019. *We Want to Do More Than Survive: Abolitionist Teaching and the Pursuit of Educational Freedom.* Boston: Beacon Press.

Myers, Walter Dean. 2010–2014. The Cruisers series. New York: Scholastic Press.

Suskind, Ron. 1998. *A Hope in the Unseen: An American Odyssey from the Inner City to the Ivy League.* New York: Broadway Books.

Williams-Garcia, Rita. 1991. *Fast Talk on a Slow Track.* New York: Puffin Books.

Winters, Mary-Frances. 2020. *Black Fatigue: How Racism Erodes the Mind, Body, and Spirit.* Oakland, CA: Berrett-Koehler Publishers.

Woodson, Jacqueline. 1992. *Maizon at Blue Hill.* New York: Puffin Books.

References

Bailey, Thomas, and Melinda Mechur Karp. 2003. *Promoting College Access and Success: A Review of Credit-Based Transition Programs.* US Department of Education, Office of Adult and Vocational Education: Washington, D.C. ccrc.tc.columbia.edu/media/k2/attachments/promoting-college-access-success.pdf.

Cotton, C.R.B, J.L. Davis, and K.H. Collins. 2021. "Hidden No More: Understanding and Addressing the Invisibility of Gifted Black Girls with Other Learning Exceptionalities." In *Giftedness & Twice Exceptionality at School,* edited by F. Piske & K.H. Collins. Curitiba, Paraná: Brazil: Juruá Editora.

Davis, Joy Lawson. 2010. *Bright, Talented, & Black: A Guide for Families of African American Gifted Learners.* Arizona: Great Potential Press Inc.

Fletcher, Edward C., Nathalie Q. Warren, and Victor M. Hernández-Gantes. 2018. "Preparing High School Students for a Changing World: College, Career, and Future Ready Learners." *Career and Technical Education Research* 43 (1): 77–97. doi.org/10.5328/cter43.1.77

Ford, Donna Y. 2010. *Reversing Underachievement Among Gifted Black Students* (2nd. ed.). Waco, TX: Prufrock Press.

———. 2013. *Recruiting and Retaining Culturally Different Students in Gifted Education.* Waco, TX: Prufrock Press.

Ford, Donna Y., Tyrone C. Howard, and J. John Harris, III. 1999. "Using Multicultural Literature in Gifted Education Classrooms." *Gifted Child Today* 22 (4): 14–21. doi.org/10.1177/107621759902200405.

Ford, Donna Y., Michelle Frazier Trotman Scott, James L. Moore III, and Stanford O. Amos. 2013. "Gifted Education and Culturally Different Students: Examining Prejudice and Discrimination via Microaggressions." *Gifted Child Today* 36 (3): 205–208. doi.org/10.1177/1076217513487069.

Ford, Donna Y., Cynthia A. Tyson, Tyrone C. Howard, and J. John Harris III. 2000. "Multicultural Literature and Gifted Black Students: Promoting Self-Understanding, Awareness, and Pride." *Roeper Review* 22 (4): 235–240. doi.org/10.1080/02783190009554045.

Ford, Donna Y, Brian L. Wright, Christopher J.P. Sewell, Gilman W. Whiting, and James L. Moore III. 2018. "The Nouveau Talented Tenth: Envisioning W.E.B. Du Bois in the Context of Contemporary Gifted and Talented Education." *Journal of Negro Education* 87 (3): 294–310. doi.org/10.7709/jnegroeducation.87.3.0294.

Gay, Geneva. 2002. "Preparing for Culturally Responsive Teaching." *Journal of Teacher Education* 53 (2): 106–116. doi.org/10.1177/0022487102053002003.

Harris III, J. John, and Donna Y. Ford. 1999. "Hope Deferred Again: Gifted Minority Students Underrepresented in Gifted Education." *Education and Urban Society* 31 (2): 225–237. doi.org/10.1177/0013124599031002007.

Ladson-Billings, Gloria. 1995. "Toward a Theory of Culturally Relevant Pedagogy." *American Educational Research Journal* 32 (3): 465–491. doi.org/10.3102/00028312032003465.

National Center for Education Statistics. 2002. *Early Childhood Longitudinal Study Kindergarten Class of 1998–99 (ECLS-K), Psychometric Report for Kindergarten Through First Grade.* Washington, DC: US Department of Education.

Nicholson-Crotty, Jill, Jason A. Grissom, and Sean Nicholson-Crotty. 2011. "Bureaucratic Representation, Distributional Equity, and Democratic Values in the Administration of Public Programs." *The Journal of Politics* 73 (2): 582–596. doi.org/10.1017/s0022381611000144.

Pierson, Ashley, Michelle Hodara, and Jonathan Luke. 2017. *Earning College Credits in High School: Options, Participation, and Outcomes for Oregon Students* (REL 2017–216). Washington, DC: US Department of Education, Institute of Education Sciences, National Center for Education Evaluation and Regional Assistance, Regional Educational Laboratory Northwest.

Scruggs, Afi-Odelia E. 2009. "Colorblindness: The New Racism?" *Learning for Justice*, 36. learningforjustice.org/magazine/fall-2009/colorblindness-the-new-racism.

Stone, James R. III, and Morgan V. Lewis. 2012. *College and Career Ready in the 21st Century: Making High School Matter.* New York: Teachers College Press.

Sue, Derald Wing, Christina M. Capodilupo, and Aisha M.B. Holder. 2008. "Racial Microaggressions in the Life Experience of Black Americans." *Professional Psychology: Research and Practice* 39 (3): 329–336. doi.org/10.1037/0735-7028.39.3.329.

Symonds, William C., Robert Schwartz, and Ronald F. Ferguson. 2011. *Pathways to Prosperity: Meeting the Challenge of Preparing Young Americans for the 21st Century.* Cambridge, MA: Pathways to Prosperity Project, Harvard University Graduate School of Education.

Thomas, Nina, Stephanie Marken, Lucinda Gray, and Laurie Lewis. 2013. *Dual Credit and Exam-Based Courses in US Public High Schools: 2010–11.* Washington, DC: US Department of Education. nces.ed.gov/pubs2013/2013001.pdf.

Whiting, Gilman. 2009. "Gifted Black Males: Understanding and Decreasing Barriers to Achievement and Identity." *Roeper Review* 31 (4): 224–233. doi.org/10.1080/02783190903177598.

———. 2014. "The Scholar Identity Model: Black Male Success in the K–12 Context." In *Building on Resilience: Models and Frameworks of Black Male Success Across the P–20 Pipeline,* edited by Fred A. Bonner II, 88–108. Sterling, VA: Stylus Publishing.

Wood, J. L., F. Harris III, and T.C. Howard. 2018. *Get Out! Black Male Suspensions in California Public Schools.* San Diego, CA: Community College Equity Assessment Lab and the UCLA Black Male Institute.

Wright, Brian L. 2019. "Black Boys Matter: Cultivating their Identity, Agency, and Voice." *Teaching Young Children* 12 (3): 4–7. naeyc.org/resources/pubs/tyc/feb2019/black-boys-matter.

Wright, Brian L., with Shelly L. Counsell. 2018. *The Brilliance of Black Boys: Cultivating School Success in the Early Grades.* New York: Teachers College Press.

Wright, Brian L., and Donna Y. Ford. 2017. "Untapped Potential: Recognition of Giftedness in Early Childhood and What Professionals Should Know About Students of Color." *Gifted Child Today* 40 (2): 111–116. doi.org/10.1177/1076217517690862.

4

Leading Gifted Hispanic Learners Toward Self-Advocacy

Dina Brulles, Ph.D.

Raul's Story

When Raul entered his second-grade classroom in January, it was his first formal experience in school. Recent immigrants from Mexico, Raul and his parents and two siblings lived in a small apartment along with his two cousins and their mother. Raul walked through the classroom door that day in January without making eye contact with anyone. He looked relieved when he realized I spoke Spanish, but he still did not speak. He spent that first day not speaking to anyone, not even the other Spanish-speaking students in the class. But I noticed his timid eyes would flash around the room when he thought it would go undetected.

The second day, Raul entered the classroom in the same way: with his head low and eyes subtly flashing around. When passing by me, however, he mumbled the word *ygriega*. I realized right away that he was referring to the daily analogy I had written on the board: 3:13 as O: _____. *Ygriega* is the Spanish pronunciation for the letter *y*. I was amazed that even though Raul had not yet learned to read in English nor was he familiar with the classroom procedures, he understood the cognitive process of analogies.

In May of that year, the principal came and read a poem to the class. He repeated the poem three times using an expressive voice, tone, and feelings, and demonstrating intensity in his words and gestures. Meanwhile, I watched Raul doodling on a piece of paper at his desk. After the principal left, Raul showed me the paper he had been doodling on. It was the poem that had so strongly grasped his attention, "We Real Cool" by Gwendolyn Brooks. After hearing it the first time, he wanted to have those words, so he'd written them down as best he could—nearly perfectly.

Raul took the Naglieri Nonverbal Ability Test (NNAT) shortly thereafter and answered every question correctly. Solving analogies, as he did on his second day of school, involves identifying relationships and making connections. Raul's keen powers of observation and ability to make connections were apparent. He was a gifted student (Brulles et al. 2008).

Introduction

This chapter is devoted to addressing the need for students of Hispanic cultures to self-advocate. We acknowledge that Hispanic students originate from many nations, and not all Hispanic students enter into schools as English language learners (ELLs). In many communities, Hispanic students are second- and third-generation citizens. The vignettes in this chapter are about specific students originating from Hispanic communities.

Raul's story is similar to the stories of thousands of gifted Hispanic learners who attend schools throughout the United States and who may struggle to advocate for themselves. In Raul's case, aside from speaking very little English, he and his parents operate under a different set of cultural norms than Raul's teachers. They view speaking up for special services as drawing unwanted attention to the family and showing disrespect for school authorities. Throughout this chapter, you will read examples describing why many Hispanic students can benefit from teachers advocating for them and why we need to help Hispanic gifted learners learn ways to self-advocate in their classrooms and schools. You will also explore ways to help Hispanic gifted students self-advocate for gifted services and extended learning opportunities.

Gifted Hispanic Students

Hispanic students have unique sociocultural and linguistic characteristics that can affect their learning and self-advocacy. Holding gifted Hispanic students to commonly held mainstream standards that contradict acculturation, their values, and their beliefs creates counterproductive outcomes for both teachers and students. Studies have shown that teachers unfamiliar with Hispanic culture perceive these students as having lower academic potential than their gifted White counterparts (Ford 2013; Leon 2018; Siegle et al. 2016).

> Brilliance can be seen in many contexts, and in many ways, regardless of cultural experiences or the languages students speak. As educators, we just need to know how to look for it.

Studies also show that teachers praise and encourage White students more often than they do Hispanic students, most likely because they misconstrue reasons for Hispanic students' observable behaviors (Brulles, Castellano, and Laing 2010). Hispanic students may feel less adequate than their peers because of the lack of learned skills and because of others' misperceptions of them. The question becomes, then, how can schools enfranchise gifted Hispanic students while honoring these students' culture?

Raul's single statement, "*Ygriega*," was a small sign that suggested he was very smart. Sharing the answer was his attempt to self-advocate—to show that he could solve a problem, even if he could not articulate it in English. All teachers have had students who have shown sparks of brilliance such as I saw with Raul. Often, teachers will see this spark when a student simply looks at a problem and comes up with a unique solution. These students see relationships that others don't, they ask insightful questions, and they have active imaginations. You may see this in mathematics, science, music, sports trivia, or knowledge of exotic plants. You see it in the child who takes apart a toy and puts it back together in no time, in the student who learns multiple languages with ease, in the learner who quickly acquires highly advanced technological skills. Brilliance can be seen in many contexts and in many ways, regardless of cultural experiences or the languages students speak (Naglieri, Brulles, and Lansdowne 2008). As educators, we just need to know how to look for it.

An Expanded View of General Ability and Giftedness

Put simply, all gifted students have high general ability, and this ability crosses over to all that they do in school. General ability is the foundation that allows people to learn. It allows people to remember facts, work with information, and understand numerous concepts. The content of the questions on a test of general ability may be verbal or visual or may require memory or recognition, but general ability is the foundation. When we think of general ability this way, we can then consider what rests on that foundation. If the foundation is weak, the learning is difficult and the rate of acquiring new information is slow. If the foundation is strong, then knowledge and skills are acquired at a fast pace and with extraordinary depth.

Regardless of the way the tests are given or the variety of the types of questions tests use to identify giftedness, all measure general ability. But someone who has not yet acquired verbal and quantitative skills because of limited opportunities or a disability will probably do poorly on a traditional ability test that relies on three scales: verbal, quantitative, and nonverbal (Naglieri, Brulles, and Lansdowne 2008).

Nonverbal Tests as a Measure of General Ability

Nonverbal measures of general ability are particularly useful for identifying gifted children from diverse populations, and especially so for those with limited opportunities to learn. And they are essential for identifying gifted Hispanic students who may have limited verbal skills in the language of the tests provided.

Given the diversity in gifted children's learning needs, it stands to reason that the identification process should vary as well as the instructional approaches teachers incorporate. There are gifted children who demonstrate high academic achievement, and there are gifted children whose academic skills may be average or even below average. Gifted children may speak various languages and come from a wide range of cultures, and for a variety of reasons, might not have been included in gifted programs. Their giftedness may not have been identified when general measures of ability that require comprehension of written language and/or quantitative test items have been used (Naglieri, Brulles, and Lansdowne 2008).

To counter this trend and make teachers aware of students' abilities, we must use identification tools appropriate for our student population. And when teachers are aware of Hispanic students' hidden potential, they will be more attuned to hearing these students' self-advocacy attempts. Less biased identification methods can be classified into two groups—those that use different tests and

ADVOCACY IN ACTION

Examine the tests and process your school uses to identify gifted students and answer the questions that follow. Do the tests and process:

- invite diversity?
- rely heavily on the English language?
- measure general ability?
- equitably identify giftedness in all student populations?

To create equitable identification practices:

- Use standardized ability tests (such as the Naglieri Nonverbal Ability Test) to eliminate bias and emphasize potential over achievement.

- Incorporate multiple measures to allow for different perspectives and expand identification opportunities when scores are not combined.

- Include identification tools that are culturally fair and linguistically unbiased to enfranchise underrepresented populations and increase equity in your identification process. Such assessments include the Raven's Matrices and the Universal Nonverbal Intelligence Test (UNIT).

those that use tests differently (Peters and Engerrand 2016). The first group includes nonverbal tests (such as the Naglieri Nonverbal Ability Test, or NNAT), broader ability tests with nonverbal sections (such as the Cognitive Abilities Test, or CogAT), and standardized performance assessments and observational protocols (such as U-STARS~PLUS.) The second group contains tools already typically used in schools (for example, academic achievement tests, rating scales, observations, and portfolios) to determine local norms. Using this information, educators can identify the most advanced students within the building who are most likely to be underchallenged and would benefit from accelerated or enriched instruction.

Admittedly, it is easier to identify and serve gifted Hispanic learners in some states due to how the gifted mandate is written. For example, reaching these goals in Arizona is easier than in some other states because the state gifted mandate has no requirement of advanced academic achievement for gifted identification; rather, identification is based solely on general ability. Schools identify giftedness based on students' potential and then work toward developing that potential. Relying on potential for the gifted identification without emphasizing academic achievement allows for students who have high ability that has yet to manifest itself as high achievement to participate in gifted programs.

While every state (and many districts within each state) may identify gifted students differently, the US federal government's definition describes gifted and talented students as those "who give evidence of high achievement capability in areas such as intellectual, creative, artistic, or leadership capacity, or in specific academic fields, and who need services and activities not ordinarily provided by the school in order to fully develop those capabilities" (US Department of Education 2004). The key word here is "capability." It is vital those who advocate for all gifted children help their constituencies identify and serve those gifted learners who currently display capability but may not yet have high achievement.

Barriers Experienced by Hispanic Students

Cultural barriers can impair Hispanic students' ability to readily understand content, which can mask high ability levels. For example, a typical word problem in mathematics may include scenarios or cultural references that are foreign to some students. Consider the following:

> While traveling across the country on a road trip, Erica's family spent two hours at a pecan farm, five hours at an amusement park, six hours at a national park exploring caverns, and nine hours at the car service center. How many total hours did Erica's family spend at tourist attractions?

To answer this math problem correctly, students would need a certain level of proficiency in the English language and would also need to know which of these activities are considered tourist attractions (Naglieri, Brulles, and Lansdowne 2008). Cultural references such as those in the math problem that are embedded into curriculum often go unnoticed by teachers but may unintentionally confuse Hispanic students. This confusion stems from the cultural reference, not from the student's intelligence or ability.

Barriers commonly experienced by Hispanic learners generally fall into two categories: in-district influences that impact opportunity, and cultural impediments to gifted services and self-advocacy.

ADVOCACY IN ACTION

Examine your upcoming lesson plans to identify areas and activities where cultural bias or barriers could interfere with Hispanic students' understanding of what is being asked. How could the lesson be modified to improve understanding for these students?

Influences That Impact Opportunity

Influences that negatively impact learning opportunities for Hispanic students in gifted education exist throughout our school structures and within daily interactions between parents, teachers, and students. We can see these influences in our interactions with parents, in our predisposed assumptions of certain groups' cultural norms, and in the ways in which we structure our learning environments and instruction. Awareness of these influences can break down the barriers that impede the self-advocacy of Hispanic students.

When structuring gifted services, we must consider:

> what educators need to know about parental influence within the school's cultural groups

> how group identity factors differ among the various underrepresented groups and their impact on the student

> how the school setting fits with students' social and cultural experiences

> how students can become partners in their education by self-advocating for what they need

Cultural Impediments to Gifted Services and Self-Advocacy

Cultural dichotomies in a school sometimes go unrecognized or underestimated by those planning instructional programs. The school structure in the United States supports gifted education for the historically dominant culture by emphasizing high standardized test scores, competitiveness, superior academic skills, achievement or other evidence of excellence, and assertiveness. These typical indicators of success may impede Hispanic gifted students' self-advocacy because they do not necessarily correlate with indicators of success for their cultures.

Teachers' perceptions and treatment of gifted Hispanic students may differ from the way they would perceive gifted White students. Teachers may assume that Hispanic students do not have the motivation or drive to accelerate their own learning because the behaviors they exhibit differ from those of other gifted identified students. This may occur because too many pre-service programs teach only the traditional characteristics of gifted learners. In other cases, it may be the result of cultural mismatch between teachers and students. Teachers who are part of the dominant culture are more familiar with, and comfortable relating to, the behaviors of the dominant culture. Such teachers may not recognize self-advocacy attempts by Hispanic students. Examples of students' indirect appeals and our possible responses to them are listed later in the chapter. (See **table 4.1** on page 52.)

The dilemma of "fitting in" for Hispanic gifted students greatly impacts their schooling options. Hispanic cultures in the United States generally strive to build connections and assimilate into the dominant culture while maintaining their own strong cultural links in their daily lives. For many Hispanic families in the United States, these values often lead families to accept placement into existing public-school programs located in their home community. Therefore, cultural values and behaviors can prevent identified Hispanic students from participating in gifted education services when these services remove students from their homeroom classes or home schools.

Consistent with cultural behaviors and values that encourage inclusion, many Hispanic families teach children not to act in ways that cause them to stand out from their peers. Leaving the general classroom for gifted education services is a visual and physical reminder of not fitting in. The inherent structure of the commonly used pull-out services model may be incompatible with Hispanic cultural values, resulting in students or families opting out of gifted services even if, and after, their students have been identified as gifted.

Another obstacle to Hispanic gifted students receiving services involves the expectation in some Hispanic families that the older children provide daily care for their younger siblings. Parents rely on older children to watch over younger children both outside and inside the home. This valued familial practice may prevent some students from receiving appropriate instruction when gifted services are provided away from the students' home school, especially if younger siblings attend the home school. It can also prevent students from participating in after-school enrichment opportunities.

Gifted Hispanic students who opt out of gifted services that are provided outside the classroom or school generally do not request other services, such as curriculum differentiation or accelerated schoolwork within their regular classroom. The desire to fit in, an emphasis on showing respect for authority, and having undocumented family members can all contribute to this opting out. School staff may be unaware of these impediments to participating in gifted services.

What can we do? We must encourage Hispanic students to self-advocate by informing teachers of the familial responsibilities, customs, or concerns that keep them from participating in gifted services. Together with students and parents, we can find the alternatives that will better address the needs of the whole child.

Initiating Change

Building sustainable gifted services designed to enfranchise Hispanic students and other underrepresented populations involves building stakeholder support, including support from parents, school staff, district administrators, and students. The students must be partners from the beginning and understand their own giftedness, rights, responsibilities, characteristics, options, and how to communicate with their advocates. This involves drawing attention to these students' specific needs and to the inequity of the existing structures. When advocating for stakeholder support, provide information to all groups associated with the school district.

The primary goal when developing effective gifted programs is to build services that reflect the school's current needs. The school's population, demographics, and goals determine those needs. Educators who become more adept at identifying gifted Hispanic students do so through a combination of traditional and nontraditional identification measures. Consider the following pertinent questions which are addressed throughout the remainder of this chapter:

> How can educators help gifted Hispanic students gain access to specialized instruction?

> What types of programs can provide gifted Hispanic students access to gifted education services?

> How can program administrators gauge whether they are appropriately serving their gifted Hispanic students?

> How can practitioners in the district encourage and support the self-advocacy of gifted Hispanic learners?

Enfranchising Hispanic gifted students really does take a village! All school personnel (including teachers, counselors, gifted specialists, Title I administrators, and ELL staff) should examine how their procedures assist with, or create barriers for, recognizing Hispanic gifted students' learning needs and serving Hispanic gifted populations and other underrepresented groups. Attention toward this goal requires a systematic approach that involves interaction and collaboration among all departments within a school system. Interactions with the Title I coordinator (whose programs serve all students from poverty), the language acquisition department, counselors, and special area teachers are key.

Title I and Language Acquisition

Interact and collaborate with the Title I coordinator and language acquisition coordinator by sharing information on gifted Hispanic students. Enlist the help of the language acquisition department by providing training in gifted education to help language acquisition assessment specialists recognize signs of giftedness in the students they test. With this understanding, these resource personnel can:

> advise classroom teachers on which ELL students to nominate for gifted testing

> provide training to ELL teachers so they can better recognize giftedness and develop potential in their students as they acquire and strengthen English language skills

> begin to encourage students to self-advocate

This represents a proactive attempt to increase proportional representation throughout gifted education programs.

Yelitza's Story

A recent immigrant from El Salvador, Yelitza is a first-grade ELL student. After training in gifted education and in the unique traits of gifted Hispanic students, the language acquisition testers at Yelitza's school recognized that "spark" indicative of giftedness and recommended her for gifted testing. She scored a 95 percent on the Naglieri Nonverbal Ability Test (NNAT). Yelitza's ELL teacher was shocked at how quickly she was acquiring English proficiency. Although Yelitza's academic achievement was understandably low, her teacher began to notice more signs of Yelitza's mental acuity. She noticed Yelitza would perceptively make connections others did not. She noticed the fine attention to detail and perspective Yelitza would include in her illustrations. And she noticed Yelitza's inquisitive nature across content areas. This inquisitiveness can be seen as attempts to self-advocate.

Special Area Teachers

Make a point to share information on giftedness with fine arts teachers and other special area teachers. Teachers of art, music, band, orchestra, and even physical education often see strengths and talents in students that classroom teachers may not notice. This is particularly true with gifted Hispanic students who may not yet be excelling academically.

Providing exposure to the traits of gifted Hispanic students can be eye-opening to special area teachers. These teachers may recognize unusually advanced, nuanced, or insightful aptitude and ability in students. Encourage special area teachers to nominate or refer students for gifted testing if teacher nominations are the practice in your school. Identifying Hispanic students as gifted via these unconventional methods can heighten classroom teachers' awareness of the advanced potential students might demonstrate in nonacademic areas. With this awareness, classroom teachers can then nurture those talents, which strengthen and become more evident through academic instruction. They can also begin to encourage students to self-advocate.

> Special area teachers often see strengths and talents in students that classroom teachers may not notice.

Rafael's Story

Rafael's family has a long history of making music. His father, uncles, and grandfather sing in mariachi bands. Rafael grew up hearing his family members sing and play their guitars and trumpets. When he started taking band at school, he wowed everyone who heard him play his trumpet. Instead of teaching Rafael how to blow the horn, fingering, and basic songs, the band teacher allowed Rafael to learn to read music, which he did with astonishing ease and speed. He was soon able to write out the music to the songs he grew up hearing his family members play. The band teacher recognized Rafael's advanced ability and built on that strength. Learning to write music gave Rafael confidence that then translated into improved achievement in his classroom. This newly found confidence helped Rafael improve his ability to self-advocate in the classroom as well.

> ## ADVOCACY IN ACTION
>
> Work with your coordinator to create a presentation for the special area teachers in your school that describes gifted students' natures and needs. Include an example in each teacher's area demonstrating how they might build on Hispanic students' strengths in that area. Explain self-advocacy and ask teachers to encourage their students to speak up and ask questions when their interests are piqued in class.

Traits to Look for in Gifted Hispanic Students

While gifted traits vary within different cultures of Hispanic students, a number of similarities exist. The list describes traits teachers can look for when nominating or referring Hispanic students for evaluation for gifted services. Being aware of these characteristics also helps teachers recognize students' self-advocacy attempts.

Characteristics that can indicate the gifted potential of Hispanic students include (Brulles and Winebrenner 2019):

> ability to learn English quickly

> articulation in role-playing and storytelling

> richness in informal language

> high interest in certain topics

> ability to learn quickly

> evidence of creative ability in thinking or problem-solving

> ability to see relationships and make connections

> ability to improvise with everyday objects

> exceptional ability in any of the fine arts

> exceptional talents in areas valued by their culture

> curiosity

> persistence

> independence

> keen observation skills

> self-directedness

> preference to not to stand out in a group

> tendency to identify and correct their own mistakes (but not others')

> ability to carry responsibilities well

> originality and imagination

> sense of responsibility to their cultural peers and family

Accessing Options

School administrators need to consider how aspects of Hispanic students' cultures might interfere with gifted service schedules. Consider two common practices among Hispanic families. First, families often prefer that their children remain at their home school. Second, many are not willing to have their children participate in gifted programs that fall outside of the regular school day. School districts that bus gifted students to a school within the district to participate in the district's gifted services, as well as those that offer gifted services after the school day, thus create obstacles for Hispanic gifted students. Hispanic families commonly rely on older siblings to accompany younger siblings to and from school and/or care for them at home when the parents are working. In these cases, gifted children are not able to participate in services offered in after-school settings.

Strategies to Encourage and Support Gifted Hispanic Students' Self-Advocacy

Providing inclusive gifted services that embrace diversity doesn't happen by accident; it requires careful consideration of student demographics, a comprehensive gifted identification process, and a continuum of options designed for serving a school district's specific student population. All schools should provide a comprehensive identification process designed to identify all students with high ability and high potential. Implementing effective gifted services in a sustainable way requires strategic planning in a manageable timeframe. Oftentimes schools take a passive approach to determining how gifted services will be offered.

Many schools seek to identify students who will be successful in existing gifted programs and do not consider specific student strengths. They then wonder how to correct underrepresentation. Consider a different approach. After identifying students as having high ability, determine if adjustments to programming or curriculum and instruction are needed to best serve those students. Include students in the planning process, listening carefully for subtle hints of self-advocacy. Letting gifted Hispanic students know what options are available encourages them to choose those that match their needs and learner profiles. This responsive approach requires that schools continually enhance their existing programs to be more inclusive and to serve all their gifted identified students.

> **ADVOCACY IN ACTION**
>
> Tips for creating a successful gifted program:
> - *First* identify students with high potential.
> - *Then* develop your services in response to student needs.
> - *And then* identify the training and curriculum needed to prepare teachers to teach in your model(s).

Factors That Influence Gifted Programming for Hispanic Students

Gifted education models and provisions commonly incorporate variations of content acceleration, enrichment, and differentiated curriculum and instruction. These instructional methods can be provided through inclusion or pull-out models. In inclusion models, students receive modifications and accommodations to curriculum and instruction in the regular classroom. In pull-out models, differentiated learning experiences are provided by a gifted education teacher outside of the regular classroom. Whether they are provided inside or outside the regular classroom, acceleration, enrichment, and curriculum differentiation benefit all gifted students. When used with culturally and linguistically diverse gifted students, these instructional methods can be more or less effective depending upon how the instruction is provided and in what setting.

School administrators and teachers must address the inherent limitations of program models or instructional methods when applied to gifted Hispanic students. For example, solely using content area acceleration for instruction in a pull-out model, or as an acceptance requirement for gifted services, denies access to gifted students who are not yet proficient in the English language. Hispanic students will not self-advocate for gifted services that they do not feel are appropriate for them. District administration can support inclusionary efforts to make sure gifted services align with the district's goals. Most districts' mission statements typically call for challenging all learners and providing equitable services for all. Given the broad range of students' achievement levels, this means that students are not all working on the same exact material at the same exact time.

Transfer that thought to how we teach gifted students. As with all students, gifted students' learning needs vary. Why would one assume then that all gifted students will be successful in a gifted program that does not distinguish between students' learning needs? With this in mind, build in methods to recognize and respond to the need to teach students at their challenge levels. (See **table 4.1.**) Ensure that students (and their parents) have reflected on their needs, are aware of their challenge levels, and understand which options are right for them. This awareness and understanding will encourage students' self-advocacy.

TABLE 4.1: Recognizing and Responding to Student Self-Advocacy	
STUDENT SAYS	**TEACHER CONSIDERS**
Can I work with _____ on my project?	Flexible grouping
Can I read ahead (of the class)?	Acceleration
I have an idea about how to . . .	Self-directed learning
I would like to learn more about . . .	Interest-based learning
I wonder how _____ works.	Enrichment Problem-based learning
I have an idea of something I'd like to study. Can I . . . ?	Project-based learning
Let me tell you about something I am working on at home.	Independent study

Be aware of students' attempts to self-advocate for differentiated learning opportunities and intentionally look for these attempts. Encourage students by hearing and responding to them. Student self-advocacy attempts may be as subtle as asking teachers questions or making statements such as those included in **table 4.1**.

ADVOCACY IN ACTION

Examine the structure of your school's or district's gifted services. Using rationale from this chapter, identify three to five areas that may interfere with how gifted Hispanic students learn. Brainstorm ways to overcome these obstacles. How can you make sure students are part of the process?

Looking at Programming Through an Equity Lens

Developing an equity mindset ensures that all students who are identified as gifted receive the services they need. This mindset propels schools to continually expand gifted services in response to identified need. It encourages flexibility in designing gifted services with a goal toward providing a continuum of services designed for the specific learning needs of the school's gifted identified students.

Schools have traditionally relied heavily on acceleration to define instruction for gifted students. Content area acceleration represents one necessary and valuable way to differentiate for most gifted students. However, gifted students, especially those from diverse cultures and those who do not demonstrate proficiency in the English language, also benefit from opportunities to extend grade-level standards and curriculum through content *enrichment*. Solely emphasizing content acceleration for gifted services may lead to teachers overlooking other learning characteristics of diversely gifted students, and especially those of Hispanic students. **Table 4.2** indicates how four prevalent gifted program models can be modified to better serve gifted Hispanic students. It is important to understand how the various models differ so we can encourage gifted Hispanic students to consider which ones to self-advocate for based on their cultural norms.

TABLE 4.2: Gifted Education Service Models Through an Equity Lens

Type of Service	Description of Traditional Model	Modifications for Hispanic Gifted Students
Cluster grouping	Grouping gifted students together at each grade level	Include in the gifted cluster class those Hispanic students who score high on a gifted test but do not formally qualify.
Self-contained programs	Highly gifted students are grouped together to learn at accelerated levels and pace	Modify entrance criteria for Hispanic gifted students so that language is not a barrier for acceptance.
Enrichment	Typically, a pull-out program where students work on projects	Ensure that the enrichment aligns with Hispanic students' cultures.
Honors	Advanced-level academics in core content areas	Use tiered lessons with varying levels of depth and complexity to support gifted English language learners.

Professional Learning Opportunities: Strengthening Student-Teacher Interactions

Professional learning opportunities targeted to address gifted Hispanic students' learning needs are critical for supporting these students. Students are more willing to open up to teachers and take academic risks when they feel accepted and understood. This can be significant for culturally and linguistically diverse students for whom school structures and customs may be unfamiliar. Once trust has been established, students are more likely to exhibit attributes reflective of their giftedness and to self-advocate. Likewise, teachers may more easily recognize these students' actual learning abilities, increasing the likelihood that instruction will build upon inherent abilities and undeveloped talents.

To promote teacher efficacy in teaching Hispanic gifted students, direct professional learning toward *how* gifted students learn and include pedagogy of teaching them. When teachers focus only on content acceleration, they direct less attention toward areas that Hispanic students need to develop in order to be successful with that content. A more effective approach includes guiding the thinking processes and communication skills necessary for developing potential in the content areas. This approach not only helps students develop their strengths, but also identifies areas where they need further attention.

Objectives for professional learning in schools serving Hispanic populations include:

> Recognize and nurture behaviors usually demonstrated by Hispanic gifted students.

> Create conditions in which all students will be stretched to learn.

> Allow students to demonstrate and get credit for previous mastery of concepts and standards, regardless of the student's level of language mastery.

> Provide opportunities for faster pacing of new material, along with reinforcement of language development.

> Incorporate students' diverse interests into their independent studies and extension lessons.

> Facilitate sophisticated student research investigations in a way that builds upon cultural influences.

> Ensure that students have the information, insights, and strategies needed to self-advocate.

Professional learning opportunities should also consider the distinctive cultural norms of the groups represented in the school. Understanding these norms helps teachers recognize when students are quietly self-advocating and when and how they can help the student move to active, intentional self-advocacy. Schools and districts can provide such professional development offerings through districtwide and site-based workshops, teacher in-services, and staff meetings, and by promoting university coursework in gifted education.

By participating in professional learning opportunities, teachers and administrators can gain information to share with Hispanic parents and students to connect families with resources that offer supplemental opportunities they may not otherwise know about. For example, state and national gifted associations, universities, and some professional organizations offer scholarships and internships for Hispanic gifted students. Educators can make sure resources such as these are available to students by researching opportunities, translating materials, and holding parent-student information nights (providing translation services, if needed). They can also share information about these resources at parent-teacher conferences and in school newsletters. Access to these resources opens new opportunities for learning and can help students and families transition throughout the school years. Once exposed to opportunities such as these, students will gain confidence in future self-advocacy.

Family Communication

As interaction between the teacher and student builds, the teacher should work closely with the parents or guardians to help inform them of the academic and social and emotional needs of their gifted children. Some parents of gifted Hispanic students may not realize the significance of their children's exceptionalities or of the possibilities and opportunities available to their children. Hispanic parents need a clear understanding of the learning potential and distinctive affective concerns of their gifted children. Helping parents develop an understanding of giftedness as it relates to the dominant culture can encourage them to advocate for services that fit with their families' customs. Some parents may feel that, for the first time, someone in the school system recognizes their children's unique talents. These parents observe exceptional behaviors exhibited through their own cultural context but may be unaware of how those behaviors translate into learning in the educational system (Brulles and Lansdowne 2009).

We need to make sure that students have this same information so that they, alone or in concert with their parents, can self-advocate for the opportunities they need. Hispanic parents rarely question authority in the schools, and they encourage this practice in their children. Families' desires to become embedded into the community extend to the school setting, and that can override potential educational benefits for gifted young people. Such parents may not question the appropriateness of the school's gifted program for their child who qualifies for services. Hispanic students learn not to judge or criticize those in authority positions. They rarely self-advocate for something different than what others have, even when they would benefit from more challenging instruction.

> **ADVOCACY IN ACTION**
>
> Create an agenda and presentation for a parent-student meeting at your school or district. Keep it simple to start. Identify a few specifics that you believe will help your Hispanic parents and students, such as the gifted characteristics of Hispanic students and what the gifted identification tells us about how these students learn.

For optimal assistance to the community, the gifted coordinator that serves students in a Hispanic community should have the ability to relate to parents in Spanish when possible. This need is vitally important to the growth and development of Hispanic gifted students whose parents may lack information about the unique characteristics and needs of their gifted children. An educator's ability to communicate clearly with students' parents also helps with family buy-in to the gifted education services offered at the school. Holding evening parent meetings in English and in Spanish supports this process and can build self-advocacy in both parents and students.

Examining Demographics

Keeping in mind that self-advocacy can conflict with Hispanic culture, it's essential to gather the demographic data showing the critical need to build self-advocacy in this population. To assist in efforts to enfranchise and build self-advocacy in Hispanic gifted learners (as well as others from disadvantaged and underrepresented populations), begin by examining the demographics. The percentage of students from any special population in the district should be roughly equivalent to the percentage of students from that population in gifted programming. When teachers are cognizant of the numbers of underidentified and underserved Hispanic learners, they become more sensitive to these students' efforts to self-advocate for their learning needs.

Analyze data at both the school and district levels. Examining the demographics of your gifted student population in relation to school and district demographics is the critical first step in creating equitable identification procedures and service models. Share the data with principals and district administration.

When looked at from a districtwide perspective, it is easy to ascertain the level of support and training needed at each school. Use this information to reach out to families to inform and enfranchise them. This effort is critical in building advocacy skills in Hispanic families and self-advocacy skills in their gifted children.

> **ADVOCACY IN ACTION**
>
> Collect and record the following data:
> - percentage of the student population identified and served as gifted, by year
> - percentage of the student population identified and served as gifted compared to the state average
> - ethnic representation of gifted students in relation to the school's or district's ethnic population
> - number and names of teachers obtaining a gifted endorsement or certification or participating in professional development offerings in gifted education

Conclusion

Effective gifted education programs should reflect the school's current needs and address its ethnic populations. This chapter recommends methods that promote equity so that Hispanic students can receive gifted services commensurate with their ability or potential. Efficacy in a school's ability to provide equitable service for gifted Hispanic students requires:

> the ability to meet the needs of all students with high potential

> documentation of students' academic growth

> increasing identification and service of gifted Hispanic students

With these goals in mind, teachers can more readily advocate for their Hispanic gifted learners and more importantly, recognize, respond to, and support these learners when they attempt to self-advocate.

Raul was very fortunate to be placed into a classroom whose teacher recognized his potential and whose school had structures and procedures in place that helped formally identify and develop that potential. Raul learned how to self-advocate for differentiated learning experiences because he felt comfortable and accepted by his teacher. Had these supports not been in place, Raul would be included in the statistics of the continually increasing number of gifted Hispanic students who have not had appropriate educational opportunities (Peters and Brulles 2017).

> **ADVOCACY IN ACTION**
>
> Give your students the writing prompt *What I want you to know about me.* All students in your class will benefit from this activity. Hispanic students, however, need you to specifically open this conversation, since many of them typically would not volunteer this personal information. When answering, students are sharing their strengths and interests because they are asked to do so. When you routinely use this activity with Hispanic students, you are encouraging them to speak up for themselves about what they want from their teachers and learning experiences.

Key Concepts

> General ability is universal among all populations.

> Cultural differences exist within Hispanic subpopulations, which help explain the challenges to self-advocacy for these groups.

> Hispanic students' self-advocacy can be fostered and supported through teachers' understanding of students' cultural values and experiences.

> Gifted programming should be established and structured in ways that enfranchise learners from diverse cultures.

> Professional learning in cultural diversity increases understanding of Hispanic gifted students' learning needs and informs instructional practices so that students feel accepted and understood, which can encourage self-advocacy.

> School districts can build support for students from diverse backgrounds through departmental collaboration, such as when interfacing gifted services with language acquisition, special education, and title school administrators.

Discussion Questions

1. When considering barriers faced by Hispanic and other underrepresented populations in gifted programs, reflect on the following questions. Do *all* our students believe that:

   - schools have their best interests at heart?

   - getting a good education will benefit everyone in the same way?

   - they can *each* pursue educational goals with the *same* outcomes in mind?

   Consider each of these questions carefully and individually. What do the answers reveal about variations among students' beliefs? Next, identify structures that exist in your school that may directly influence these differences and possible outcomes.

2. Reflect on and discuss how parental influence, group identity factors, and the impact of the school setting affect gifted Hispanic students. Delve into these three areas by answering the following questions as pertaining to your school or school district.

   a. Parental Influence
   - How does parental influence differ among the ethnic groups in your school or district?

   - How does parental influence in various groups impact the gifted student at school?

   - What do educators need to know about parental influence in the school's cultural groups?

   b. Group Identity Factors
   - What is fundamental with all identity groups?

   - Why are these identity group designations important? How do group identity factors differ among the various underrepresented groups?

   - How do group identity factors impact the child at school?

   - How does this impact student groups, both socially and cognitively, in the learning environment?

c. School Setting
- How does the school setting fit with Hispanic students' social and cultural experiences?
- What do educators need to know to better support Hispanic children's education?
- What specific steps can your school take to alter the course of action?

3. Either individually or as a group in your school or district, explore and identify specific resources and tools that can support the goal of identifying and serving gifted Hispanic students. How can you find and implement them?

Recommended Resources

Brulles, Dina, and Karen L. Brown. 2018. *A Teacher's Guide to Flexible Grouping & Collaborative Learning: Form, Manage, Assess, and Differentiate in Groups.* Minneapolis: Free Spirit Publishing.

Brulles, Dina, Jaime A. Castellano, and Peter C. Laing. 2011. "Identifying and Enfranchising Gifted English Language Learners." In *Special Populations in Gifted Education: Understanding Our Most Able Students from Diverse Backgrounds*, edited by Jaime A. Castellano and Andrea Dawn Frazier. Waco, TX: Prufrock Press.

Equity in Gifted/Talented Education. gtequity.org.

Naglieri, Jack, Dina Brulles, and Kim Lansdowne. 2021. *Naglieri Ability Tests: Verbal, Quantitative, and Nonverbal.* Toronto: Multi Health Systems.

National Association for Gifted Children. n.d. "Diversity Toolbox." nagc.org/resources-publications/resources /timely-topics/including-diverse-learners-gifted-education-program-1.

National Association for Gifted Children. n.d. "Increasing Equity in Gifted Education Programs and Services." nagc.org /resources-publications/resources/timely-topics/including-diverse-learners-gifted-education-programs.

Ritchotte, Jennifer, Chin-Wen Lee, and Amy Graefe. 2020. *Start Seeing and Serving Underserved Gifted Students: 50 Strategies for Equity and Excellence.* Minneapolis: Free Spirit Publishing.

Texas Education Agency, Equity in Gifted Education. 2006. "True or False?" gtequity.org/docs/self_assessment /trueorfalse.pdf.

References

Brulles, Dina, and Kim Lansdowne. 2009. "Enfranchising Gifted Hispanic English Language Learners Through Cluster Grouping." In *Encyclopedia of Giftedness, Creativity, and Talent,* edited by Barbara Kerr, 144–147. Thousand Oaks, CA: SAGE Publications.

Brulles, Dina, Scott J. Peters, and Rachel Saunders. 2012. "Schoolwide Mathematics Achievement Within the Gifted Cluster Grouping Model." *Journal of Advanced Academics* 23 (3): 200–216. doi.org/10.1177/1932202X12451439.

Brulles, Dina, and Susan Winebrenner. 2019. *The Cluster Grouping Handbook: A Schoolwide Model: How to Challenge Gifted Students and Improve Achievement for All.* Minneapolis: Free Spirit Publishing.

Ford, Donna Y. 2013. "Multicultural Issues: Gifted Underrepresentation and Prejudice—Learning from Allport and Merton." *Gifted Child Today* 36 (1): 62–67. doi.org/10.1177/1076217512465285.

Ford, Donna. 2015. "Multicultural Issues: Recruiting and Retaining Black and Hispanic Students in Gifted Education: Equality Versus Equity Schools." *Gifted Child Today* 38 (3): 187–191. doi.org/10.1177/1076217515583745.

Ford, Donna, and Jack Naglieri. 2005. "Increasing Minority Children's Participation in Gifted Classes Using the NNAT: A Response to Lohman." *Gifted Child Quarterly* 49 (1): 29–36. doi.org/10.1177/001698620504900104.

Leon Leal, Melissa I. 2018. "Underrepresentation of Hispanic Bilingual Students in Gifted and Talented Programs: The Role of Teacher Expectations." The University of Texas Rio Grande Valley: ProQuest Dissertation Publishing.

Matthews, Michael S., and Scott J. Peters. 2018. "Methods to Increase the Identification Rate of Students from Traditionally Underrepresented Populations for Gifted Services." In *APA Handbook of Giftedness and Talent,* edited by Steven I. Pfeiffer, Megan Foley-Nicpon, and Elizabeth Shaunessy-Dedrick, 317–331. Washington, DC: American Psychological Association Press.

Naglieri, Jack, Dina Brulles, and Kim Lansdowne. 2008. *Helping All Gifted Children Learn: A Teacher's Guide to Using the NNAT2.* San Antonio, TX: Pearson Assessments.

Peters, Scott J., and Dina Brulles. 2017. *Designing Gifted Education Programs and Services: From Purpose to Implementation.* Waco, TX: Prufrock Press.

Plucker, Jonathan A., Scott J. Peters, and Stephanie Schmalensee. 2017. "Reducing Excellence Gaps: A Research-Based Model." *Gifted Child Today* 40 (4): 245–250. doi.org/10.1177/1076217517723949.

Siegle, Del, E. Jean Gubbins, Patricia O'Rourke, Susan Dulong Langley, et al. 2016. "Barriers to Underserved Students' Participation in Gifted Programs and Possible Solutions." *Journal for the Education of the Gifted* 39 (2): 103–131. doi.org/10.1177/0162353216640930.

US Department of Education. 2004. "Title IX—General Provisions." ed.gov/policy/elsec/leg/esea02/pg107.html.

5

Emerging from the Shadows: Self-Advocacy of Gifted American Indian and Alaska Native Learners

Marcia Gentry, Ph.D., and Anne Gray, Ph.D.

There is no need
for you to give
back to us
what we already own

—Eric Gansworth, S·ha-weñ na-sae? (Onondaga, Eel Clan), 2018

American Indian and Alaska Native (AIAN) students are overlooked and underserved in gifted education and viewed from a deficit perspective in education in general. Their cultures are invisible or appropriated, and unless they are among the 8 percent of AIAN young people who attend Bureau of Indian Education (BIE) schools, they likely attend classes where neither educators nor other students know about or understand their cultures. To effectively educate these young people, teachers need to educate themselves about their AIAN students' cultures and Nations. Teachers need to see their students and listen to them as they describe their wants and needs, while genuinely caring about and connecting to them.

AVOIDING ESSENTIALIZATION

In this chapter, American Indians and Alaska Natives have been referred to collectively. This is due in part to the construction of seven racial categories and their use in the collection of data in the United States, and the similarities in how Native Nations experienced settler colonialism. There are currently 573 federally recognized, and approximately another 60 state-recognized, Native Nations. Each has a unique history, origin story, language, and traditions. And within a Nation's shared culture and traditions, there can be found variations from one home to the next. It's critical for educators to see that each AIAN student is a unique individual who cannot and must not be treated as a number or reduced to a stereotype. When helping gifted AIAN students self-advocate and achieve their potential, it is of utmost importance that we listen to their voices and their stories and avoid essentialization.

Kate's Story

Please meet Kate, a sixteen-year-old Diné girl, who grew up on the Navajo Nation where she attended a BIE elementary school with about four hundred other Diné students. Identified with gifts and talents, Kate thrived in this school, performing in the top 15 percent on standardized tests using national norms. However, as she entered middle school, her family moved away from the reservation and enrolled her in a Midwestern public middle school with about one thousand students. Kate went from being surrounded by other Diné students to being one of four Native students in her new school. BIE schools rank among the lowest performing schools in the United States, and Kate had significant gaps in her knowledge as she started middle school. She was given a single placement test at the start of sixth grade for math and science and, based on her scores, was denied access to the gifted and talented program at her new school. After extensive conversations with the principal and gifted coordinator at the school, Kate and her parents felt it would be better for her to be in the general education classes, anticipating that the staff's attitude of indifference to Kate's educational background would continue. However, this meant that Kate was "no longer gifted"—a message that adversely affected her self-esteem.

During middle school, Kate's grades went up and down. She would begin each quarter with As and Bs, but then she would falter mid-quarter and struggle to regain her grades before finals. She finished middle school with a 2.8 GPA on the 4-point scale, at which time the school counselor referred her to a remedial program, rather than encouraging her to take classes to prepare her for college. Kate was distressed by this placement and reported to her parents that the majority of students referred to the remedial program were brown like her.

Kate's parents appealed this placement, never receiving an acceptable justification from the school for why Kate would benefit from this remedial program. They won the appeal process, and Kate attended a regular high school program. Nevertheless, this entire process was detrimental to Kate's self-esteem, self-efficacy, and self-confidence in the school environment. Although she thrived in out-of-school enrichment, including at a summer camp she had attended for years, school for her became an endless challenge.

Kate continued to struggle to understand some math and science content and actively sought help from her teachers. This was difficult for her because she felt intimidated approaching White teachers who often only repeated the same information rather than helping her understand the material. Despite the fact that Kate was a talented leader and a wise young woman with aspirations to become an environmental scientist, her interests and talents went unrecognized and unnurtured in high school. Kate's teachers seemed to lack an understanding of her potential and interests, and she was invisible.

| Self-advocacy requires reciprocity. |

When Kate entered her sophomore year, she began to self-advocate and applied to a BIE college preparatory school. She gave the rigorous application process her best effort and found motivation in the opportunity to return to learning that embraced her culture and language and that provided an opportunity to work with teachers who would see and nurture her strengths. The opportunity to attend this school motivated Kate to work hard during her sophomore year, and she and her parents recently moved back to her reservation so she could attend the college prep school with other Diné students. Kate's confidence is returning as she thrives in a rigorous and culturally relevant college preparation program in which educators see her and believe in her.

Kate has continually self-advocated throughout her educational journey. For example, in sixth grade she self-advocated through accommodation (Masta 2018b) by entering the general education program, rather than setting herself up for failure by insisting she be admitted to the gifted program. She did this because it was clear to her that the school staff cared little about her academic ability or the differences in her educational background. In addition, she protected her self-identity by participating in traditional ceremonies and stepping into leadership roles in out-of-school activities. Kate self-advocated for assistance from teachers, but to no avail. When she had the opportunity to attend a school with a more rigorous academic program and culturally competent staff, she raised her grades to meet the academic criteria, studied, and passed the exams for admission. Kate's story shows how self-advocacy efforts from students must be received by teachers who are open to these efforts. Self-advocacy requires reciprocity.

Violet's Story

Violet is a Diné woman in her early twenties. Her family lives on the Navajo Nation on one of the checkerboard sections.* When Violet was ready to enter kindergarten, her older sister was attending the local BIE school. Their parents were very concerned about the low performance of students attending this school and the lack of academic rigor at the school. Violet's parents made the difficult decision to transfer their daughters to a public school district in which students had much higher academic performance. During her K–12 school years, Violet had a ninety-minute daily bus ride each way to and from school. Because of the distance and the resulting transportation issues, if the girls missed the bus, they missed school that day. This was the case for most of the Diné students from the area who attended these schools.

In second grade, Violet was tested for admission into the gifted and talented program, but she missed the cutoff score by a few points. Her advanced academic ability never came up again. Throughout elementary and middle school, Violet was always at the top of her class in all subjects. But she was one of "those kids" from the reservation. In general, teachers had low expectations of, and what appeared to be apathy for, "those kids." Staff and non-Native students were always surprised to learn how well Violet did in school.

Violet's first overt act of self-advocacy was registering for AP classes during her freshman year of high school. Despite Violet's record of academic achievement, none of her teachers nor her guidance counselor recommended or encouraged her to take AP courses. In fact, none of the staff expected any of "those kids" to go to college.

In middle school, Violet was limited to extracurricular activities that met during school hours, but in high school her parents were able to juggle their schedules to give her one day a week for after-school activities. She used this opportunity to pursue her academic goals and joined the National Honor Society, the Mathematics, Engineering, Science Achievement (MESA) program, and the Society for Advancement of Chicanos/Hispanics and Native Americans in Science (SACNAS). Despite Violet's self-advocacy, advanced course load, and consistently high GPA, her teachers, counselors, administrators, and peers continued to underestimate her intelligence and motivation.

In her junior year, Violet heard about the College Horizons program, and in another act of self-advocacy, immediately applied for their summer college preparation program.† At College Horizons, Violet was mentored by Native college graduates who supported and encouraged her higher education goals. She worked with these adult mentors together with other Native students who had similar drive and motivation to attend college. With her mentors' assistance, guidance, and encouragement, Violet was able to complete applications on time for all the schools she selected.

---

*Some of the land of the Navajo Nation is interspersed with land that is not part of the reservation. On a map this creates a pattern similar in appearance to a checkerboard.

†College Horizons is a national nonprofit that provides college admissions workshops for American Indian, Alaska Native, and Native Hawaiian students in tenth and eleventh grades.

The one not-so-great experience she had in this program was with a non-Native mentor who was provided after the summer program concluded to assist Violet with the remaining parts of her applications. The writing prompt for one of the essays was, "Describe a difficult moment in your life." The mentor rejected Violet's idea for the essay and wanted her to write about her experiences and struggles in a way Violet felt exploited her personal trauma. Instead of following her mentor's directive, Violet, in an act of self-advocacy and self-determination, decided to write about the terrible accident her father had experienced earlier that year and the importance of family. She wrote about how her mother had spent long days at the hospital, relying on Violet and her older sister to care for their two younger brothers, and how new responsibilities and continuing transportation issues led to numerous absences from school during this family crisis. She continued to self-advocate as she asked her English teacher to help her edit and finalize her admissions essay. After she read Violet's essay, the English teacher began helping her with other applications, finding her resources such as application fee waivers and giving her support and encouragement to finish her senior year academically strong. This teacher saw Violet not as one of "those kids," but as an intelligent young woman with strong family ties and some difficult life situations. The teacher received Violet's self-advocacy and responded with reciprocity.

AIAN Students: Description and Context

American Indian and Alaska Native students with gifts and talents are often overlooked and misunderstood across the United States. Nationally, AIAN young people comprise 1.04 percent of the public-school student population. Because this is a small percentage, many researchers simply omit AIAN students from their inquiry and many educators lack cultural competencies needed to effectively connect with AIAN students in their classrooms.

Thus, researchers and educators are complicit in perpetuating the narrative about AIAN peoples that most Americans have been exposed to in history books and by the entertainment industry. This is a narrative of American Indians and Alaska Natives existing in the historical past or, when portrayed as contemporary, having deficits such as poverty, substance abuse, and low achievement. This is a narrative in which AIAN people are blamed for the barriers they experience because they continue to resist assimilation (Masta 2018a). An extensive review of the extant literature revealed that these deficit perspectives dominate the literature on AIAN students (Gentry and Fugate 2012). Invisibility and negative stereotypes perpetuated by omission and deficit perspectives combine to maintain the myth that giftedness among this group is near nonexistent (Gentry et al. 2014).

A truthful and contemporary narrative describes AIAN people as contributing citizens of the United States who participate in all professions and are active members of their Nations. This narrative fosters recognition of the gifts and talents of AIAN people as evidenced through their contributions to the sciences, mathematics, literature, politics, sports, and the arts, while simultaneously honoring their traditions, languages, and relations to land, water, and kin. Further, educators must understand that AIAN students are not a homogenous group; rather, they come from 573 federally recognized sovereign Native Nations, each with its own histories, traditions, and language.[++] The 573 Native Nations are spread across thirty-five states, yet AIAN students are educated in all fifty states (National Congress of American Indians 2020). There are 334 American Indian reservations in the United States (National Congress of American Indians 2020); however, in 2010, 78 percent of people who identified as AIAN did not reside on a reservation (US Census Bureau 2010). **Figure 5.1** depicts the percentage of AIAN young people in each state.

[++]There are more than 600 sovereign Native Nations in the United States. As of this writing, 573 are federally recognized, others are state recognized, and some are recognized only among other Native Nations (Reclaiming Native Truth 2018).

FIGURE 5.1: Percentage of AIAN Young People in State Student Populations

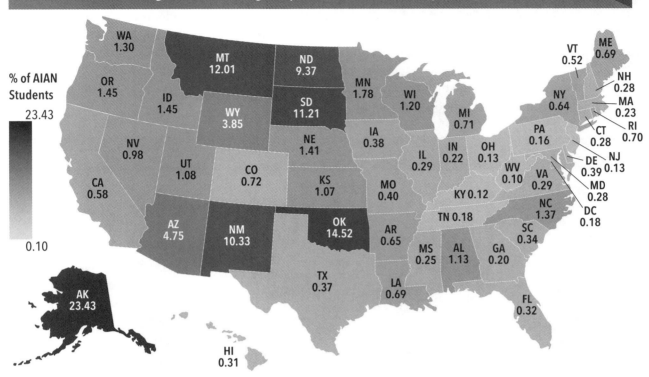

Used by permission. Gentry, Marcia, Anne Gray, Gilman W. Whiting, Yukiko Maeda, and Nielsen Pereira. 2019. *System Failure: Access Denied. Gifted Education in the United States: Laws, Access, Equity, and Missingness Across the Country by Locale, Title I School Status, and Race.* Report Cards, technical report, and website. West Lafayette, IN: Purdue University; Lansdowne, VA: Jack Kent Cooke Foundation.

Overview of the Current Status of AIAN Students in Gifted Education

Gentry, Gray, Whiting, Maeda, and Pereira (2019) analyzed the current status of AIAN students with gifts and talents using restricted data from the Civil Rights Data Collection (CRDC) by the Office of Civil Rights. In this review, they examined access, equity, and absence of data nationally and for each state. AIAN students' access to schools that identify students with gifts and talents is at only 0.92 the rate of other races. Nationally, 80 percent of AIAN students attend Title I schools compared to 68 percent of all students. So not only do AIAN students attend schools with fewer resources at a higher rate, but Title I schools also identify gifted and talented students at a lower rate (7.86 percent) than non-Title I schools do (13.46 percent).

Further, 92 percent of AIAN students are educated in twenty-seven states. Although equity exists in Oklahoma and Alabama, underrepresentation is pervasive and severe in South Dakota, Alaska, Arizona, Montana, New Mexico, and Minnesota—all states with large proportions of AIAN young people—with representation indices (RIs) ranging from 0.26 to 0.61. (Ideally, if a school is made up of 5 percent AIAN students and the gifted program is made up of 5 percent AIAN students, then the RI would be 1.00.)

Although 25,954 AIAN students were identified with gifts and talents nationally during 2015–2016, between 24,290 and 44,663 learners were missing from identification due to underidentification in schools that identify students or attendance in schools that do not identify students (see **figure 5.2**). Thus, 48 to 63 percent of potentially talented AIAN students were not identified. Further, AIAN students are largely invisible in gifted education research and within calls for equity in gifted education (Gentry et al. 2014). Because of their small numbers, due in part to genocide, their diverse cultural groups, and stereotypes that relegate them to the historic past, AIAN students are virtually invisible in educational research in general, as well as in the schools they attend.

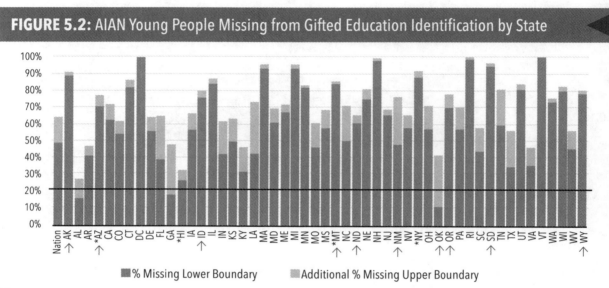

FIGURE 5.2: AIAN Young People Missing from Gifted Education Identification by State

■ % Missing Lower Boundary　　■ Additional % Missing Upper Boundary

Notes

- In states with an asterisk, the state average identification rate is higher than the state average non-Title I school identification rate. In these cases, the bars for "% Missing Lower Boundary" and "Additional % Missing Upper Boundary" are reversed.

- States indicated by an arrow (→) have the ten largest proportions of AIAN students in their student enrollment among schools that identify students with gifts and talents.

- The line at the 20% mark indicates a "passing" mark on missingness.

Used by permission. Gentry, Marcia, Anne Gray, Gilman W. Whiting, Yukiko Maeda, and Nielsen Pereira. 2019. *System Failure: Access Denied. Gifted Education in the United States: Laws, Access, Equity, and Missingness Across the Country by Locale, Title I School Status, and Race.* Report Cards, technical report, and website. West Lafayette, IN: Purdue University; Lansdowne, VA: Jack Kent Cooke Foundation.

Barriers to Identification

Barriers to the identification of AIAN students' gifts and talents include a lack of culturally competent educators, low expectations, teachers as gatekeepers, a lack of cultural peer groups and cultural role models, and the invisibility many AIAN students experience in public schools where there are few other AIAN students (Gentry and Fugate 2012).

Returning to Kate's Story

The barriers Kate and her parents experienced were not due to a lack of knowledge or understanding of giftedness. Rather, they were symptomatic of the invisibility of American Indians and Alaska Natives as contemporary peoples and of the power educators have, as gatekeepers, over students' academic advancement. It is very difficult to self-advocate when one is invisible.

Before Kate took the sixth-grade math and science placement tests, her parents had spoken to the middle school's administration and the teachers involved in the gifted education program. They detailed to the staff how Kate had qualified for the gifted program through her scores on standardized tests, how she excelled in her classroom, and that they expected she would have gaps in her content knowledge due to differences between the states' standards, the documented underperformance of BIE schools, and the lack of access to advanced curriculum at the small rural BIE school she had previously attended. Needless to say, Kate's parents were not surprised when her scores on the math and science placement tests were not high enough to qualify her for the gifted program. What did surprise them was the staff's lack of willingness to work with Kate to fill in her knowledge gaps. These educator-gatekeepers behaved with indifference to Kate's demonstrated high ability, which, due to lack of educational opportunities and resources, was not displayed in this one-time performance.

Kate and her parents were confronted with a difficult choice: press the school to admit Kate into the gifted program with no guarantee that the teachers would recognize her abilities and help her fill her knowledge gaps or concede and do their best to provide Kate with enrichment opportunities themselves. Their experience of the intractability of the school staff indicated that a change in attitude toward Kate's knowledge gaps was unlikely. This experience with unsupportive school adults, in addition to her struggles to adjust to the new learning environment, led Kate to believe she was "no longer gifted." However, she retained her identity as a young Diné woman, and her resiliency was not affected.

When Kate was placed in the remedial program for high school, she and her parents took immediate action. With no explanation for the placement, and only fluctuating classroom grades as a possible reason for it, Kate's parents appealed. The family's expectation was, and had always been, that Kate would go to college. Not only was placement in the remedial program a denial of Kate's abilities, but it would also not provide her with the coursework or diploma she needed to pursue a college education. Once again, educators were acting as gatekeepers and blocking Kate's access to the opportunities necessary to reach her goal of being an environmental scientist. Kate and her parents refused to agree with this remedial placement and enrolled her in the regular high school college preparatory program.

Kate had the same academic record her freshman year of high school that she had in middle school: fluctuating classroom grades while scoring at or above grade level on standardized tests. When the opportunity to apply to a BIE college preparatory school arose, Kate put every effort into the rigorous application process. She knew that at this school she would be with other Diné students and have teachers who would see and value her abilities. She knew educators at this school would recognize and support her efforts to self-advocate, open doors to opportunities that would help her pursue her career goals, and respect the value of her identity as a Diné woman. Kate worked hard her sophomore year, improved her grades, and was admitted as a junior to the International Baccalaureate program at the BIE preparatory school.

Returning to Violet's Story

Stereotyping and apathy were barriers that plagued Violet throughout her K–12 public school experience. Violet and the other Diné students at her school were regularly referred to as "those kids" by educators who had an underlying belief in the stereotype of AIAN students as intellectually and academically deficient (Lomawaima and McCarty 2006). This deficit perspective was so ingrained in the culture of the school that it had developed into educator apathy toward the students from the reservation. Even with clear evidence that Violet was very bright, it was not until she connected with an English teacher at the end of her high school education who developed a more personal understanding of her that Violet received any recognition for her advanced intellect and academic abilities.

Strategies for Educators

Educators have power and influence, and most intend to do good things for their students. Because there are precious few AIAN educators, most AIAN children are educated by teachers who are unfamiliar with their cultures. But teachers can learn and can relate to their students, and they hold the ability to inspire, to encourage, and to provide opportunities. Some of the steps they can take to encourage their AIAN students' self-advocacy and to help them reach their potentials follow.

Bring Visibility

One of the pressing issues for AIAN people is their invisibility. The most common social representations of Native peoples, if there are any, are ones that portray them in the historical past. Pocahontas and sports team mascots top the list of the most common images. There are few, if any, modern portrayals of Native peoples. How can AIAN students relate to these representations of Native people and construct ideas of their future selves from an image that conveys the message that people like them are not present in contemporary society, that people like them are extinct? Teachers and curriculum designers are in a position to change this error. Additionally, students from other cultural groups in classrooms across the nation receive this same message, which furthers the myth that AIAN people do not exist in contemporary society.

Educators can bring contemporary representations of Native peoples to all students. Curriculum can be enriched with the works of AIAN writers, poets, artists, musicians, politicians, dancers, scientists, environmental activists, human rights activists, lawyers, and more. Some resources are included in the recommended resources section of this chapter, but you will find that it often takes effort to locate the work of AIAN people in many professions. This is due to the societal invisibility and continued lack of opportunities experienced by AIAN people. However, providing these exemplars of contemporary Native people encourages AIAN students to see themselves in those roles and to self-advocate for broader, richer opportunities.

Acknowledge Native Nations and Their Ancestral Lands

Forty states currently have federally or state-recognized Native Nations within their borders, and the entirety of the United States exists on the ancestral lands of Native peoples. For example, Purdue University is located on the ancestral lands of the Bodéwadmi (Potawatomi), Myaamiaki (Miami), Shawnee, and Lenape (Delaware) Nations. Land acknowledgments can be done at the beginning of the year, as part of a daily opening routine, or to open school events. A land acknowledgment is a way to recognize the pre-colonial contact, post-colonial contact, and contemporary histories of the Native peoples upon whose ancestral land your building or community sits and aid in creating a classroom community that is welcoming of all students. For example, at Purdue, a non-Native professor might begin class by saying, "I would like to acknowledge that Purdue University is built upon the ancestral and unceded lands of the Bodéwadmi, Myaamiaki, Shawnee, and Lenape peoples. As a visitor to these lands, I would like our class to pay respect to the elders and their descendants who have stewarded these lands and waters since the beginning." Think how empowering this simple acknowledgment would be for your AIAN students.

Develop Cultural Competence

It is up to students if they want to reveal their tribal affiliation to the class, whether directly or through the sharing of stories about their life outside of school. If students have shared about their Nation, culture, or traditions, and you want to know more, do your own research. There are many resources for information listed in the recommended resources for this chapter. Do not ask your students to teach you about their cultures. This is not their role in your classroom, and it is a tiring activity for AIAN people who are confronted by uninformed and misinformed people on a regular basis. As pointed out earlier, within a Nation's shared culture and traditions can be found variations from home to home. Accept what you learn as a wide-angle view, a clue of how things *may* be in your students' families. It is appropriate to invite an AIAN student to participate in a general classroom conversation on holidays or traditions their families have. But all students should be allowed the right to not participate in this type of disclosure.

Keep an open mind and listen. Self-advocacy among AIAN students may not appear the same as it does among students from other cultures. For example, in eighth grade, Kate and her parents notified her teachers and the school administrators in advance that she would need her assignments for a week because she would be returning home to have her womanhood ceremony. The teachers and administrators suggested to Kate and her parents that requesting an absence such as this meant that the family did not understand the importance of school attendance. They told the family that if Kate exceeded the allowable days of absences for the quarter, she would have to repeat the classes. The school staff did not have an open mind nor the cultural competence to understand that the importance of a ceremony could outweigh the importance of class attendance for Kate and her family. In addition, they did not recognize the value Kate and her family placed on education when they requested her assignments well in advance of the ceremony nor did they consider that Kate had had no prior attendance issues.

Take an Asset Perspective

As with all historically marginalized groups, it can be easier to find or focus on information on what is going wrong within AIAN communities than it is to find information on what is going right. Although these negative factors exist within their environment and are worth being noted, it cannot be assumed that they directly affect your student. An asset perspective is not a denial of the barriers students bring with them to school. Rather, it is a strengths-based focus that identifies and builds on what is working well for the student. Nonassimilation into the majority culture is not a deficit, nor is assimilation necessary for the success of AIAN students with gifts and talents. Students who believe that you see their assets are more apt to turn to you as an advocate.

For Violet, this did not happen until her senior year in high school. Notably, even a short period of support and advocacy affected Violet in positive ways. She experienced the support of one teacher who took an interest in who she was as a student and as a person. Support such as this, in which educators care about, advocate for, and believe in their students, can make all the difference in the academic lives of AIAN students.

Conclusion

Because of the lack of factual information, the wealth of misinformation, and their invisibility in American society, AIAN people are overburdened with filling in the knowledge gaps of others on a daily basis. Allies standing *with* AIAN students can start by educating themselves, seeking information about Native peoples *from* Native people, and finding teachable moments in which to share what they have learned with and from students, colleagues, and others.

> AIAN students do not define themselves by their challenges; American society does. Rather, these students define themselves by their cultures, traditions, and relations—the assets in their lives.

AIAN students do not define themselves by their challenges; American society does. Rather, these students define themselves by their cultures, traditions, and relations—the assets in their lives. Gifted education also has an assets perspective, seeking out and nurturing the high abilities, potentials, and talents of students. Bringing visibility to AIAN students means staying aware of and catching the moments that reveal students' high ability. It could be in an area you did not expect, from a child you did not expect, or well-hidden. For AIAN students, breaking barriers not only means having the same opportunities as others, but also having their choices regarding those opportunities valued by others. As educators, we can support students' choices and encourage their self-advocacy.

Future Outlook

The future for AIAN students is bright! Just as Eric Gansworth said in the poem at the beginning of this chapter, AIAN students do not need us to give them back what they already have. Yet without increased visibility, greater knowledge of their histories and cultures, and contemporary representations of AIAN professionals, their participation in gifted education will likely remain low. Educators will strive to meet the educational needs of the majority culture, and AIAN students with gifts and talents will be under-identified and underserved because their abilities will continue to go unseen. Thus, awareness, action, and advocacy are key to mitigating this trend of underrepresentation and underidentification in gifted programs across the country.

Keys to discovering and developing talent among AIAN young people include increasing the number of AIAN teachers, increasing allies in education, and increasing opportunities for these students with high potential in schools across the country. As Gentry et al. (2014) suggested, more researchers need to include AIAN students in their research. Doing so will increase these students' visibility in the literature and, ultimately, in educational programming, including gifted education. AIAN youth may be invisible in schools, but they are increasingly visible on social media, bringing attention to the challenges they face and the creative solutions they have developed to overcome them.

Kate Epilogue

In the first month of her junior year, Kate was admitted to the gifted education reading and science programs at her school and joined an environmental science student group. Wednesdays are Traditional Clothes Days when students can choose to wear pieces or full outfits of traditional clothing from their Native Nations. Kate takes great pride in showing off the blouses and skirts her aunty made for her, the moccasins and leg wraps her parents gave her, and the rug-weave purse she was gifted by a family friend. None of her friends from her previous school ever saw these clothes. Now Kate gets to share the significance of these items and how they connect her to her relatives and her ancestors with little explanation needed.

Violet Epilogue

The high school staff and students were shocked when Violet was named as salutatorian of her senior class. Not until after graduation did Violet learn that the valedictorian had beaten her GPA by only one one-thousandth of a point. Violet was accepted to twelve of the fifteen colleges and universities to which she applied. She chose to attend a Northeastern Ivy League college and graduated with a Bachelor of Arts degree in Ethnic Studies in 2018. She is currently completing her first year of graduate school in American Studies at a state university.

Self-Advocacy

The focus of this book is self-advocacy, but self-advocating is difficult when one is invisible. Self-advocacy takes strength, courage, and resolve, and it is challenging for populations that have experienced marginalization, genocide, and invisibility. For example, despite her parents' advocacy for her, Kate had to leave the large public school and enroll in a school that would honor her culture. Kate self-advocated for her needs by moving across the country to attend a school where her culture is seen and celebrated, and she is now thriving. This is not possible for all AIAN students in public schools. Moreover, such drastic moves should not be necessary. Perhaps by sharing this chapter and by speaking up, you can strengthen the voices of allies and help create changes that can positively affect gifted AIAN students. As these students continue to achieve despite adversity, lack of understanding, and invisibility, they pave the way for others who follow them. Developing a supportive environment takes allies, perseverance, and resolve. Advocacy involves all stakeholders.

Key Concepts

> American Indian and Alaska Native students are overlooked and underserved in gifted education and viewed from a deficit perspective in education in general.

> Keys to discovering and developing talent among AIAN students include increasing the number of AIAN teachers, increasing allies in education, and increasing opportunities for these young people with high potential.

> Allies standing *with* AIAN students can educate themselves, seek information about Native peoples *from* Native people, and find teachable moments in which to share what they have learned with and from students, colleagues, and others.

Discussion Questions

1. What do you currently know about American Indians and Alaska Natives, and where did this information come from?

2. How can educators identify and serve AIAN students with gifts and talents?

3. What is the connection between the visibility of AIAN students and a land acknowledgment?

4. Which suggestions in the Strategies for Educators section resonate with you and why?

5. Is it okay for a non-Native person to dress up as an AIAN person for Halloween? Why or why not?

Recommended Resources

This section contains resources for educators. First, **table 5.1** lists professionals who are AIAN. These individuals can serve as models and examples for students. Following the figure are lists of online resources, books, and articles. None of these lists is comprehensive. Rather, they are starting points for educators to consider. Additionally, in many cities, you can find local nonprofit organizations that serve AIAN community members from many Nations. These organizations often have websites or social media sites. (For example, check out the Albuquerque Indian Center at abqindiancenter.org, the American Indian Center of Chicago at aicchicago.org, and the United Indians of Milwaukee, Inc. on Facebook.) You can check your local area for similar organizations. Finally, most university communities have Native American student organizations that serve the AIAN students on their campuses. These organizations might provide a link to the K–12 community as well as present mentorship opportunities for students to spend time with role models similar to them who are succeeding in college.

TABLE 5.1: American Indian and Alaska Native Professionals

NAME	PROFESSION
Lori Alvord	Surgeon, author
Ron Baker	Professional basketball player
Twyla Baker	President, Nueta Hidatsa Sahnish College
Ryneldi Becenti	Professional basketball player
Fred Begay	Nuclear physicist
Notah Begay III	Professional golfer
Sam Bradford	NFL football player
Bryan Brayboy	Professor of indigenous education and justice at Arizona State University
Gregory Cajete	Author, professor of Native American studies and language literacy sociocultural studies at University of New Mexico
Tom Cole	Oklahoma US Representative
Sharice Davids	Kansas US Representative
Walter Echo-Hawk	Speaker, author, attorney, and indigenous rights activist
Jacoby Ellsbury	Professional baseball player
Louise Erdrich	Author, poet
Dallas Goldtooth	Environmental activist, Dakota language instructor
Joy Harjo	Poet Laureate, musician, playwright
Sterlin Harjo	Filmmaker

continued >

TABLE 5.1 American Indian and Alaska Native Professionals (continued)

NAME	PROFESSION
Deb Haaland	New Mexico US Representative, Secretary of the Interior under the Biden administration
Ryan Helsley	Professional baseball player
Adrienne J. Keene	Assistant professor of American studies and ethnic studies at Brown University, podcast producer, blogger
Winona LaDuke	Writer, environmentalist, economist
Terese Marie Mailhot	Author, journalist, educator
Stephanie Masta-Zywicki	Assistant professor of curriculum studies at Purdue University
N. Scott Momaday	Author, poet
Markwayne Mullin	Oklahoma US Representative
Migizi Pensoneau	Television and film writer, producer
Ryan RedCorn	Graphic artist, photographer
Kali Reis	Professional boxer
Luana Ross	Associate Professor Emerita of gender, women, and sexuality studies at University of Washington
Mary Golda Ross	Engineer
Shoni Schimmel	Professional basketball player
Maria Tallchief	Prima ballerina
James Welch	Author
Matika Wilbur	Educator, photographer, podcast producer, blogger
Bobby Wilson	Visual artist, actor
Chris Wondolowski	Professional soccer player
Stephen Wondolowski	Professional soccer player

Websites

American Indian College Fund collegefund.org

American Indian Science and Engineering Society aises.org

Center for Native American Youth at the Aspen Institute cnay.org

College Horizons collegehorizons.org

Indigenous Environmental Network ienearth.org

Honor the Earth honorearth.org

Indian Country Today: Digital Indigenous News indiancountrytoday.com

The ISLA Project islaproject.org

National Congress of American Indians ncai.org

National Indian Education Association niea.org

Native American and Indigenous Studies Association naisa.org

Native Land native-land.ca

NDNSPORTS ndnsports.com

The Nihewan Foundation for Native American Education nihewan.org

Project 562 project562.com

Reclaiming Native Truth rnt.firstnations.org

SACNAS: Advancing Chicanos/Hispanics and Native Americans in Science sacnas.org

Well for Culture wellforculture.com

Books and Articles

Dunbar-Ortiz, Roxanne. 2019. *An Indigenous Peoples' History of the United States for Young People.* Boston: Beacon Press.

Ford, Donna Y. 2013. *Recruiting and Retaining Culturally Different Students in Gifted Education.* Waco, TX: Prufrock Press.

Lo Wang, Hansi. June 24, 2014. "The Map of Native American Tribes You've Never Seen Before." NPR. npr.org/sections/codeswitch/2014/06/24/323665644/the-map-of-native-american-tribes-youve-never-seen-before.

US Department of Arts and Culture. n.d. "Honor Native Land: A Guide and Call to Acknowledgment." usdac.us/nativeland.

References

Battistich, Victor, Daniel Solomon, Dong-il Kim, Marilyn Watson, and Eric Schaps. 1995. "Schools as Communities, Poverty Levels of Student Populations, and Students' Attitudes, Motives, and Performance: A Multilevel Analysis." *American Educational Research Journal* 32 (3): 627–658. doi.org/10.3102/00028312032003627.

Clotfelter, Charles T., Helen F. Ladd, Jacob L. Vigdor, and Justin Wheeler. 2007. "High-Poverty Schools and the Distribution of Teachers and Principals." *North Carolina Law Review* 85 (5): 1345–1379.

Fryberg, Stephanie A., and Nicole M. Stephens. 2010. "When the World Is Colorblind, American Indians Are Invisible: A Diversity Science Approach." *Psychological Inquiry* 21 (2): 115–119. doi.org/10.1080/1047840X.2010.483847.

Fryberg, Stephanie A., and Sarah S. M. Townsend. 2008. "The Psychology of Invisibility." In *Commemorating* Brown: *The Social Psychology of Racism and Discrimination*, edited by Glenn Adams, Monica Biernat, Nyla R. Branscombe, Christian S. Crandall, and Lawrence S. Wrightsman, 173–193. Washington, DC: American Psychological Association.

Gansworth S·ha-weñ na-sae², Eric. 2018. "Repatriating Ourselves." In *New Poets of Native Nations,* edited by Heid E. Erdrich, 245. Minneapolis: Graywolf Press.

Gentry, Marcia, and C. Matthew Fugate. 2012. "Gifted Native American Students: Underperforming, Under-identified, and Overlooked." *Psychology in the Schools* 49 (7): 631–646. doi.org/10.1002/pits.21624.

Gentry, Marcia., C. Matthew Fugate, Jiaxi Wu, and Jaime A. Castellano. 2014. "Gifted Native American Students: Literature, Lessons, and Future Directions." *Gifted Child Quarterly* 58 (2): 98–110. doi.org/10.1177/0016986214521660.

Gentry, Marcia, Anne Gray, Gilman W. Whiting, Yukiko Maeda, and Nielsen Pereira. 2019. *System Failure: Access Denied. Gifted Education in the United States: Laws, Access, Equity, and Missingness Across the Country by Locale, Title I School Status, and Race.* Report Cards, technical report, and website. West Lafayette, IN: Purdue University; Lansdowne, VA: Jack Kent Cooke Foundation.

Gentry, Marcia, Anne Gray, Gilman Whiting, Yukiko Maeda, and Nielsen Pereira. 2019. "Equity of Student Populations Identified as Gifted by Race, Rurality, Income, and ELL Status Across the United States." *Jack Kent Cooke Foundation Report*.

Hodges, Jaret, Juliana Tay, Yukiko Maeda, and Marcia Gentry. 2018. "A Meta-Analysis of Gifted and Talented Identification Practices." *Gifted Child Quarterly* 62 (2): 147–174. doi.org/10.1177/006986217752107.

Kettler, Todd, Joseph Russell, and Jeb S. Puryear. 2015. "Inequitable Access to Gifted Education: Variance in Funding and Staffing Based on Locale and Contextual School Variables." *Journal for the Education of the Gifted* 38 (2): 99–117. doi.org/10.1177/0162353215578277.

Lomawaima, K. Tsianina, and Teresa L. McCarty. 2006. *To Remain an Indian: Lessons in Democracy from a Century of Native American Education*. New York: Teachers College Press.

Masta, Stephanie. 2018a. "'I Am Exhausted:' Everyday Occurrences of Being Native American." *International Journal of Qualitative Studies in Education* 31 (9): 821–835. doi.org/10.1080/09518398.2018.1499984.

———. 2018b. "Strategy and Resistance: How Native American Students Engage in Accommodation in Mainstream Schools." *Anthropology & Education Quarterly* 49 (1): 21–35. doi.org/10.1111/aeq.12231.

McInnes, Brian D. 2017. "Preparing Teachers as Allies in Indigenous Education: Benefits of an American Indian Content and Pedagogy Course." *Teaching Education* 28 (2): 145–161. doi.org/10.1080/10476210.2016.1224831.

Myers, Samuel L., Hyeoneui Kim, and Cheryl Mandala. 2004. "The Effect of School Poverty on Racial Gaps in Test Scores: The Case of the Minnesota Basic Standards Tests." *The Journal of Negro Education* 73 (1): 81–98. doi.org/10.2307-3211261.

National Congress of American Indians. 2020. "Tribal Nations and the United States: An Introduction." ncai.org/tribalnations/introduction/Indian_Country_101_Updated_February_2019.pdf.

Reclaiming Native Truth. 2018. "Changing the Narrative About Native Americans: A Guide for Allies." firstnations.org/publications/changing-the-narrative-about-native-americans-a-guide-for-allies.

29 C.F.R. §1607.3 (2019)

29 C.F.R. §1607.4 (2019)

US Census Bureau. 2012. "The American Indian and Alaska Native Population: 2010." census.gov/history/pdf/c2010br-10.pdf.

US Department of Education. 2018. "Improving Basic Programs Operated by Local Educational Agencies (Title I, Part A)." www2.ed.gov/programs/titleiparta/index.html.

Vanderhaar, Judi E., Marco A. Muñoz, and Robert J. Rodosky. 2006. "Leadership as Accountability for Learning: The Effects of School Poverty, Teacher Experience, Previous Achievement, and Principal Preparation Programs on Student Achievement. *Journal of Personnel Evaluation in Education* 19: 17–33. doi.org/10.1007/s11092-007-9033-8.

Wisconsin Department of Public Instruction. 2016. "Title I Status of Wisconsin Schools for 2015–16 School Year." dpi.wi.gov/sites/default/files/imce/focus-schools/pdf/List%20of%20Title%20I%20Schools%202015-16.pdf.

Yoon, So Yoon, and Marcia Gentry. 2009. "Racial and Ethnic Representation in Gifted Programs: Current Status of and Implications for Gifted Asian American Students." *Gifted Child Quarterly* 53 (2): 121–136. doi.org/10.1177/0016986208330564.

6

Opening the Doors for Gifted English Language Learners Through Self-Advocacy

Jaime Castellano, Ed.D., with Robert Robertson, Ed.D.

Introduction

No one can refute the challenges we face in educating English language learners (ELLs) in the United States. In lectures and conversations with both my graduate and undergraduate students, I maintain that the problems are all too real and are easily documented through local, state, and national achievement data. Furthermore, the enrollment of ELLs in our nation's schools is outpacing the schools' readiness and infrastructure required to effectively educate and prepare them for a successful future. There is an urgency to teach this now-mainstream population to self-advocate, and particularly to self-advocate for their advanced academic needs. Using parents, teachers, school and district administrators, and community resources to promote hope, inspiration, and self-efficacy in gifted ELLs is fundamental to changing the status quo for them. This level and quality of engagement is foundational to promoting a culture of achievement in the form of advocacy, participation, and shared decision-making.

Lucas's Story

I first met Lucas when he was a three-year-old Spanish-speaking immigrant from Venezuela. His parents enrolled him in our federal Head Start program. In the beginning, he would yell, scream, hit, kick, and attempt to run away as his parents walked him to his classroom. There were many days when I had to literally peel Lucas off his mother's leg. Eventually, though, he settled in and would greet me each day with a hug and a smile. One year later, Lucas was leading circle time, reading books in English to his classmates, and devouring all the content his Head Start teachers provided.

Before Lucas left the program for a public kindergarten, his parents began asking questions about what they should do. They knew their child was exceptional; all assessments, observations, and achievement data confirmed it. They wanted to advocate for Lucas but didn't know how. One day, in a conversation with Lucas's parents, I asked if they were considering a gifted kindergarten education program for him. They did not know what that was or how to move forward. They informed me that during the kindergarten roundup for their community, this was never mentioned, nor was information provided. They inquired whether the program was free. They asked if it would meet his needs.

Lucas started the new school year in a regular kindergarten program and immediately started to display problem behaviors. Everything was simply too easy, and he became a handful. The teacher was constantly calling his parents about his behavior. In advocating for their child, Lucas's parents returned to the center to ask me more explicit questions about the district's gifted education program. I provided them the information they wanted and they, in turn, made a request to have Lucas tested. As it turned out, Lucas was assessed by a bilingual psychologist, which, surprisingly, Lucas himself requested, and he surpassed all the scores needed for eligibility. By watching his parents advocate for him, Lucas learned to advocate for himself as a six-year-old. Not only did he request a bilingual psychologist, but he convinced his parents to enroll him in a gifted program outside of his community. They agreed reluctantly but are now glad they did. The family's shared decision-making paid off. Lucas is flourishing in a second-grade gifted program and looks forward to what the future brings.

English Language Learners

Students who are classified as English language learners (ELLs) are one of several populations who traditionally have been underrepresented in programs for academically advanced learners.

There is no question that English language ability is a key to students' success in the United States. Unfortunately, many people who are fluent only in English (as most US citizens are) tend to view proficiency in their majority language as synonymous with intelligence and assume that those who are not yet proficient in English must not be very smart. Of course, this is a fallacy, but these widespread fallacious beliefs often prevent bright learners who are not proficient in English from receiving an education at the advanced levels they are capable of mastering.

ELLs are not monolithic. They are defined as students who are unable to communicate fluently or learn effectively in English, who often come from non-English-speaking homes and backgrounds, and who typically require specialized or modified instruction in both the English language and in academic courses. Roughly three-quarters of students with limited English proficiency in US public schools said they spoke Spanish as their primary language at home, making it by far the most commonly reported language, according to the US Department of Education. The remaining students spoke a wide variety of languages, including Arabic, Chinese, and Vietnamese (each spoken by around 2 percent of all English language learners) (US Department of Education 2017). While most of my professional experience is with Spanish-speaking ELLs, the potential barriers to self-advocacy and the strategies to overcome them shared in this chapter are applicable to all ELL students.

> The unique needs of ELLs who immigrate to the United States make self-advocacy critical for their success.

The unique needs of ELLs who immigrate to the United States make self-advocacy critical for their success. Michael Matthews and I wrote in 2014 that changing demographics bring numerous challenges, but they also present multiple opportunities (Matthews and Castellano 2014). Improving education for ELL students will lead not only to positive long-term outcomes in terms of economic productivity and effective citizenship, but also to a more satisfied populace who understand and are able to meet their own needs for personal growth and for professional and life satisfaction. Teaching ELLs self-advocacy skills and strategies will aid them in this endeavor.

While there are no simple solutions to meeting the needs and supporting the strengths of every ELL, this chapter offers ideas, strategies, and practices that highlight the importance of teaching ELLs skills to share their own stories and ask for what they need in advanced academic programs. Fostering shared beliefs about the importance of self-advocacy among stakeholder groups, along with communication and collaboration, allows for a targeted approach to focus on developing the talent and potential ELLs possess.

Overview of the Current Status of ELLs in Gifted Education

As an award-winning and nationally recognized scholar, researcher, trainer, consultant, and speaker, and as a university professor and practitioner at the school and district level, I can say with confidence that, yes, the status of ELLs in gifted education has improved over the past several years (Castellano 2018; Castellano 2020). The National Center for Research on Gifted Education (2018) supports this assertion. They visited sixteen elementary and middle schools across three states that were selected for their exemplary identification of gifted English language learners. Although ELLs continue to be underrepresented in gifted and talented programs in the three states studied, each state has mandates for identifying and providing programming for diverse gifted and talented students, decreasing the extent of the underrepresentation. The sixteen schools in the study had documented percentages of ELL students identified for gifted and talented programming that were proportionally representative of their overall populations of ELL students.

This example offers hope, but the field of gifted education still has a long way to go. According to the National Center for Educational Statistics (2018), ELLs accounted for approximately 10 percent of the total number of students enrolled in US public schools in the 2014–2015 school year, or about five million students. However, the United States Department of Education Office for Civil Rights (2014) reported that only 2 percent of ELLs (or 100,000 students) are enrolled in gifted and talented programs.

If the glass is half-empty, the current status of ELLs in gifted education continues to reflect a history of inequity, lack of access, and missed opportunity for identifying and serving ELLs. The education of our gifted and talented ELLs is of paramount importance to the future of the United States (Castellano 2018). Furthermore, it is clear that talents that go unrecognized, or that remain underdeveloped, represent a tremendous waste of human capital for the individual, as well as a failure of progress for the society in which they live (Garn, Matthews, and Jolly 2010 and 2012). Relatedly, the economic or national competitiveness argument, whose goal is the development and utilization of mental resources for the benefit of the country and of humanity in general (Dixon et al. 2016), also recognizes the importance of capitalizing on the contributions of talented ELLs.

If the glass is half-full, then those school districts mentioned above offer a glimmer of hope. Zhou (2018) adds that more ELLs are taking and passing advanced placement exams. Champions for identifying and serving gifted ELLs exist at the local, state, and national levels. More than ever before in the history of gifted and talented education, this population is often a featured subgroup at state and national conferences, a target for quantitative and qualitative research, and a topic that informs advocacy, action, and inclusion. As a building principal, district gifted education coordinator/director, and state department of education specialist/expert in the field, I can attest that participation in gifted education is a game-changer in the lives of ELLs that offers a positive trajectory for their futures. It is incumbent on us to continue to move forward in this advocacy for identifying and serving gifted ELLs.

Barriers for ELLs in Gifted Education and Other Advanced Academic Programs

Key to moving our advocacy forward is recognizing the barriers that often prevent ELLs from accessing gifted education and other advanced academic programs. The most common obstacles include the following (Castellano 2018):

> Language proficiency

> Poverty

> Unstable home

> Adverse childhood experiences

> The challenge of identity

> Lack of life experiences

> Identification procedures

> Assessment procedures

> Inadequate policies

> Lack of access to advanced academic programming at the primary grades

> Historic patterns of underachievement

> Inability to participate in extracurricular activities that may serve as a source of enrichment or acceleration

> Limited background knowledge and negative perceptions of the classroom teacher about under-served populations

From 2014–2018, I was the assistant director of the Luciano Martinez Child Development Center with the Hispanic Human Resources Council, Inc., in West Palm Beach, Florida. In this capacity, I had the opportunity to engage with hundreds of parents and families. My experiences included counseling monolingual Spanish-speaking parents of gifted and high-ability children. Some parents were uneducated and illiterate, and the vast majority of them had absolutely no conception of what gifted education meant, although they had received written communication in Spanish from their children's schools. Some had no idea their children were highly intelligent, gifted, or different from the other ELL students in their communities. In these situations, I would sit with the parents, and sometimes families, and explain what gifted education is and what it would mean for their children. I would answer any questions families had. It was common for them to ask if there was a cost involved with a gifted program or if they had to provide government documents so their children could participate. These questions helped me realize that there was a disconnect in the communication between the school and the parents. Information is power. If parents don't have information, or if it is not provided in a fashion that is easy for them to understand, they remain in the dark, rendering them unable to make informed decisions that are in the best interests of their children and keeping them from encouraging their children's decision-making and self-advocacy.

More than a decade ago, Aguirre and Hernandez (2011) issued a call to action, submitting that we cannot wait until ELLs reach proficiency in English to place them in gifted and talented programs—and yet that call has still not been sufficiently answered. If these students are not challenged and motivated, they will become frustrated and conclude that schools do not offer solutions or possibilities for their future. Many bright, gifted ELLs have dropped out of school because they sensed rejection and felt alienated from their teachers and peers.

Aguirre and Hernandez also suggest that stereotyping the characteristics of gifted students makes it very difficult to refer ELLs who are potentially gifted. ELLs may manifest their gifts in unique ways; when students are culturally or linguistically diverse, it can be difficult to recognize their strengths. Discrepancies exist between how a teacher expects a gifted child to behave and how a culturally or linguistically diverse gifted student may behave. One example of this is the advanced verbal skills and ability of gifted students from the dominant culture. Most White gifted children in the United States are encouraged to be verbal and express themselves, yet this may not be a characteristic that is present in gifted ELLs, who are mostly taught to speak only when spoken to.

Challenges for promising English language learners include a structural barrier that limits the availability of gifted programs in schools serving low-income neighborhoods, where the families of a disproportionate number of ELLs live. In informal interviews with parents and families who chose not to have their children participate in gifted education, reasons included a desire to keep children (especially girls) in the neighborhood school, satisfaction with the child's current program, concern about undue pressure, communication barriers, and conflicting advice from school personnel. However, a family's decision to decline opportunities for a student to participate in programs for the gifted may result in lower achievement (Kitano 2008).

As a new elementary school principal in the mid-1990s, I inherited a school in a primarily Hispanic community in one of the nation's largest school districts, where about 65 percent of the students were ELLs. We were a Title I Schoolwide Project, with a history of low academic achievement and where remediation and compensatory instruction were the norms. Because of my work in the gifted education field, I coordinated a year-long professional development program for all teachers that was focused on identifying gifted Hispanic/Latino students and gifted ELLs. As teachers began to apply their new knowledge, referrals to gifted education increased. What we did not anticipate at the time was that once a student became eligible, they would need to be bussed to a different school outside the community to receive services because there were no gifted programs in our low-income community. Some parents declined the services for their gifted child for the very same reasons Kitano identified ten years later. Cultural norms also posed barriers. For example, most families did not want their children to attend schools outside of the neighborhood school and did not favor having their girls participate in specialized programs.

This narrative occurred in the mid-1990s; Kitano's research was conducted approximately ten years later. The point is that structural barriers for low-income neighborhood schools have existed for a very long time and are often difficult to overcome. In our case, to combat these structural barriers, in 1996, Palmetto Elementary School in West Palm Beach, Florida, started one of the first gifted education programs for ELLs in the state and the nation. The program exists to this day.

Overcoming the Deficit Model

In spite of immigration issues that dominate the media and the perception that the United States is being inundated with undocumented immigrants, the fact is that most ELL students are American citizens. According to the US Department of Education's National Center for Education Statistics (2018), 85 percent of ELL students in prekindergarten to grade 5 and 62 percent of ELL students in grades 6 to 12 were born in the United States. The majority of ELLs will receive most, if not all, of their education in the American school system. They are valued members of our school communities and need to be recognized as such. Unfortunately, they are often seen through a deficit-model lens in our education system.

Traditionally, schools divide their student populations into low, middle, and high performers. Ability grouping helps organize the class into manageable groups for the teacher. The general education teacher normally teaches to the middle, with low performers and high achievers pulled out for intervention and enrichment or leaving the teacher to differentiate instruction and give interventions and enrichment to their students in the classroom. There are many variations on how schools tackle these issues—some successful and some not. Gifted ELLs fall in the zone of needing both language support (intervention) and opportunities to challenge themselves (enrichment and acceleration). More often than not, teachers' focus is placed on gifted ELLs' language deficits since that supports the school's academic goals. Therefore, ELLs are often seen as having a deficit that needs to be fixed, at the expense of not seeing their potential.

Initiating Change Despite the Obstacles

Educators must teach ELLs the linguistic competencies needed to be successful academically and help them see how valuable they are as bilingual and multilingual citizens. Just teaching them English is not enough. Unfortunately, this is not a skill that is taught to educators. Most teacher education programs nationwide focus only on content and general education practices. They often omit best practices for ELLs, which leaves teachers with little to no knowledge on how to educate these students, much less how to advocate for them or help them self-advocate.

> Educators must take responsibility for looking deeper than classroom academic goals and measures and seeing the real needs—and potential—of their students.

Another obstacle is the fact that over thirty states do not require any ELL training for general classroom teachers beyond the federal minimum requirement. Although federal law states that school districts must provide research-based professional development to any teachers, administrators, and staff who work with ELLs (Education Commission of the States 2014), the practice of teaching ELL students in separate classrooms can often circumvent that mandate.

Nevertheless, most teachers are well-versed at their craft and focus their attention on academic achievement. Many are skilled at best instructional practices, curriculum and assessment design, and differentiation techniques. In addition, there are any number of teaching methodologies, protocols, and instructional tools to support ELLs in the classroom, including:

> structured English immersion (SEI) and bilingual education methods

> sheltered instruction observation protocol (SIOP)

> specially designed academic instruction in English (SDAIE)

> curriculum and educational software products

All of these resources can assist teachers with their instructional practice, but what lies at the heart of advocacy is the teacher's passion for working with students. If teachers have no intrinsic belief that their students can achieve great things, then they are just going through the motions and are less likely to be successful at educating ELLs. Educators must take responsibility for looking deeper than classroom academic goals and measures and seeing the real needs—and potential—of their students. They must see themselves as advocates and change agents for the challenges they see before them. The advocacy can be challenging, and not every teacher feels or has the intrinsic desire to advocate for students.

Fenner (2014) states that educators tend to advocate more actively for ELLs who fit into a category of obvious need, such as:

> new arrivals to the United States

> those who are at lower levels of English language proficiency

> those who come from lower socioeconomic groups

> those who are from families who do not know their rights or the community resources available to them

> those who have undergone trauma

> those who come from families with limited or interrupted educational backgrounds

Though this list is not exhaustive, it gives an idea of the students and their circumstances that teachers most often and naturally advocate for. But what about those ELLs who do not have an obvious need? Those in the gifted ELL category or those born in the United States who grow up speaking English alongside their home language, yet never quite reach full proficiency? The following case study shows how one teacher worked with exactly this group of students and recognized her own need to advocate for them.

Viewing Advocacy Through a Teacher's Lens

Clarissa, a first-year teacher in a high school with a heavy concentration of ELLs, had been struggling to make inroads with her ELL students and their families. As their tenth-grade English teacher, she worked all year to get students' academic language skills up to a proficient level so they could be more successful on the state exam the coming year. All her students were proficient speakers of English, but they struggled with writing and vocabulary. She also identified public speaking as an area in which they were very weak.

Outside of becoming familiar with students' academic needs, Clarissa had not really gotten to know her students the way she wanted to. She had concentrated all her efforts on being the best teacher she could be, which she defined as helping her students achieve academically. She was also overwhelmed with the duties and responsibilities of a first-year teacher. As a result, by the time winter break came around and she gave herself time to reflect, Clarissa realized that she had only met two of her students' parents at the beginning of the year during the rather poorly attended parent night that was organized by the school. She decided that when she got back from break, she needed to meet with her students individually to talk about their academic progress and to get to know them better on a personal level.

These one-on-one meetings were eye-opening for her. She learned that over half of her thirty-two ELL students wanted to go to college after graduation but had no idea how to make that happen. They did not think they would have the money to pay for it, so it was just a dream. She learned that most of her ELL students had two working parents and came from large families where they were expected to go home after school and participate in the raising of younger siblings and cousins. She also learned that each of them had their own challenges, from boyfriend problems to ill and dying family members.

All this information brought Clarissa closer to her students, and she was upset with herself for not having done this sooner. She set about immediately making an academic plan for each student that included more individual meeting time during lunch and after school to go over their writing assignments and weekly mini-presentations where they could report on current affairs to increase their confidence in public speaking. She also met with the school's guidance counselor to find out what opportunities there were for college scholarships and post-high school programs for English language learners. She learned that the district had a Spanish interpreter on staff who could support her to give a talk to her students' parents about college and trade school opportunities. She set up a meeting date and invited her students' families to come to the school for a special family night to learn about post-high school education opportunities specifically for English language learners.

Even though only half the families came, Clarissa felt the evening was a success. Those who did come were very interested in learning more and had questions around college applications and funding opportunities. They were also interested in what other programs the school offered to help get their students college ready. Energized by their interest and enthusiasm, Clarissa told the guidance counselor that evening that she wanted to set up meetings with her colleagues in other content areas to see how they might provide support and enrichment in math, science, history, and other subjects to help her students before they graduated. The guidance counselor quickly let her know that ELLs were normally on a specific track all through high school that simply got them through the basic coursework in each content area while they were learning English. Clarissa was surprised to hear this, and upon further investigation realized that many of her students were not being given an opportunity to take the more challenging college-ready courses that other students had access to. She made it her mission that year to start a conversation with her principal and colleagues about changing the tracking system for ELLs and allowing them to take the courses they wanted to take while supporting their language development needs.

As this story illustrates, Clarissa became an advocate for her students by doing a few simple things:

> identifying needs academically, socially, and emotionally

> being a voice for her students with the guidance counselor

> getting to know her students and their families so she could better support them

> changing the conversation at her school about course opportunities for ELLs

> encouraging her students to find their own voices and speak up for what they needed

A Model for Advocacy

How to define advocacy is up to each individual; Clarissa's story shows how one teacher defined it for herself. By being proactive and determining the needs of her students both academically and personally, she was able to bridge the gap for the students and their families with an education night geared specifically for them. In the process, she learned who her school allies were and what resources were available to her in her efforts to empower ELL students.

The National Education Association outlines a five-step approach that teachers can follow to advocate for their ELL students and increase the chances that students will eventually self-advocate (National Education Association n.d.):

1. **Isolate the issue:** Determine what the needs are.

2. **Identify your allies:** Know who to go to for support and resources.

3. **Know the rights of ELL students:** Know the laws and rules surrounding ELL issues so you can be a well-informed advocate.

4. **Organize and educate others:** Inform your audience of what they need to know.

5. **Identify your outlets for change:** Determine what you can do to make a difference.

All teachers must decide for themselves how they want to define their own advocacy. It must come from an intrinsic desire to want to help, but it can be learned. Teachers must be taught to not only educate their students effectively, but also help them advocate for themselves, see themselves as valuable and worthy, and support them with the tools they need to be successful. Ultimately, English language learners must learn to advocate for themselves to attain their academic and career goals. Role models like Clarissa can help them get there.

Helping Gifted ELLs Self-Advocate

Matthews (2014) maintains that student motivation can present one of the most problematic issues for teachers of students with gifts and talents. What can a teacher do with a student who obviously has a high aptitude for the course content but does not want to complete homework or assigned class tasks? A related issue, relevant specifically for ELLs, is that some teachers may assume that these students are not going to achieve academically regardless of any additional help the teacher may offer. One may hear statements such as, "These students are just going to drop out when they get to high school, so why should we make any extra efforts to help them achieve?" or, "Their families are going to move away as soon as the peach crop is harvested," or, "Those parents just don't value the education we are offering their children." There is perhaps a kernel of truth to these views: Latino students (the largest ELL group in the United States) in general do have greater high school dropout rates and lower college attendance rates than most other groups of underrepresented students. But there are also many ELL students who have had academic success, completed graduate degrees, and become eminent scholars, professionals, and leaders in their adult lives. In my experience, the influence of a single committed teacher, family member, or mentor often is what made the difference for these individuals. Encouraging and promoting self-advocacy was a crucial part of the relationship between the student and the committed adult.

Access to gifted education and other advanced academic programs is a right of every student who demonstrates high ability through assessments and prior classroom performance. To recognize their right to access information and advanced programs and services designed for gifted learners, gifted ELLs must be able to navigate a system that historically has excluded them from these advanced programs. Self-advocacy is a lifelong skill, and for most, it begins with their K–12 education. **Table 6.1** shows common areas where gifted ELLs have successfully advocated for themselves, either individually or as a group. It is important to restate that their success with self-advocacy is often reliant on collaborating with trusted and respected adults.

TABLE 6.1: Gifted ELLs: Areas of Self-Advocacy	
IDENTIFICATION AND ASSESSMENT	**CURRICULUM AND INSTRUCTION**
• Self-nomination	• Use of heritage language
• Culturally relevant characteristics	• Placement in advanced academic programs
• Types of IQ tests administered	• Content and grade acceleration
• Use of heritage language	• Evaluation of progress
• Choice of English-speaking, Spanish-speaking, or bilingual psychologist	• Choice of teachers (culturally competent)
• Testing accommodations or modifications	• Culturally relevant materials
	• Demonstration of mastery
	• Access to community resources

Student Motivation and Self-Advocacy

In general, high-ability learners report higher levels of intrinsic motivation than do average-ability learners (Garn, Matthews, and Jolly 2010 and 2012). But as noted earlier, some gifted ELL students may not appear self-motivated if they haven't yet gained insights into themselves as learners. Their internal motivation is related to their belief in self, their belief in their power to personally change and to control and overcome circumstances, and their resiliency and optimism. According to Matthews (2014), theorists have long recognized a distinction between two broad types of motivation: internal (intrinsic) and external (extrinsic). In essence, intrinsic motivation is when one does something for the enjoyment of it, while extrinsic motivation is when an external factor (such as a reward or threat of punishment) causes one to do something. Intrinsic motivation is considered the healthiest form and is associated with a variety of positive long-term academic and mental health outcomes. It is plausible that gifted ELLs who advocate for themselves do so because they are intrinsically motivated to access advanced academic programs that best meet their needs.

Resiliency theory refers to a trait of those individuals who demonstrate high achievement or who otherwise thrive despite encountering obstacles, adversities, and challenges that would harm or severely hamper the average person's ability to succeed in life. For ELLs, challenges may take the form of traumatic memories of the immigration process, economic hardship in a family due to relocation, or stresses related to the immigration status of themselves or other family members, in addition to the many other stressors they share in common with non-ELL children (Matthews 2014). Regardless of race, ethnicity, socioeconomic status, or home language, characteristics typically associated with resiliency theory include high levels of motivation, commitment to education, advanced academic achievement, ability to thrive, social and intellectual competence, developed self-esteem, and access to at least one psychologically healthy adult, among others. These same characteristics are complementary to, or are embedded in, the advocacy areas identified in **table 6.1** on page 85.

Mindset is the term used by psychologist Carol Dweck (2016) to describe how individuals view their own intelligence and other abilities. Based on my experience as a scholar, researcher, and practitioner in gifted education, I've found that high-ability ELLs are more aligned with an incremental mindset, rather than a fixed mindset. Individuals who have an incremental (or growth) mindset believe that intelligence and other abilities can be developed through study and other efforts to practice. They believe that working hard is more important in improving intelligence than innate ability is. Matthews (2014) describes how mindset in gifted ELLs is important to understand because it influences how the students react to failure and because it is malleable and therefore can be influenced through the use of appropriate teaching strategies and through relationships with others with whom the gifted ELL identifies.

It should be evident that there is a connection between motivation, resilience, and mindset in ELLs of any ability. Importantly, motivation and its connection to gifted ELLs should be viewed as a state of mind. Motivation depends heavily on the specific situation, whatever it may be, and it also is subject to change; teachers and other caring adults can foster the development of motivation in gifted ELLs so that they achieve the success they are capable of.

Strategies for Student Self-Advocacy

As defined by Davis and Douglas in their framework for this book, self-advocacy is the dynamic process that enables high-potential students to claim their right to an education that addresses their unique intellectual, academic, psycho-social, and cultural needs. For ELL students to recognize their needs and their strengths and weaknesses, and to become aware of how to support themselves through self-advocacy, they need teachers to explicitly guide them to this understanding. Good educators usually know what their students' strengths and weaknesses are. But once students can identify their own strengths and weaknesses, are they able to ask for help and know where to get it?

In my own experience as a teacher of English language learners, I often saw that my students struggled with basic language issues. I could generally handle those issues in the classroom through direct instruction and oral language exercises. One year, however, I had three Spanish-speaking eighth graders who were struggling with their communication skills. Their English was fine. They functioned at an

> Good educators usually know what their students' strengths and weaknesses are. But once students can identify their own strengths and weaknesses, are they able to ask for help and know where to get it?

intermediate level in academic English, were studious, and made decent grades in class. They tended to hang together and speak Spanish with one another whenever they could. They were very shy with the adults in the school and were hesitant to ask for assistance of any kind. When they did need help with anything at school, they went through the school's Spanish interpreter, who would talk for these students even though each was more than capable of speaking and understanding English. Yet they were hesitant to communicate directly with the English-speaking adults on campus, including me.

I noticed this as a problem and recognized that as eighth graders, they would naturally be shy and struggle with their self-esteem. But this seemed extreme, so I asked the school's Spanish language interpretor for her advice and learned that she was growing frustrated with the students for continuously using her as a crutch for communication. All three of the students had the same free period in the morning, so I decided to put them on a work detail in the front office during this time two days a week. They were asked to answer the phone for the secretaries. At first, they were not too keen on this idea, but I said they could do it together and that I would give them extra points on their oral language assignments if they did this. They agreed, and we practiced how to answer the phone and what to say when they needed to hand the call off to one of the secretaries. After two weeks, I could see a difference in both their language skills and their comfort level speaking with English speakers. The front office secretaries loved having the help and quickly built a great rapport with these three students, who started loving this period of the day. They went from working in the front office twice a week to doing it every day during their free period.

Not long after, they started to assist the translator with some of her work translating documents from English to Spanish, and by the second semester of the year, they were serving as a student mentors to new English language learners who were enrolling in the school. They went from never asking for help to being that help and support for other students. It was an amazing transformation, and I saw their confidence and self-worth grow in leaps and bounds.

What this taught me was that as an educator, it is my duty to empower my students to advocate for themselves by scaffolding their experience. By answering the phones, these three students learned everything about the school, the bus routes, what every teacher's name was, who taught what, and where to send people for the right answers and help. At the same time, they built relationships with staff members that they may never have interacted with otherwise. As a result, they quickly they became leaders and advocates for other students.

Fenner (2014) talks about scaffolded advocacy in *Advocating for English Learners* and describes it as being much the same as scaffolded instruction. Engaging ELL students as partners in advocacy efforts makes sense. The benefits of doing this outweigh any excuses not to. This may require involving others who speak students' home language, who share similar backgrounds and upbringing, or who can serve as advisors and mentors. As cultural brokers, these individuals can help students explore options, increase their motivation, and help bring their voices to the decision-making process. Douglas (2018) supports this partnership between teachers and students and identifies the following key benefits of self-advocacy for students:

> more appropriate academic challenge (in English or the student's home language, for example)

> increased motivation

> greater independence and self-direction

> improved academic performance

> greater equanimity and less frustration

Through this partnership, teachers also benefit by growing their cultural competency and gaining a better understanding of each of their students.

The more proficient students become in English, the fewer language scaffolds they need in accessing challenging content. The same is true for advocacy. To get on the same educational footing as native English speakers, ELLs need fewer advocacy scaffolds as they and their families improve their English, learn to navigate the US education system, and find their own voices as self-advocates. It is our job as educators to both connect ELL students and their families with the resources they need and support them in using those resources to be successful in our schools and communities. Until ELL students are able to advocate for themselves, educators must advocate for them and show them the way.

Conclusion

Although it may seem contradictory, the journey of self-advocacy often begins with collaboration, most typically between the home and the school. Teaching gifted ELLs to advocate for themselves gives them a voice in their education, beyond lip-service. It empowers them to ask questions and make decisions that are unique to who they are and their local context. Teaching gifted ELLs to ask key questions of the right person helps them access information that can influence their decision-making.

Reflection is another part of the self-advocacy process. Through reflection and self-assessment, gifted ELLs are able to identify and understand their own needs and beliefs. In turn, they communicate these thoughts with others they trust and respect with an expectation of feedback that is authentic. This is, in part, the journey to self-advocacy.

For adults who are part of the gifted ELL self-advocacy experience, cross-cultural perspectives on gifted education are important. Culturally competent adult educators who "get it" when working with gifted ELL students put themselves in a position to make a difference based on their ability to use relational pedagogy, which means the use of empowerment strategies and activities that promote both increased academic achievement and mastery of learning, as well as a connection that encourages students to advocate for themselves. Gifted ELLs who self-advocate put themselves in a position to take control of their own narratives and demonstrate their ability to persevere, be resilient, and, with the assistance of key adult collaborators, rise above challenges that stand in their way.

Key Concepts

> In order to develop the gifts, talents, and self-advocacy skills of ELLs, stakeholder groups must follow a collaborative and collegial approach rooted in clear communication and respect for the challenges faced by ELL students.

> In promoting student self-advocacy, teachers and administrators develop positive relationships with students, reinforcing qualities that are key to resilience. They also share personal examples of resilience, perseverance, and advocacy. They become models and mentors for gifted ELLs.

> Self-advocacy may involve making difficult decisions that impact family dynamics, friendships, and other such relationships. This is not selfish behavior. Rather, self-advocacy is an attempt to actualize the gifts, talents, and potential that one possesses and is a way to take ownership of one's educational future.

> Improved parent awareness is critical to gifted ELL self-advocacy. Through collaborative efforts, parents receive one collective message rather than multiple, possibly conflicting messages.

> Using schools and classrooms to promote gifted ELLs' self-advocacy is fundamental to changing the status quo for them and their parents, families, and communities. This advances a culture of influence in the form of advocacy, participation, and shared decision-making that informs equity, access, and opportunity.

Discussion Questions

1. How can teachers learn to be better advocates for ELL students?

2. Who else could be part of the advocacy team?

3. When do educators stop advocating and start allowing their students to advocate for themselves?

4. What are some of the most effective ways to teach ELL students to self-advocate?

5. In what ways can educators support students' efforts?

Recommended Resources

Ballantyne, Keira Gebbie, Alicia R. Sanderman, and Jack Levy. 2007. *Educating English Language Learners: Building Teacher Capacity. Roundtable Report.* National Clearinghouse for English Language Acquisition.

Ireson, Judith, and Julie Hallam. 2001. *Ability Grouping in Education.* Thousand Oaks, CA: SAGE Publications.

Lee, Andrew M.I. n.d. "The Importance of Self-Advocacy for Kids Who Learn and Think Differently." *Understood.* understood.org/en/friends-feelings/empowering-your-child/self-advocacy/the-importance-of-self-advocacy.

Little, Catherine A., Jill L. Adelson, Kelly L. Kearney, Kathleen Cash, and Rebecca O'Brien. 2018. "Early Opportunities to Strengthen Academic Readiness: Effects of Summer Learning on Mathematics Achievement." *Gifted Child Quarterly* 62 (1): 83–95. doi.org/10.1177/0016986217738052.

Roberts, Julia Link, and Tracy Ford Inman. 2006. "Effective Advocates: Communicate Effectively." *Parenting for High Potential*, 8–9.

References

Aguirre, Nilda M., and Norma E. Hernandez. 2011. "Differentiating the Curriculum for Gifted Second Language Learners: Teaching Them to Think." In *Special Populations in Gifted Education: Understanding Our Most Able Students from Diverse Backgrounds*, edited by Jaime A. Castellano and Andrea Dawn Frazier. Waco, TX: Prufrock Press.

Castellano, Jaime A. 2018. *Educating Hispanic and Latino Students: Opening the Doors to Hope, Promise, and Possibility.* West Palm Beach, FL: Learning Sciences International.

———. 2020. "Serving Gifted, Advanced, and High-Ability Latino Students: Programming for Success." In *High-Achieving Latino Students: Successful Pathways Toward College and Beyond*, edited by Susan J. Paik, Stacy M. Kula, Jeremiah J. González, and Verónica V. González, 231–246. Charlotte, NC: Information Age Publishing.

Dixon, Lauren, Bravetta Hassell, Sarah Fister Gale, and Frank Kalman. December 2, 2016. "Welcome to the Talent Economy." *Talent Economy.* chieflearningofficer.com/2016/12/02/talent-valuable-resource.

Douglas, Deb. 2018. *The Power of Self-Advocacy for Gifted Learners: Teaching the 4 Essential Steps to Success.* Minneapolis: Free Spirit Publishing.

Dweck, Carol. 2016. *Mindset: The New Psychology of Success.* New York: Ballantine Books.

Education Commission of the States (ECS). 2014. "What ELL Training, if Any, Is Required of General Classroom Teachers?" ecs.force.com/mbdata/mbquestNB2?rep=ELL1415.

Fenner, Diane Staehr. 2014. *Advocating for English Learners: A Guide for Educators.* Thousand Oaks, CA: Corwin.

Garn, Alex C., Michael S. Matthews, and Jennifer L. Jolly. 2010. "Parental Influences on Academic Motivation of Gifted Students: A Self-Determination Theory Perspective." *Gifted Child Quarterly* 54 (4): 263–272. doi.org/10.1177/0016986210377657.

———. 2012. "Parents' Role in the Academic Motivation of Students with Gifts and Talents." *Psychology in the Schools* 49 (7): 656–667. doi.org/10.1002/pits.21626.

Kitano, Margie K. 2008. "Poverty, Diversity, and Promise." *Gifted Education Communicator* 39 (4): 16–19.

Matthews, Michael S. 2014. "Motivation and the Academically Able English Learner." In *Talent Development for English Language Learners: Identifying and Developing Potential*, edited by Michael S. Matthews and Jaime A. Castellano. Waco, TX: Prufrock Press.

Matthews, Michael S., and Jaime A. Castellano. 2014. "Thoughts for the Future." In *Talent Development for English Language Learners: Identifying and Developing Potential*, edited by Michael S. Matthews and Jaime A. Castellano. Waco, TX: Prufrock Press. 217–228.

National Center for Research on Gifted Education. 2018. *Exploratory Study on the Identification of English Learners for Gifted and Talented Programs.* Storrs: University of Connecticut. ncrge.uconn.edu/wp-content/uploads/sites/982/2020/09 /NCRGE-EL-Report.pdf.

National Education Association. n.d. "5 Steps to ELL Advocacy." useaut.org/home/63594.htm.

US Department of Education, National Center for Education Statistics. *Common Core of Data, Local Education Agency (School District) Universe Survey Data.* nces.ed.gov/ccd/pubagency.asp.

US Department of Education, National Center for Educational Statistics. 2017. *SY 2015–2016 Consolidated State Performance Reports Part I.* www2.ed.gov/admins/lead/account/consolidated/sy15-16part1/index.html.

US Department of Education, National Center for Education Statistics. *English Language Learners in Public Schools.* nces.ed.gov/programs/coe/indicator_cgf.asp.

US Department of Education, Office for Civil Rights. 2014. *Civil Rights Data Collection, Data Snapshot: College and Career Readiness.* www2.ed.gov/about/offices/list/ocr/docs/crdc-college-and-career-readiness-snapshot.pdf.

VanTassel-Baska, Joyce. 2018. "Achievement Unlocked: Effective Curriculum Interventions with Low-Income Students." *Gifted Child Quarterly* 62 (1): 68 –82. doi.org/10.1177/0016986217738565.

Zhou, Amanda. 2018. "More Students Are Taking AP Exams, but Researchers Don't Know if That Helps Them." *Chalkbeat.* chalkbeat.org/posts/us/2018/08/03/more-students-are-taking-ap exams-but-researchers-dont-know-if-that-helps-them.

7

Empowering Gifted Students from Low-Income Households

Tamra Stambaugh, Ph.D.,
and Timothy W. Stambaugh, Ph.D.

Introduction

Many gifted students from low-income households have difficulty self-advocating for their needs. Perhaps they have been told that adults have full authority and that they should never question those in charge. Maybe students have tried to self-advocate, but it did not go well, and they gave up after consistently feeling unheard. Perhaps students are unaware of opportunities for which they need to self-advocate. Consider the following stories of two gifted students.

Sam's Story

Sam is a White student who lives in a rural area in the foothills of the Appalachian Mountains. He loves working with his hands and making models to demonstrate the concepts he learns in physics class, but he does not enjoy reading. He gets good grades in general and is definitely advanced in science. However, Sam's teachers are more focused on his lack of interest in reading than his strengths in science. Sam's mom wants to encourage him and wants Sam to pursue his strengths, but she doesn't understand his science homework and doesn't have the time to investigate options for him (or the financial resources to support his interests). Sam's parents are divorced, and his dad lives in another town. Sam's dad admittedly doesn't understand Sam and makes fun of him and his "brainy talk." Though Sam lives with his single mom, she is always working to make ends meet, so Sam spends most of his time with his grandparents, who criticize him for "trying to show off" when he talks to them about science or uses advanced vocabulary. Sam's grandparents, the adults most active in his life, think that Sam is doing well since he gets decent grades and the school has not called about any problems. Therefore, they have not stepped up to advocate for him. That leaves Sam with two options at school: either endure comments about his lack of reading prowess while teachers ignore his interest in science or speak up for himself, a skill he has not yet learned.

Kindra's Story

Kindra is a gifted Black girl in an urban school. She gets good grades overall, but is particularly advanced in English language arts, where assignments are often too easy. Kindra tried to self-advocate by asking her teacher about options for higher level assignments but was rebuffed and told she needed to stop distracting her classmates and just wait for them to catch up. Kindra's parents would like to come to school to discuss Kindra's concerns. But because their jobs are not flexible, attending a meeting during school hours is not an option. In

> Gifted and potentially gifted low-income students may not always show their unique talents in the ways we expect.

the evenings, there are younger children at home who need support, and a babysitter is too expensive. Kindra has asked her teacher to Skype with her parents after they get home from work, but the teacher hasn't responded yet. Her parents said it is important to address Kindra's concerns, but they don't have time to initiate something right now since there are other family needs to address and since Kindra is getting good grades. Meanwhile, Kindra is becoming more frustrated. She is trying creative options to find relief, but she feels adults are being inflexible. She is beginning to shut down as her attempts at self-advocacy are consistently not welcomed or attended to as quickly as she would like.

Current Status of Low-Income Gifted Students

When you envision a gifted student from a low-income household, what immediately comes to mind? For some, the words *gifted* and *low-income* are rarely used in the same phrase. But why? Perhaps it is because gifted and potentially gifted low-income students may not always show their unique talents in the ways we expect. The US Census Bureau reported that 16.2 percent of young people under the age of 18 were living in poverty in 2018. Students who are identified as being in poverty come from all race and ethnicity backgrounds. According to the National Center for Children in Poverty (NCCP), students of color in the United States have higher rates of poverty than White students do. Their 2016 figures show the following percentages of young children living in poverty (Jiang and Koball 2018):

> 65 percent of American Indian and Alaska Native children

> 64 percent of Black children

> 61 percent of Hispanic children

> 31 percent of White children

> 28 percent of Asian children

Moreover, gifted students of color living in poverty are 250 percent less likely to be identified as gifted in school (National Center for Research on Gifted Education 2019). If students are going to be supported, they need advocates and self-advocacy strategies. Since teachers are rarely taught about the special learning needs of gifted students in their preservice training, it is no wonder the unique qualities of a gifted student from poverty are too often missed. Academically advanced low-income students differ from one another as much as they are alike. While there are many lists of characteristics available, these lists are widely based on educators' personal experiences and may not be true of all populations of low-income students or necessarily correlated with giftedness in all regions, cultures, or races and ethnicities.

TABLE 7.1: Characteristics and Potential Manifestations

CHARACTERISTIC OF GIFTEDNESS	POSSIBLE MANIFESTATIONS AMONG STUDENTS FROM LOW-INCOME HOUSEHOLDS
Advanced problem-solving or reasoning	Ability to navigate multiple systems and problems at home and school
	May take care of younger siblings or cook meals at earlier ages than peers and with success
	Navigates bus or train schedules independently and earlier than same-age peers
	Solves adult and practical life problems in creative ways (how to get home, to get to the library, or to negotiate food or income sources)
Communication and leadership skills	Family may rely on the student for support and help for sophisticated and real-life problems and solutions
	Student is able to negotiate with adults to get what they want—especially for their own basic needs and wants and those of others they care about
	May have leadership positions in community-based activities near their home (church, theater, agricultural clubs, jobs)
	May have poor grammar or writing skills but innovative ideas and a strong grasp of abstract concepts
	Easily builds relationships or will garner relationships to achieve goals
	Is trusted or sought after by others in their specific community
Advanced vocabulary	Uses advanced vocabulary and technical language in areas of exposure and interest (uses mechanical or agricultural language if interested and exposed to those areas)
Above-average ability and rate of learning	Shows significant growth in areas of interest after exposure (even if not the highest in the class)
	May show an uneven testing profile across subtests and achievement areas
	Can learn information quickly when interested or applied to practical life situations or relationships
	Wins contests or has success in community-based events (4-H, church groups)
Creativity or innovation	Uses materials and ideas available to achieve goals
	May prefer hands-on and practical ways of learning and demonstrating advanced concepts
	Solves real-world problems in ways that promote success
Curiosity	Asks a lot of questions if interested in the content, if the content is relevant, and if they trust or have a relationship with that adult

Table 7.1 combines many of the common traits, behaviors, and descriptions of gifted students along with possible ways these behaviors may be manifest in low-income students. Many of the characteristics were adapted from the HOPE Scale (Peters and Gentry 2010) which is a statistically validated checklist of behaviors designed with low-income learners in mind, and TABS (Traits, Aptitudes, Behaviors

Scale; Frasier et al. 1995) which recently has been used in modules created by the National Association for Gifted Children (NAGC) to support teachers in observing and finding students from diverse backgrounds, including low-income households.

It must be noted that these characteristics are generalizations, and other considerations such as language, race, ethnicity, and geography must also be considered and will vary by school population and region. Using **table 7.1**, think about the potential characteristics from your own school population, including how the general traits may be seen in students from your school context, considering your unique population and other information provided in this book. Additionally, the following list of questions can aid you in reframing conceptions about low-income students.

Ask yourself which students in your classroom:

> show the most growth over time based on pre–post data (by subject area and even by individual units within subject areas)?

> are able to attain information quickly once it's explained even if they did not know the content ahead of time?

> have insightful ideas but may not be able to communicate those ideas concisely or using mainstream vocabulary?

> are able to convince others to conform to an idea or activity (even if that activity is not appropriate for school)?

> show problem-solving or reasoning skills and responsibility through home or community connections and at earlier ages than their same-age peers? (For example, navigating bus schedules, taking care of younger siblings at earlier ages than typical, or planning meals.)

> participate in and are recognized for or have leadership roles in events or organizations outside of school? (For example, 4-H, dance clubs, church groups, community theater clubs, or traveling teams.)

> are able to design new methods or ideas for completing a task or creating something new using minimal materials or combining what is available in unique ways?

Barriers to Successful Self-Advocacy and Ways to Address Them

Students cannot learn to speak up for themselves unless they are taught to do so and have supportive adults who also know how to appropriately advocate for them. Even if educators understand how students may manifest talent in unique and varied ways, there are several barriers to success that advocates need to be aware of so they can be a voice for their gifted low-income students at the individual, school, and community levels and, more importantly, enable students to find their own voice. Of course, a major barrier to success is lack of adequate money and, therefore, basic needs going unmet. So as you read about and examine some of the barriers to success for gifted low-income students, consider your circle of influence and what you have control over, coupled with the things you can grab onto immediately and work toward changing or advocating for with the child and their family, school, and community. Though eradicating poverty is a worthy goal, educators must take action in the short term with the resources and knowledge currently available to them. The key barriers discussed in this chapter are barriers to understanding giftedness, accessing identification and service options, understanding rights and responsibilities, and connecting with advocates. To help students overcome these barriers, advocates must:

> ❯ reframe misconceptions and incorrect assumptions about gifted low-income students
> ❯ advocate for evidence-supported schoolwide identification of students with high ability
> ❯ encourage gifted low-income students' access to advanced programs with scaffolds and supports
> ❯ build relationships and connections with gifted low-income students and their families

Next, each of these strategies is discussed in more detail.

Reframing Misconceptions and Incorrect Assumptions

Before you can advocate for students or teach them self-advocacy skills, you need to:

> ❯ know who and what you are advocating for and why
> ❯ know your own beliefs and biases about gifted students from low-income backgrounds
> ❯ understand the populations for whom you work in order to advocate for them
> ❯ understand your own beliefs about income and giftedness and recognize that your experiences may not always be the same as those of your students; you can use your personal experiences to relate to students but must take care not to project your own experiences upon them

Advocacy also requires helping others reframe misconceptions about gifted low-income students. Since these students may not always show their giftedness in traditional ways, we must figure out alternative methods for identifying and supporting them. Additionally, we must help students see themselves as capable. It is challenging to advocate for yourself if you don't believe in your ability or you don't know what you need. Similarly, if you do not know your students or your population, how can you advocate for them? Determining characteristics and alternative ways in which gifted students from low-income households may show their talents is only the beginning. Giftedness and advocacy are more than recognizing a list of behaviors. We must also understand barriers to successful advocacy. These barriers include:

> ❯ a lack of understanding about gifted low-income students
> ❯ having inadequate school-based systems in place for finding and serving those students
> ❯ denying access or not providing access (intentionally or unintentionally) to appropriately matched learning opportunities
> ❯ not connecting with students and their families and failing to inform them of ways to access information and services
> ❯ mistaking a lack of access, opportunity, and resources for a lack of giftedness

One of the most important things advocates can do is help others understand the population they are working with. You may have heard frustrated educators and leaders from schools that primarily serve low-income students say, "We don't have any gifted kids in our school," or "Parents in our school don't care about achievement because they don't attend events." But are statements like these true? Perhaps the observations that few students have been identified and few parents attend events are true. But the question is, *why?* Jansorn (2020), an advocate from a nonprofit organization that supports gifted low-income students, asked parents how they support their child's learning. She found that few parents of gifted students from low-income schools felt they had healthy communication from schools. Most parents chose to support their child at home by helping with homework or by providing for their basic needs so that the child would have an environment that is away from the chaos of neighborhood dysfunction or crime and that, therefore, is a safe place to learn. This is important to note because many times as educators we think parents are disengaged if they are not helping at the school when, in reality, they have prioritized their child's learning by working a second job to keep food on the table and provide sustenance for their child as a way to maximize potential. Jansorn (2020) also reports that many families also utilize free community resources to support their child's quest for knowledge, such as going to the local library.

Most parents have competing demands for their time, and when these demands are coupled with a lack of financial resources and access, even harder decisions must be made about how to best spend limited resources. Regardless of income level, most parents want the same for their children—an opportunity for the child to be the best person possible and achieve as much as possible while leading a happy and productive life. Some families are able to nurture talent and achievement and access impactful opportunities in a more direct way due to the resources they have, while other families must choose between providing their children with a home environment that allows them to safely learn and attending school events.

Advocate for Evidence-Supported Schoolwide Identification Systems

As previously mentioned, students in poverty may not demonstrate the cultural and social norms generally anticipated among wealthier high-ability students. Additionally, students from low-income households are more likely to have discrepant and varied testing profiles, meaning that they may show advanced work in one area but not another (depending upon their access and exposure) and are less likely to score advanced on state assessments (Stambaugh and Olszewski-Kubilius 2020).

In addition to being identified as gifted less frequently, students who attend low-income schools have fewer opportunities overall. Title I schools:

> have more beginning teachers (Stambaugh and Olszewski-Kubilius 2020)
> have more low-level classes
> are less likely to offer AP and honors classes (Plucker and Peters 2018)
> have lower scores on AP tests (Gagnon and Mattingly 2015)

Gifted low-income students have a right to have the same access to high-quality teachers, curriculum, clubs, extracurricular activities, and services as students in non-Title I schools in their district or neighboring districts have. Therefore, they often must shoulder the burden of advocating for this access.

Recognition and access will eventually help gifted low-income students self-advocate. How, then, do we promote equitable systems that ensure recognition of gifts and talents and access to services for students from low-income households when they may not perform or score in a way that shows their potential? Schools will recognize more low-income learners if they use:

> talent-spotting systems (Robinson et al. 2018; Horn 2015)
> local norms (Peters and Engerrand 2016)
> universal screening as opposed to teacher referrals (McBee 2006)

> holistic student profiles instead of rigid cut-off scores (Horn 2015)

> multiple opportunities for assessment and determination of student strengths (Olszewski-Kubilius and Clarenbach 2012)

Some of these approaches may be more familiar than others. You can explore them further by checking out the references for this chapter.

Encourage Access to Services with Scaffolds and Strengths-Based Supports

Douglas (2018) explains that gifted students have two main rights: to understand their giftedness and to have an appropriately challenging curriculum.

Many curricula and service provisions are available and have been successful in supporting gifted low-income students. On a systems level, Horn (2015), an administrator and researcher in a large school district, found success in adopting a model in which a menu of services is provided to meet a variety of student needs. All students have access to higher level thinking skills and opportunities in the classroom, many students may receive enrichment opportunities while some may need to be pulled out of the regular classroom and provided more extensive support, and a few students may need grade skipping or more intensified services. The services are labeled instead of the child. Opportunities for free out-of-school options are also available and strongly encouraged for students who are from diverse or low-income backgrounds and who need a few more supports to fill in gaps and enjoy enrichment. All students have access to the same higher level thinking models when teachers are taught to be talent scouts.

Curriculum-based approaches that support scaffolding of instruction from lower to higher level skills are necessary to fill in gaps in exposure while also helping students "catch up" or keeping them challenged through the provision of higher-level thinking skills. Supplemental curriculum such as the Jacob's Ladder framework (VanTassel-Baska and Stambaugh 2008)—designed with gifted students in Title I schools in mind—provides a scaffolded approach for leading students from lower to higher level skills as they "climb" a ladder (Stambaugh 2018). Other curricula recommended for low-income students include Mentoring Mathematical Minds from the University of Connecticut, STEM Starters+ from the University of Arkansas Little Rock, and the English language arts and science curricula from the College of William and Mary.

After a review of Javits grants focused on curriculum design and implementation for high-ability students from low-income households, Stambaugh (2010) compared features across all curriculum that positively impact the achievement of students attending low-income schools and found the following features consistent across all materials:

> high-level curriculum tasks with built-in scaffolding

> relevant and conceptually based content that includes ways for students to relate to and experience the content, including opportunities to create experiences for students as needed for exposure

> the explicit and consistent use of models and frameworks to guide student thinking

> modeling of processes and vocabulary of experts

Also present were systems for administrative support, accountability, teacher coaching, and fidelity of implementation.

As part of advocacy, educators can level the playing field through access to high-level curriculum with scaffolding and the teaching of advanced-level skills. Some schools have even used advanced curriculum as a way to find more students for gifted programs, teaching everyone higher level thinking-skill strategies and observing students who are able to learn and apply these skills more quickly after exposure, eventually assessing them for additional and more advanced services in gifted education. Instead of reinventing the wheel, perhaps schools could adopt or adapt high-level curricula found successful with high-ability students in Title I schools as a first step toward promoting equity and access. This is important to consider as currently many Title I schools have course offerings that are less rigorous than those in wealthier school districts (Plucker and Peters 2018).

Build Relationships and Connections with Students and Their Families

Without relationships, advocacy approaches are destined to fail. Relationships are important in general, but they seem to be even more important for those from low-income households. Students from low-income backgrounds are more likely to engage and do work if they like you and believe that you like and respect them, regardless of whether they have interest or ability in that subject area (Richards and Stambaugh 2015; Budge and Parrett 2018).

In a qualitative study, Milacci and Zabloski interviewed gifted students from low-income and rural settings who dropped out of school. They found that the presence of positive relationships was the most important mitigating factor. The researchers concluded that:

> Review of the interview transcripts showed us that the majority of conversation with these gifted dropouts centered around relationships both good and bad. The interviewees placed much less emphasis on academics in the discussions than they did on who delivered the academics, how they delivered it, and why they liked or disliked the person doing so. For example, if they spoke of boredom, they explained who was boring more than what was boring. (Milacci and Zabloski 2012, 187)

Students participating in this study also explained that they did not have advocates or positive relationships with schools or other significant individuals in their lives to know where to turn for support. In fact, the majority of students experienced negative relationships, no advocates, and relational trauma in middle school. These experiences were cited as a catalyst for major behavior changes that led to them dropping out.

Relationships with families, not just students, are another critical component for advocacy and overall success in Title I schools. However, Jansorn (2020) found that some families she worked with were not comfortable going to the school for support. Rather, they found access through community agencies or dealt with concerns on their own. Some schools have had success engaging families through creative opportunities such as those recommended by Parrett and Budge (2012):

> opening free laundry facilities during the school day

> volunteering space for meetings

> providing space for food pantries

> ensuring that child care and food are available during meetings

> providing time for families to get to know each other

In my time as a gifted coordinator in Title I schools, some of my most well-attended parent meetings included those where I incorporated learning activities for families and provided care for young children. I have also solicited donations from companies in the local area to offer gas cards to pay for transportation or other door prizes such as school supplies, snacks, or learning games. Other schools have had success engaging families through activity nights where students and families work together on integrated unit activities and packets that students can take home later (Coleman and Shah-Coltrane 2011).

Until trust is built, a champion or other person who is respected or known by the families may need to act as a spokesperson. This person might help with phone calls, emails, or parent meetings to discuss possible opportunities for the student or even attend home visits as appropriate. One personal story comes to mind. I was launching a program through a generous gift to support low-income gifted students in reading. Participating students were to be provided with free books, in-class services, and an opportunity to attend Saturday and summer enrichment and accelerated programs on a college campus. My colleagues and I sent permission slips for participation and scheduled a pizza party for students and their families to get together to learn more about the project.

> Trust comes with time, and for many families it is built through ongoing positive experiences and relationships.

Because we were not known individuals in the school, fewer than 2 percent of invitees confirmed their attendance. We then decided to add another layer of communication and provided a choice of a sweet treat or a school supply to any students who returned their notification letter confirming or denying their attendance at the event. Many students reported that they did not bring back their notifications because their parents were afraid the offer was too good to be true, because they didn't know us and would not attend, or because they were afraid there would be a later "ask" for money.

After talking with the principal, guidance counselor, and a favorite teacher of many of the students, it was decided that the teacher and guidance counselor would make individual calls to families since these school adults had already built strong relationships. Additionally, during car-rider pick-up duty, one of the teachers individually spoke with parents about the opportunity. By the time the parent meeting and event was ready to take place, over 70 percent of families had agreed to attend.

Over the four years we worked in the school, most of the families eventually reached out to call or email us directly and stopped going through the teacher or guidance counselor when questions arose. It took time to develop relationships and build trust, and we had to follow through on our promises. We also had to make sure the meetings we provided were efficient and met families' expectations and needs in addition to our own.

Trust comes with time, and for many families it is built through ongoing positive experiences and relationships. When parents trust the system and the individuals within the system, they are more apt to encourage their children to self-advocate.

Evidence-Supported Advocacy Models

How do we develop talent through an advocacy lens for low-income students? What matters in the development of talent? When should we teach students to self-advocate, and when should we advocate on their behalf? Talent needs to be recognized and nurtured to be developed. The trajectory from ability to expertise (leading to creative performance) is based on many factors including ability, motivation, opportunities taken, developed social skills, opportunities offered in and out of school, access to financial resources with social and cultural capital, and developed psychological strength, including resilience, self-confidence, efficacy, and mindset (Subotnik, Olszewski-Kubilius, and Worrell 2011). This means that advocates need to support low-income students in developing or accessing opportunities, skills, and resources that lead to ongoing social, emotional, and academic growth.

Each year at my office, we lead a conference focused on academically advanced students from under-represented groups. We generally host a panel composed of students from low-income households who are attending colleges and universities. I ask students to reflect on their years in school and to discuss what factors supported or inhibited their talent development processes and made a significant difference in their current trajectory. Without fail, everyone mentions a person who helped show them the way. This advocate may not have even known that they were influential or played such a huge role in students' lives.

The panelists share numerous stories about how a teacher, coach, or community member noticed their talent and helped with tangible and intangible support. Advocates provided transportation to important events, helped students find financial support for attending specialized programs to develop their talent outside of school, showed them how to navigate school systems, made them aware of programs available, sat with them as they completed paperwork for a scholarship, or just noticed a struggle and asked what they could do to help. Some students mention individuals who showed them the ropes and provided emotional support or helped them believe in themselves and their abilities, giving them the confidence to step out and try something new or different from their family norm.

One student said a combination of many small things led to her success. She explained that in order to survive a really tough advanced class in high school, the students formed study groups that met after school at a local coffee shop. Everyone would buy coffee and study. This particular student needed the peer support of the study group but did not have the money to buy coffee and was embarrassed to show up without purchasing anything. When she stopped attending the group, she really missed the camaraderie and her grades started to suffer. The teacher noticed the dilemma and without saying a word, transformed her classroom into a makeshift coffee shop complete with coffee beans and a grinder, fancy creamers, and comfortable seating. The student appreciated the gesture and was able to rejoin the study group with success. For other panelists, simple but powerful words like, "You belong here," or "I know you can do this," were enough to keep them going.

Panelists also note that they were not aware of outside activities or courses available to them, and it was generally a teacher or family friend who told them how to navigate school systems, sign up for advanced classes, or join after-school clubs with promises of support with transportation or entrance fees. Many students said that even if they were aware of advanced opportunities, they were worried about signing up because of hidden costs. They were also concerned about required commitments that were not always known up front that could keep them from fully participating or feeling as if they were part of the group. Things that educators take for granted, such as candy sale requirements, buying a required t-shirt for an event, contributing food, gathering materials for a project, or coming to school for practice on a weekend, proved to be barriers that kept some gifted low-income students from engaging. Having relationships with teachers or another adult to whom they felt comfortable disclosing this information and who would not judge or shame them was important. When students stepped out and did participate in accelerated and appropriate options, it was because they trusted the individual in charge.

Another common finding from panelists was their internal psychological strength. Panelists had to learn how to be their own advocates. They had to be motivated enough to search for information on their own since their parents, while generally supportive, often did not know where to turn or how best to guide them to available options. The group also noted their own resiliency, perseverance, and mindset as contributing to their success. Even if a teacher or advocate told them about an opportunity, they had to have the motivation and discipline to seek it and put in the time and effort to pursue it on their own. This often required doing double or triple the work of some of their more well-informed and wealthier peers in gathering information, explaining processes and opportunities to their parents, and negotiating other family obligations or outside jobs in order to participate. Yet students did not regret this effort. They said that as a result they had better time-management skills, study habits, problem-solving skills, practical knowledge, and work ethic than some of their counterparts. They were proud of their prior experiences, practical knowledge, and hard work.

So how do we help students self-advocate and gain access necessary to develop their amazing talents? Douglas (2018) outlines four steps in self-advocacy for gifted learners that include:

1. Understanding one's rights and responsibilities
2. Assessing and reflecting on one's learner profile
3. Investigating options and opportunities based on student strengths
4. Connecting with adults who can help them accomplish the goal

Others who study self-advocacy for students with disabilities have found that self-advocacy involves the following components:

1. Knowledge of self
2. Knowledge of rights
3. Communication of needs
4. Leadership or advocacy for themselves and others (Test et al. 2005)

Advocates are responsible for helping students become independent in their own self-advocacy. However, gifted students often fail to ask for what they need without support and prompting (Douglas 2018)—something that is even more true of students from low-income households. They need support as they move through the process.

So far, we have discussed a talent development model as well as two self-advocacy models. Just as frameworks for scaffolding and instruction for low-income learners are important, frameworks for advocates are important too. The American Counseling Association and the American Association of School Counselors outline a model for advocacy that includes specific competencies for advocates (Ratts, DeKruyf, and Chen-Hayes 2007). Distinctions are made between advocating *on behalf of* and advocating *with* students; both are needed, but the goal is to move students along a continuum toward their own independence in self-advocacy through empowerment. Specific competencies outlined include:

> ways to negotiate for services
> teaching self-advocacy skills
> working with students to develop goals and action plans for attaining goals
> identifying strengths and needs in the school and the student
> recognizing possible external factors that can impede or support student growth
> developing connections and alliances within the family, school, and community

Advocates support students at the individual student level (helping the student realize and access opportunities and advocate on their own), the school and systems level (change procedures that have negative unintended consequences for a particular population or connect with other community agencies to garner support), and in the public arena (educating others and supporting positive change in political arenas and supportive agencies) (Ratts, DeKruyf, and Chen-Hayes 2007). **Table** 7.2 combines talent development features with self-advocacy components and outlines ideas for educators to support students in their self-advocacy efforts.

TABLE 7.2: Strategies for Advocates to Support Talent Development in Students from Low-Income Households

	SELF-AWARENESS	KNOWLEDGE OF RIGHTS	COMMUNICATION AND CONNECTION
Ability	Explain what giftedness is and is not to families, students, and educators, including how it might manifest in various populations. Emphasize the impact of hard work, access, and opportunity as part of realizing ability. Provide strengths-based approaches and interest surveys to help students understand and capitalize on their strengths instead of focusing on deficits.	Make identification practices transparent. Make sure everyone receives information annually about how to access services and identification. Follow an inclusion model with the assumption of giftedness unless proven incorrect instead of requiring students to prove their intelligence first. Explain that all students have a right to learn something new every day and a right to have the same access to higher level curriculum, quality teachers, and clubs as students from wealthier schools in their same or neighboring districts. Be transparent about policies and laws that govern identification, service, and appeal processes within the state and district.	Explain what giftedness looks like in your particular school population. Design multi-leveled approaches and services to accommodate a variety of ability and content-area performances—connecting students to appropriate services matched to their ability with opportunities to fill in gaps due to lack of access as needed. Provide opportunities to connect with knowledgeable adults or mentors in areas of strength and interest to nurture abilities.
Opportunities taken	Help students set goals that include opportunities that will develop their strengths and help them carry out these goals.	Help students gain access to appropriate resources.	Communicate opportunities. Examine systems within your school or district to ensure that opportunities are equitably available to all students.

continued >

TABLE 7.2 Strategies for Advocates to Support Talent Development in Students from Low-Income Households (continued)

	SELF-AWARENESS	KNOWLEDGE OF RIGHTS	COMMUNICATION AND CONNECTION
In-school and out-of-school accelerated opportunities	Match student abilities and strengths to services available. Inform families and students of services matched to their ability. Consider grade-level and advanced opportunities to support and realize talent.	Help students navigate needs such as transportation, taking care of siblings, or asking for time off from a job to attend a program.	Ask someone the student and family trust to make personal phone calls to explain opportunities that are available, including potential hidden costs, available scholarships and financial aid, and expected commitments. Support continuing self-advocacy strategies if students are moving out of their immediate school district for program participation. Visit the program ahead of time or connect the student and family with a leader or another participant from the program.
Psychological strength	Provide students with tools and resources to continue to develop their self-awareness.	Incorporate the 6 Cs of Resiliency and Motivation into lessons and school-based approaches.	Communicate and practice ways to deal with self-doubt, resistance, belonging, and mindset.
Mentoring	Discuss what students want in a mentor and how that relationship can help them realize their goals.	Explain the give-and-take of mentoring relationships and the rights and responsibilities that students and their mentors have.	Help students communicate their needs, weaknesses, goals, and strengths with mentors. Connect students to others who are able to support their content-based strengths and show them how to navigate systems.
Communication and self-advocacy	Help students understand how they communicate effectively in a variety of settings.	Help students understand the importance of self-advocacy and how to communicate their needs.	Provide sentence stems or practice ways to communicate and self-advocate through simulations of typical events.

Strategies for Educators

Several strategies have been discussed throughout this chapter while considering an advocate's circle of influence. Review **tables 7.1** and **7.2** for information about creating systems for identification, curriculum, and instructional approaches that support advocacy, and how to support your own advocacy within a talent development framework. Then focus on how to help students do the same. The ultimate goal is to help students become self-advocates. This takes time, deliberate development of relationships and psychosocial skills, and access to advanced content with scaffolds. Here are some additional strategies for educators to support gifted low-income students in becoming self-advocates and to develop advocacy skills:

1. **Understand and acknowledge your personal beliefs about gifted students and low-income gifted students.** What we believe about gifted students from low-income households determines who we will see (or not) and to what extent we can advocate for these students. Context, culture, beliefs, and personal experiences may impact our conceptions and attitudes about gifted low-income students. Acknowledge these, and continue to reframe your misconceptions, as necessary.

2. **Develop strengths-based identification and service-delivery systems.** Consider the unique characteristics and strengths students from your district bring to the school and capitalize on those, understanding that problem-solving may manifest itself in taking care of younger siblings or navigating competing priorities. Provide opportunities for students to have access to high-quality curriculum, instruction, services, and teachers. Encourage your district to conduct a school equity scan to determine if services across buildings are aligned and available for all eligible students, not just those in wealthier parts of the district.

3. **Follow a strength-based model.** In their book *Disrupting Poverty*, Budge and Parrett (2018) explain that to best advocate for students, teachers need to understand each student's unique living conditions, the strengths and cultural capital they bring to the classroom, their level of reliance on school services, and what is done when they do not master the content. They suggest that educators make a list of the students in their classrooms and respond to each consideration for each student. This will help them determine which students are most at risk, consider students' home situations, and outline strengths-based plans for supporting their achievement. I recommend adding one more consideration to support gifted low-income students: examine ways in which students' strengths and mastery of content might be masked by other factors and develop opportunities for them to show their skills within the context of their environment. While living in poverty certainly creates multiple barriers, we need to focus on what schools can do to mitigate these factors as much as possible and provide support. **Table 7.2** on page 103 provides more ideas within a talent development framework to enhance services and promote access and opportunity.

4. **Develop trust and relationships with students and families through school-based partnerships.** We discussed earlier the importance of working and communicating with families and building trusting relationships. Parrett and Budge (2012), in their book *Turning High-Poverty Schools into High-Performing Schools*, explain that schools that are the hub of community life are more likely to have fewer students who are truant, fewer disciplinary and special education referrals, and higher achievement. A school as a hub might mean offering adult education classes for families based on community needs, such as ELL or GED classes. It also means visiting or calling families to check in with positive messages and no-cost opportunities and offering service learning and mentorship opportunities to students as ways to build relationships so that everyone is part of the community and successfully contributes. Additionally, Berkowitz and colleagues (2017), in a synthesis of research, reported that "feelings of belonging" was another major difference between students from wealthy and low-income households. Developing ways to help families and students feel like they belong is another critical component for building relationships. Belonging entails feeling connected, committed, and supported in endeavors (Anderson-Butcher and Conroy 2002). Stambaugh (2017), when surveying gifted students on their perceptions of boredom, belonging, number of friendships, and the impact of each on anxiety and depression, found that when students felt like they belonged, they reported lower anxiety and depression and less disruptive behavior. Moreover, when gifted students were in settings that were appropriately challenging and felt satisfied with their friendships, they reported higher belonging.

5. **Teach psychosocial skills such as resiliency, mindset, motivation, and goal-setting.** Work with your guidance counselor and others to help students develop goal-setting skills, understand the importance of hard work and effort as a central component to developing talent, and motivate themselves. Wang and Han (2010) outline what they call the six Cs of motivation: choice, challenge, control, collaboration, constructing meaning, and consequences. These features can be embedded within a curriculum for low-income students, ensuring that they know how to take control of their learning in relevant and important ways that motivate them within their unique context and circumstance. As a low-income gifted learner, it may be difficult to be motivated by long-term outcomes and abstract ideas presented in class when the present-day issue is lack of food. However, a curriculum that provides challenge through debatable questions about world hunger and connects that information to science and chemistry or service learning within the community can allow for challenge, choice, and collaboration. And while we are on the Cs in the alphabet, let's also examine resilience. Ginsburg and Jablow (2015) outline the following ways to help students become more resilient: competence, confidence, connection, character, contribution, coping, and control. While these principles are not specific to low-income students, groups who support such students have used them with success, providing students with ways to develop confidence through small successes and scaffolding when necessary, creating connections to others who care about them and their community, and providing opportunities for students to have control in something that matters to them. The Center for Parent and Teen Communication video "The Seven C's of Resilience" can be viewed at youtube.com /watch?v=DTmi4kHor_s. Finally, setting personal and content-based short- and long-term goals is important and part of psychosocial development in which advocates can play a role. Many times, students from low-income households struggle with setting long-term goals. They may not always know what the next day holds or how they can plan for the future.

6. **Provide mirrors and windows.** Bishop (1990) first discussed the idea of children's books as windows and mirrors and explained that students need windows into worlds with which they are not familiar and mirrors reflecting the world in which they are living. In this way, books and biographies can provide mirrors and windows for students to see stories and characters who are like them and who differ from them. Community mentors can also provide mirrors and windows and are an important part of talent development (Subotnik, Olszewski-Kubilius, and Worrell 2011). Mentors for low-income students include not only content-based mentors and experts in a field, but mentors who are able to help students navigate systems. Students also need individuals whom they can emulate, especially individuals from their own communities or backgrounds who are willing to share their stories, failures, and successes. The Jacob's Ladder Affective Framework (VanTassel-Baska and Stambaugh 2018) provides reading prompts, biographies, and poems for students to read and discuss in a safe way, through the lens of a character rather than as themselves, while focusing on strategies around goal-setting, perfectionism, identity, motivation, resiliency, developing empathy, and achievement orientations. The framework integrates reading achievement outcomes with proactive social and emotional need discussions in a safe way in the classroom.

Putting It All Together

The STARR Model in **figure 7.1** may be helpful to summarize the contents of this chapter, bringing together the various strategies discussed into one holistic approach to teaching gifted students from low-income households to self-advocate. All components of the STARR model need to be considered by the advocate and the self-advocate. Reflect on the questions for you and your school in each area of the model and equip your students with the resources to ask their own questions too.

Self-Determination

Self-determination for gifted low-income students is defined as having perseverance, resiliency, goal-setting, and motivation.

Ask yourself:

> Are students equipped with the skills and opportunities to persevere?

> Do they have opportunities to work on areas of interest and things that motivate them?

> Am I teaching students skills to persevere when things become challenging?

> Am I providing scaffolds so that students can enjoy small successes?

> How can I help students set small goals that will help them realize their larger goals?

Ask your students:

> What are you interested in?

> How can you find ways to do more of those things?

> What strategies do you have to persevere when things get challenging?

> How do you ask for help when you need it?

> When is it appropriate to ask for help?

> What do you feel competent in?

> How can you build skills in areas in which you do not yet feel competent?

> What do you have control over, and how can you focus on those things?

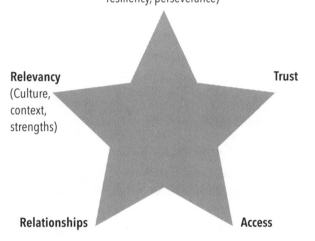

FIGURE 7.1: STARR Model for Teaching Self-Advocacy to Gifted Students from Low-Income Households

Self-Determination
(Psychosocial skills: Motivation, resiliency, perseverance)

Relevancy
(Culture, context, strengths)

Trust

Relationships

Access

Trust

Trust involves feeling connected, committed to others or a cause, supported in endeavors, and belonging to various groups.

Ask yourself:

> How am I helping students build relationships with each other in positive ways?

> Are there enough opportunities in my classroom for students to feel like they belong to a variety of groups?

> Am I mixing up groups to support interests as well as abilities?

> Does everyone have an opportunity to experience success?

> What service-learning opportunities are available to help students engage in areas of interest in positive ways?

> What barriers need to be removed for students to engage in service-learning opportunities?

> Am I reliable? Do I do what I say I will do so that students can trust me?

> Am I consistent in my responses for all students?

> Do I inadvertently give some students preferential treatment?

> Do the classroom rules apply to everyone equally?

> Does everyone get the benefit of the doubt?

> Am I approachable?

> Do I stop negative comments or counter erroneous beliefs about students from low-income households?

Ask your students:

> Who can you go to when _____? (Insert a variety of scenarios here and encourage students to seek out various people as they build a circle of support. This list will increase from a family or school unit to others outside the family as students get older.)

> What does trust mean to you and what do you look for in someone you can trust? How are you a trustworthy person?

> Where are places you feel like you belong? What do these places have in common?

> What do you do if you don't feel like you belong but want to be involved? What could you say or do, or who could you talk to?

Access

Access is defined as having opportunities, knowing about those opportunities, and taking advantage of them. Ask yourself:

> Are there similar opportunities for enrichment at my school as there are at wealthier schools?

> Do the opportunities that are provided encourage success and strengths, or are they deficit focused?

> How do I communicate opportunities to all students so they all have an equal chance of access?

> What can be done during the regular school day to increase students' access, as opposed to after school when travel and cost may be more of a barrier?

> Are there community agencies that can fund enrichment opportunities after school?

> Are free transportation or ride-sharing lists an option?

> How can I best encourage students and their families to take advantage of opportunities or ask for help when finances are a barrier to access?

> Who in my class has not signed up for enrichment opportunities but would benefit from them?

> How can I provide personal support to students and their families to encourage them to take advantage of the opportunities provided?

> Does my school provide food or child care for meetings?

> Are meetings offered at convenient times and locations?

> Are there alternatives for communicating information besides a meeting at school?

Ask your students:

> How can you find out what enrichment opportunities are available during or after school that might be of interest to you? Who can you ask?

> How can you ask for financial help when you know there are opportunities that your family cannot afford?

> What do you do if you have other job or sibling responsibilities that conflict with enrichment opportunities?

> When do you sacrifice short-term gain (after-school job and extra money) for long-term gain (taking part in a school club that will help you advance in your future career)?

Relevancy

Relevancy is broadly defined to include relevant curriculum (mirrors and windows, goal valuation) and relevant context (community application) as well as strength-based approaches.

Ask yourself:

> Am I providing examples of successful community members or other individuals who have similar backgrounds and experiences as my students?

> Am I providing role models for students to emulate (whether through literature or real people)?

> Am I making appropriate connections from the curriculum to student goals and life examples?

> Am I connecting and scaffolding instruction and creating experiences for students who do not have personal experiences to draw from?

Ask your students:

> What are your personal goals?

> How does this class content help you reach your personal goals?

> Who are your heroes and how might their words and actions help you reach your goals?

> What community connections are available to help you with your goals? How can you find connections?

> If something does not seem to apply to you, how can you ask for ways to make it more relevant?

Relationships

Without relationships it is difficult, if not impossible, to support gifted low-income students. Relationships matter for ongoing success. This includes how individuals communicate as well as how trusting, healthy, and supportive relationships are formed and cultivated. Relationships need to be cultivated between the student and teacher, the teacher and family, the family and school, and so forth.

Ask yourself:

> How can I get to know each of my students better?

> Can I name at least one thing each student in my classroom is interested in?

> How do I convey to my students that they matter and that they can come to me as a resource?

> Am I fair and consistent when talking with all students?

> How can I find mentors or others in the school or community to help me advocate for or build relationships with my students and their families?

> Do I ask families about their needs and dreams for their children, or do I assume or make judgments based on where students live or other factors?

> Do my nonverbal cues relay something different than my verbal communication does?

> Do families of gifted low-income students know that I am a resource and support for their children's education?

> Do I listen?

> Are the meetings at my school school-centric or child/family-centric?

> Is the school a place where families feel comfortable showing up?

Ask your students:

> Who are the teachers or other adults in this school that you know you can ask for help?

> How are you cultivating positive relationships? What does that look like?

> Who are your friends and how often do you get to hang out? How can you develop more friendships?

> What does it mean to be a friend?

> What does it mean to be a student?

> When and how might you approach a teacher or parent to develop a positive relationship?

> Are you perceived as someone who wants positive relationships? If yes, why? If not, why not, and what can you do to develop this skill set?

> Why are positive relationships with others important?

> How might you communicate in a way that showcases your strengths and talents?

> What does positive communication look like?

Sam and Kindra

Let's go back to the beginning of this chapter and think about Sam and Kindra. While their life situations were very different, their needs and the systems around them were similar. What do you think these two students have in common? How have their families and schools supported or helped them thus far? What additional support do they need in order to successfully self-advocate? If you were invited to consult on their situations, what information from this chapter would inform your first and next steps?

Both of these students are in low-income families and low-income schools with cultural and social barriers to success. Both seem to have found school personnel who want to be helpful. Sam has access to a physics class, and Kindra has a language arts class she loves. But they also need help. To effectively advocate for Sam and Kindra, teachers must understand these students' social and cultural contexts to build relationships and be perceived as being invested. Teachers can then validate Sam's and Kindra's feelings and life experiences with expertise to build trust. Sam needs to know that he is allowed to be intelligent and that he has a right to higher level classes. Kindra needs a curriculum that allows her to progress at her own pace. Both students have educational rights, but they may not know what these are. They need adults to advocate on their behalf and teach them to advocate for themselves. The adults also need to encourage and applaud Sam's and Kindra's attempts to ask for help, even if their requests are not always communicated in ways that school staff are expecting or watching for.

Looking at the STARR Model, access, relationships, and self-determination are key factors educators need to develop with Sam. They can help him build resiliency and communicate his strengths and interests as well as how he feels when his family does not understand him. Role-playing conversations or providing sentence stems would be beneficial. The teacher and Sam could initiate a meeting with Sam's family, including his grandparents, to explain Sam's strengths and interests and provide a menu of opportunities that Sam has already expressed interest in. The teacher can listen to the family's concerns and provide doable and affordable options that allow Sam and his family to have ownership over Sam's education and not feel talked down to. Assisting Sam in better understanding himself through validation and acceptance of his strengths and weaknesses will also be helpful. A strengths-based approach would include offering Sam access to experts in physics to affirm his interests, assistance finding online learning options for new coursework that the school doesn't offer, or mentoring in a content area he chooses.

> While we may not be able to eradicate poverty for each learner, we can take action each day to provide resources, information, and encouragement that supports their self-advocacy.

For Kindra, recognizing what she has done herself to affirm her perseverance will be empowering. A teacher would continue in the STARR Model by supporting Kindra's family's interest in her education. Determining creative ways to connect the family and the school would be helpful in building trust and would allow Kindra and her parents to communicate her academic needs more easily. Perhaps communication through technology could be a viable way to create dialogue and teamwork between the family and school. Kindra may be aware of her strengths, but she would benefit from encouragement and empowerment to ask for what she wants and needs from a teacher with whom she has a positive relationship. Kindra's teacher may work with Kindra's parents to find flexible conference times that fit into their schedules while affirming the complexity of the family's responsibilities and demands on their time. Since Kindra already feels a connection to her language arts teacher, she might consider whether there is another class or independent study offered by the same teacher that has more rigor.

Finally, both Sam and Kindra would likely benefit from skill building around social and emotional themes, such as resiliency, self-confidence, and self-efficacy (Choi 2017).

Conclusion

The key barriers to gifted low-income students' self-advocacy include misunderstandings about giftedness, an inability to access identification and service options, unfamiliarity with rights and responsibilities, and lack of connection to advocates. In order to help these students break through such barriers, educators can take four important steps: reframe misconceptions and incorrect assumptions about gifted low-income students; advocate for evidence-supported schoolwide identification of students with high ability; encourage gifted low-income students' access to advanced programs with scaffolds and supports; and build relationships and connections with gifted low-income students and their families. While we may not be able to eradicate poverty for each learner, we can take action each day to provide resources, information, and encouragement that supports their self-advocacy.

Key Concepts

> Low-income students have the same rights as other students to an appropriate education and to access to quality teachers, curriculum matched to their strengths and abilities, and in- and out-of-school opportunities for enrichment and acceleration.

> Relationships with families and students matter, and they can powerfully impact student trajectories, psychosocial skills, and belonging.

> The systems schools put in place for identification, services, and community outreach matter.

> Explicit attention to psychosocial skills matters.

> The selection and implementation of curriculum and instructional resources matter.

> You, as an advocate, matter.

> Students' voices matter, and students may need your help finding theirs.

> Self-advocacy needs to and can be taught through modeling and direct instruction.

Discussion Questions

1. How does self-advocacy for gifted low-income students differ from self-advocacy for other groups of students discussed in this book? Select another group and create a Venn diagram.

2. How might gifted low-income students in your district or building show their abilities in ways that may be atypical or need advocate support?

3. What training in your school needs to take place so that educators and leaders can be better advocates for gifted low-income students?

4. What are you doing well to support gifted students from low-income households, according to this chapter? What else do you need to do or implement? Create an advocate plan based on data from your building.

5. Do all gifted or potentially gifted students in your district have the same level of opportunity to access high-quality teachers, advanced coursework, and advanced in- and out-of-school opportunities? If not, why not? If so, what systems are in place to support that access?

6. How might the STARR Model be applied in your context? Provide specific examples for how it can be used to enhance your advocacy and support the self-advocacy of your students.

Recommended Resources

Borland, James. 2005. "Gifted Education Without Gifted Children: The Case for No Conception of Giftedness." In *Conceptions of Giftedness,* 2nd ed., edited by Robert J. Sternberg and Janet E. Davidson, 1–19. New York: Cambridge University Press.

Lohman, David F. 2005. "An Aptitude Perspective on Talent: Implications for Identification of Academically Gifted Minority Students." *Journal for the Education of the Gifted* 28 (3–4): 333–360. doi.org/10.4219/jeg-2005-341.

———. 2005. "The Role of Nonverbal Ability Tests in Identifying Academically Gifted Students: An Aptitude Perspective." *Gifted Child Quarterly* 49 (2): 111–138. doi.org/10.1177/001698620504900203.

Lohman, David F., and Joni Lakin. 2008. "Nonverbal Test Scores as One Component of an Identification System: Integrating Ability, Achievement, and Teacher Ratings." In *Alternative Assessments with Gifted and Talented Students*, edited by Joyce VanTassel-Baska. 41–66. Waco, TX: Prufrock Press.

Loveless, Tom. 2009. *Tracking and Detracking: High Achievers in Massachusetts Middle Schools.* Washington DC: Thomas B. Fordham Institute.

Mayer, Roger C., James H. Davis, and F. David Schoorman. 1995. "An Integrative Model of Organizational Trust." *The Academy of Management Review* 20 (3): 709–734. dx.doi.org/10.2307/258792.

Mofield, Emily, and Megan Parker Peters. 2018. *Teaching Tenacity, Resilience, and a Drive for Excellence: Lessons for Social-Emotional Learning for Grades 4–8.* Waco, TX: Prufrock Press.

VanTassel-Baska, Joyce L., and Tamra Stambaugh, eds. 2007. *Overlooked Gems: A National Perspective on Low-Income Promising Learners.* Washington DC: National Association for Gifted Children and Center for Gifted Education, College of William and Mary.

References

Anderson-Butcher, Dawn, and David E. Conroy. 2002. "Factorial and Criterion Validity of Scores of a Measure of Belonging in Youth Development Programs." *Educational and Psychological Measurement* 62 (5): 857–876. doi.org/10.1177/001316402236882.

Berkowitz, Ruth, Hadass Moore, Ron Avi Astor, and Rami Benbenishty. 2017. "A Research Synthesis of the Associations Between Socioeconomic Background, Inequality, School Climate, and Academic Achievement." *Review of Educational Research* 87 (2): 425–469. doi.org/10.3102/0034654316669821.

Bishop, Rudine Sims. 1990. "Mirrors, Windows, and Sliding Glass Doors." Ohio State University. *Perspectives: Choosing and Using Books for the Classroom* 6 (3).

Budge, Kathleen M., and William H. Parrett. 2018. *Disrupting Poverty: Five Powerful Classroom Practices.* Alexandria, VA: ASCD.

Choi, Nayoung. 2017. "The Effect of an Empowerment Program for Children in Poverty." International Information Institute (Tokyo), 20, no. 3(A): 1613–1620. search.proquest.com/openview/fd2e58d0186638f1333edf80c2741fce/1?pq-origsite=gscholar&cbl=936334.

Coleman, Mary Ruth, and Sneha Shah-Coltrane. 2011. *U-STARS~PLUS: Professional Development Kit Manual.* Arlington, VA: Council for Exceptional Children.

Douglas, Deb. 2018. *The Power of Self-Advocacy for Gifted Learners: Teaching the 4 Essential Steps to Success.* Minneapolis, MN: Free Spirit Publishing.

Frasier, Mary M., Scott L. Hunsaker, Jongyeun Lee, Vernon S. Finley, Jaime H. Garcia, Darlene Martin, and Elaine Frank. 1995. *An Exploratory Study of the Effectiveness of the Staff Development Model and the Research-Based Assessment Plan in Improving the Identification of Gifted Economically Disadvantaged Students.* Storrs: University of Connecticut, The National Center for Research on the Gifted and Talented.

Gagnon, Douglas J., and Marybeth J. Mattingly. 2015. "Limited Access to AP Courses for Students in Smaller and More Isolated Rural School Districts." *Carsey Research, National Issue Brief* 80.

Ginsburg, Kenneth R., and Martha M. Jablow. 2015. *Building Resilience in Children and Teens: Giving Kids Roots and Wings,* 3rd ed. Elk Grove Village, IL: American Academy of Pediatrics.

Horn, Carol V. 2015. "Young Scholars: A Talent Development Model for Finding and Nurturing Potential in Underserved Populations." *Gifted Child Today* 38 (1): 19–31. doi.org/10.1177/1076217514556532.

Jansorn, Natalie Rodriguez. 2020. "Tapping Into Family Resources to Support Gifted Learners from Low-Income Backgrounds." In *Unlocking Potential: Identifying and Serving Gifted Students from Low-Income Households,* edited by Tamra Stambaugh and Paula Olszewski-Kubilius, 263–284. Waco, TX: Prufrock.

Jiang, Yang, and Heather Koball. 2018. "Basic Facts about Low-Income Children Under 9 Years, 2016." New York: National Center for Children in Poverty, Columbia University Mailman School of Public Health. nccp.org/publication/basic-facts-about-low-income-children-children-under-9-years-2016.

———. 2018. "Basic Facts about Low-Income Children Under 18 Years, 2016." New York: National Center for Children in Poverty, Columbia University Mailman School of Public Health. nccp.org/publications/pub_1194.html.

McBee, Matthew T. 2006. "A Descriptive Analysis of Referral Sources for Gifted Identification Screening by Race and Socioeconomic Status." *Journal of Secondary Gifted Education* 17 (2): 103–111. doi.org/10.4219/jsge-2006-686.

Milacci, Fred, and James Zabloski. 2012. "Gifted Dropouts: Phenomenological Case Studies of Rural Gifted Students." *Journal of Ethnographic and Qualitative Research* 6 (3): 175–190.

National Association for Gifted Children and the Council of State Directors of Programs for the Gifted. 2011. "State of the States in Gifted Education 2010–2011." Washington, DC: Author.

National Center for Education Statistics. "National Teacher and Principal Survey." Retrieved from nces.ed.gov/surveys/ntps. Accessed September 2019.

National Center for Research on Gifted Education. 2019. "Four Years' Research Results from the NCRGE." Presented at the World Council for Gifted and Talented Children, Nashville, TN. July 2019. ncrge.uconn.edu/wp-content/uploads/sites/982/2019/07/NCRGE-First-Four-Years-World-Conference-Presentation.pdf.

Olszewski-Kubilius, Paula, and Jane Clarenbach. 2012. *Unlocking Emergent Talent: Supporting High Achievement of Low-Income, High-Ability Students.* Washington DC: National Association for Gifted Children.

Olszewski-Kubilius, Paula, Tamra Stambaugh, and Susan Corwith. 2020. "Poverty, Academic Achievement, and Giftedness: A Literature Review." In *Unlocking Potential: Identifying and Serving Gifted Students from Low-Income Households,* edited by Tamra Stambaugh and Paula Olszewski-Kubilius, 3–26. Waco, TX: Prufrock Press, 2020.

Olszewski-Kubilius, Paula, Saiying Steenbergen-Hu, Dana Thomson, and Rhoda Rosen. 2017. "Minority Achievement Gaps in STEM: Findings of a Longitudinal Study of Project Excite." *Gifted Child Quarterly* 61 (1): 20–39. doi.org/10.1177/0016986216673449.

Parrett, William H., and Kathleen M. Budge. 2012. *Turning High-Poverty Schools into High-Performing Schools.* Alexandria, VA: ASCD.

Peters, Scott J., and Marcia Gentry. 2010. "Multi-Group Construct Validity Evidence of the HOPE Scale: Instrumentation to Identify Low-Income Elementary Students for Gifted Programs." *Gifted Child Quarterly* 54 (4): 298–313. doi.org/10.1177/0016986210378332.

Peters, Scott J., and Kenneth G. Engerrand. 2016. "Equity and Excellence: Proactive Efforts in the Identification of Underrepresented Students for Gifted and Talented Services." *Gifted Child Quarterly* 60 (3): 159–171. doi.org/10.1177/0016986216643165.

Plucker, Jonathan A., and Scott J. Peters. 2018. "Closing Poverty-Based Excellence Gaps: Conceptual, Measurement, and Educational Issues." *Gifted Child Quarterly* 62 (1): 56–67. doi.org/10.1177/0016986217738566.

Ratts, Manivong J., Lorraine DeKruyf, and Stuart F. Chen-Hayes. 2007. "The ACA Advocacy Competencies: A Social Justice Framework for Professional School Counselors." *Professional School Counseling* 11 (2): 90–97. doi.org/10.1177/2156759X0701100203.

Richards, Zachary J., and Tamra Stambaugh. 2015. "National Context of Rural Schools." In *Serving Gifted Students in Rural Settings,* edited by Tamra Stambaugh and Susannah M. Wood, 1–21. Waco, TX: Prufrock Press.

Rivkin, Steven G., Eric A Hanushek, and John F. Kain. 2005. "Teachers, Schools, and Academic Achievement." *Econometrica* 73 (2): 417–458. doi.org/10.1111/j.1468-0262.2005.00584.x

Robinson, Ann, Jill L. Adelson, Kristy A. Kidd, and Christine M. Cunningham. 2018. "A Talent for Tinkering: Developing Talents in Children from Low-Income Households Through Engineering Curriculum." *Gifted Child Quarterly* 62 (1): 130–144. doi.org/10.1177/0016986217738049.

Stambaugh, Tamra. 2018. "Scaffolding of Instruction is Necessary for Gifted Students, Too." *Teaching for High Potential.* Washington DC: National Association for Gifted Children.

Stambaugh, Tamra. 2010. "Curriculum and Instructional Strategies for Working with Promising Students of Poverty." Webinar. Washington DC: National Association for Gifted Children.

Stambaugh, Tamra, and Paula Olszewski-Kubilius, eds. 2020. *Unlocking Potential: Identifying and Serving Gifted Students from Low-Income Households.* Waco, TX: Prufrock Press.

Stambaugh, Timothy Willard. 2017. "Gifted Students and Mental Health: The Role of Boredom, Belonging, Friendship, Service Delivery, and Academic Challenge." Ph.D. dissertation, Trevecca Nazarene University. proquest.com/openview/896b177149dc13c4b797ac5968c215fa/1?pq-origsite=gscholar&cbl=18750&diss=y.

Subotnik, Rena F., Paula Olszewski-Kubilius, and Frank C. Worrell. 2011. "Rethinking Giftedness and Gifted Education: A Proposed Direction Forward Based on Psychological Science." *Psychological Science in the Public Interest* 12 (1): 3–54. doi.org/10.1177/1529100611418056.

Test, David W., Catherine H. Fowler, Wendy M. Wood, Denise M. Brewer, and Steven Eddy. 2005. "A Conceptual Framework of Self-Advocacy for Students with Disabilities." *Remedial and Special Education* 26 (1): 43–54. doi.org/10.1177/07419325050260010601.

VanTassel-Baska, Joyce, and Tamra Stambaugh. 2018. *Affective Jacob's Ladder Reading Comprehension Program (Grades 4–5): Social-Emotional Intelligence.* Waco, TX: Prufrock Press.

———. 2008. *Jacob's Ladder Reading Comprehension Program, Level 1.* Waco, TX: Prufrock Press.

Wang, Shiang-Kwei and Seungyoen Han. 2010. "Six C's of Motivation." In *Emerging Perspectives on Learning, Teaching, and Technology,* edited by Michael Orey, 267–270. textbookequity.org/Textbooks/Orey_Emergin_Perspectives_Learning.pdf.

US Census Department. 2019. "Historical Poverty Tables: People and Families—1959 to 2019." census.gov/data/tables/time-series/demo/income-poverty/historical-poverty-people.html.

US Department of Education, Office of Educational Research and Improvement. 1994. "National Excellence: A Case for Developing America's Talent: An Anthology of Readings." Washington, DC: Author.

8

Moving Beyond Disabilities: Twice-Exceptional Students and Self-Advocacy

Megan Foley-Nicpon, Ph.D.,
and Charles Cederberg, Ph.D.

David's Story

David is a seventh grader with a longstanding diagnosis of ADHD. In the third grade, he was placed on a 504 Plan, which provides accommodations for students with disabilities, following teacher concerns with his behavior and ability to sustain focus. In preparation for his triennial 504 Plan team meeting, David underwent an assessment by an independent psychologist. Testing showed that David continued to meet diagnostic standards for ADHD; however, his profile also indicated significant areas of strength, including superior overall intellectual abilities and strong performances in reading comprehension and mathematics achievement. On questionnaires completed for his evaluation, David's teachers reported that he was frequently inattentive and was increasingly becoming a behavioral concern in class. For instance, they often observed David distracting his peers during structured work time, leaving his desk excessively, and pushing boundaries when his teachers set behavioral limits and provided directions to tasks. One of David's teachers explained, "David is clearly a bright boy who seems to struggle with completing his work and following directions. He is definitely not performing to the level at which he is capable." Another teacher added, "I often catch David misusing classroom technology, where I find him on the internet reading about robotics and other science-related topics instead of working on the assigned project." David's 504 Plan was subsequently renewed following the recommendations of the evaluating psychologist and the continued concerns expressed by David's teachers and parents regarding his inconsistent academic progress.

Shortly thereafter, on a particularly challenging school day, David confided to one of his teachers that he frequently feels bored in class and feels like he is always "phoning it in" because he rarely feels challenged. When his teacher asked for an example of when he *hadn't* felt this way with his learning, David enthusiastically described an experience competing in a LEGO robot competition the previous summer. David lit up, explaining how exciting robotics was to him and how the experience was even more rewarding because of the positive relationships he had developed with his classmates and instructors during that time. David added that he wished there were more hands-on opportunities to learn about science at his school. Touched by David's story, the teacher emailed his parents about the conversation. Later that evening, David and his parents discussed how he might advocate for opportunities to gain such experiences at school. David decided to personally reach out—with the support of his parents, teachers, and psychologist—to his school's principal and the gifted education coordinator for his district to inquire about accelerated science programming opportunities at his school. The principal responded by citing a broad school policy to retain students on individualized accommodation plans rather than offer accelerated programming; however, the principal conceded that this was a unique situation, since it was clear that this policy presented an unfair bias to bright students such as David who happened to have a coexisting disability. The principal therefore decided in conjunction with the gifted education coordinator to grant David's request.

Once David gained access to accelerated science coursework, his behavioral and attentional issues greatly improved, with the additional supports afforded by his 504 Plan. David's academic performance also began to align more closely to his intellectual abilities, and his teachers noted a marked improvement in his disposition toward others and in his attitude toward school.

Twice-Exceptionality

David's story is a common one encountered by educators who work with high-ability students who have a coexisting disability—that is, students who are twice-exceptional learners. Students identified as *twice-exceptional* (2e) demonstrate high ability in one or more areas while also meeting eligibility requirements for one or more disabilities as defined by state and federal criteria (Reis, Baum, and Burke 2014). This combination of high ability and disability in turn creates a unique set of circumstances that impact a student's academic performance and gifted identification. It also presents important implications for educational programming and professional development (Baldwin et al. 2015). Although educators and scholars are increasingly recognizing the unique needs of 2e students, research investigating self-advocacy within this population is presently scarce. What's more, many 2e students who receive Individualized Education Programs (IEPs) or 504 Plans are excluded from accelerated or talent development programming if their school places a greater emphasis on remediating their disability than developing their potential (Barnard-Brak et al. 2015). In other cases, school systems that use a Response to Intervention (RTI) model to identify and provide services for students with disabilities may overlook 2e students whose curriculum-based assessment scores fail to fall below eligibility thresholds that allow for remediation in areas for growth (McCallum et al. 2013). These challenges highlight what is described as a masking phenomenon, where a student's talent may serve to "hide" their disability or vice versa (Assouline, Foley-Nicpon, and Whiteman 2010). Therefore, it is important that educators and researchers alike collectively articulate a sound definition of twice-exceptionality to accurately understand the needs of this population so that empirically informed educational programming can effectively and simultaneously address students' areas of talent and deficit.

Related Theories and Models

Definitions of twice-exceptionality proposed by Reis, Baum, and Burke (2014) and Baldwin et al. (2015) aim to articulate high ability and disability and the way they manifest simultaneously in one student. These definitions help explain how a coexisting talent and disability may affect a student's academic performance in the classroom, reference the masking phenomenon, outline challenges with identification, and offer guidelines for providing educational programming. Consistent definitions are also necessary to enable parent, teacher, and student advocacy efforts. The goals of such definitions are to:

> expand recognition of twice-exceptionality in schools

> allow for a broader scope of students to be included within its definition (Reis, Baum, and Burke 2014)

> enhance and optimize professional development opportunities for educators (Foley-Nicpon 2015)

> facilitate greater cohesion among researchers and practitioners (Baldwin et al. 2015)

> heighten awareness for twice-exceptionality among caregivers and constituency groups (Foley-Nicpon 2015)

The Social-Ecological Systems Theory

This theory (Bronfenbrenner 1977) provides a valuable lens for conceptualizing the realities and challenges facing 2e students with self-advocacy since it accounts for the diverse array of individuals (family members, teachers, school personnel, counselors) who might interact with 2e students across multiple contexts (Foley-Nicpon and Candler 2018). The social-ecological model argues that child development occurs within a context of systemic relationships developing within the child's environment, where understanding the development of each person must account for all aspects through which they relate to their environment. In David's case, the psychologist who diagnosed him with ADHD and discovered his high ability only did so after obtaining information from his parents and teachers, making observations, and interpreting test scores in comparison to what would be expected for his age. Without this information, an accurate picture of David's strengths and areas for growth could not have been obtained.

There are unique contextual factors that have potential to contribute to a 2e student's capacity to self-advocate. For instance, many twice-exceptional students may encounter a lack of awareness of their own personal strengths and weaknesses. This confusion may be compounded by a lack of teacher awareness about twice-exceptionality. A dearth of empirical evidence and a "one-size-fits-all" approach have implications for identification and service provision and allow for well-intentioned educators to implement ineffective procedures. For instance, in many schools, the order in which a disability or talent is identified may have consequences in determining whether a student is offered services for gifted education or special education, such as a situation where a student who was initially provided an official accommodation plan is overlooked for talent development programming (Schultz 2012; Crim et al. 2008).

> Many twice-exceptional students may encounter a lack of awareness of their own personal strengths and weaknesses.

Further, contextual challenges arise regarding the differences among diagnostic backgrounds of 2e students. For example, a student's disability may be related to a learning, psychiatric, neurodevelopmental, behavioral, or physical difference. Twice-exceptional learners may also encounter differing degrees of amenability to their efforts to self-advocate for tailored educational experiences. High-ability students with ADHD, for instance, often possess high levels of creativity and tend to benefit from greater opportunities to engage in activities that emphasize divergent thinking and problem-based learning (Fugate, Zentall, and Gentry 2013). Therefore, the receptiveness of educators and the degree of inclusivity contained within school policy to provide educational opportunities that allow gifted students with ADHD to use their creativity can affect whether these students feel empowered or discouraged to self-advocate.

Megamodel of Talent Development

Self-advocacy among 2e students can be further informed by the megamodel of talent development (Subotnik, Olszewski-Kubilius, and Worrell 2011), which is a proposed theory of talent development that integrates the most compelling components of previously established models. The megamodel of talent development posits that all domains of talent follow developmental trajectories with different starts, peaks, and end times. The construct of giftedness is determined in terms of ability in relationship to other people. The development of talent involves transitions from initial potential to demonstrated achievement and finally eminence (Subotnik, Olszewski-Kubilius, and Worrell 2011, 34).

Regarding 2e students, the systemic component necessary for cultivating "abilities into competencies, competencies into expertise, and expertise into eminence" (Subotnik, Olszewski-Kubilius, and Worrell 2011, 33) may not exist due to a lack of awareness among educators that students with disabilities can participate in accelerated educational opportunities and services including lessons, school programs, and extracurricular activities (Schultz 2012). In David's case, he shared with a sensitive and inquisitive teacher his excitement for a LEGO robot competition. His teacher, in turn, shared this information with David's parents. David's parents then helped him self-advocate for more in-school opportunities like the LEGO competition. The timing was right for David to be enrolled in accelerated science programming, and his talents were recognized on a systemic level when the school principal supported David's move to the advanced class. David's behavioral challenges decreased when he was afforded opportunities to practice and develop skills in his talent domain.

> Educators play a valuable role in training and coaching 2e learners as they work to develop self-advocacy skills and effectively meet inevitable challenges along their educational paths.

The megamodel of talent development is also unique in that it emphasizes the intentional development of noncognitive characteristics, namely psychosocial skills (Olszewski-Kubilius, Subotnik, and Worrell 2015). As the talent development process evolves, high-ability students are expected to build a personal sense of responsibility for their learning and a heightened awareness for their personal strengths and growth areas. Therefore, it is important that 2e students are afforded an educational environment where they may assume ownership over their learning by advocating for opportunities that enable choice and flexibility in selecting topics of interest, individually tailored teaching methods, and expectations for assessment that are congruent to their individual learning preferences (Willard-Holt et al. 2013).

However, some 2e learners may struggle with the psychosocial demands required to effectively self-advocate in their educational setting. For example, gifted students diagnosed with ADHD or ASD often possess weaknesses with social skills that can create challenges in navigating dynamic relationships with mentors and teachers. Thus, educators play a valuable role in training and coaching 2e learners as they work to develop self-advocacy skills and effectively meet inevitable challenges along their educational paths.

Research in Self-Advocacy and Twice-Exceptionality

The onus of advocating for a twice-exceptional student almost always falls on the student's parent. This important role is often challenging, yet it is crucial to the child's educational achievement (Cooper, Ness, and Smith 2004; Speirs Neumeister, Yssel, and Burney 2013). It is not uncommon for parents to report needing to advocate for their child annually as teachers and/or schools change. In Speirs Neumeister, Yssel, and Burney's qualitative study of parents of 2e students (2013), parents discussed the importance of preparing their children to eventually take charge of their learning. They also noted that self-advocating is a skill that is developed over time. In the study, parents reported initially doing the advocating but teaching their children that they will eventually need to identify and self-advocate for the strategies they need to be successful.

Self-advocacy is a concept talked about and studied both in gifted education and disability studies, but less is known about self-advocacy for 2e students specifically. What we do know comes from investigations of how students can advocate for themselves as they develop and enter postsecondary education. For example, Dole (2001) conducted a narrative study of four college students with high ability who also had a learning disability. Through their stories, it was discovered that self-knowledge, self-advocacy, self-acceptance, and self-determination were all themes that helped the students be efficacious personally and educationally. Additionally, by gaining experience advocating for themselves, the students had greater confidence to advocate for others.

Reis, McGuire, and Neu (2000) conducted a similar study of high-ability students with learning disabilities who were successful in college. One of several factors students listed as important to their educational matriculation was self-advocacy. The same was true in a mixed-methods study of 2e students ages ten to twenty-three who reflected on which learning strategies were facilitators and which ones were barriers in their educational journeys. One strategy students reported as being helpful was having choice and flexibility in their learning, yet they also reported that this was not often afforded to them. This speaks to 2e students' desire for more influence in their own education.

Self-advocacy does not develop independently. In studies of college students with disabilities (Kimball et al. 2016) and with twice-exceptionality (Dole 2001), participants noted overwhelmingly that their parents taught them self-advocacy skills through modeling. Students watched their parents advocate for them during their K–12 education, which taught them to later apply these skills to a variety of causes in higher education. Many of the students transferred their self-advocacy skills to activism in other areas, such as the environment, LGBTQ issues, and poverty (Kimball et al. 2016).

Barriers to Self-Advocacy

The editors of this book, Joy Lawson Davis and Deb Douglas, created their own unique definition of self-advocacy for gifted students:

> Self-advocacy is the dynamic process that enables high-potential students to claim their right to an education that addresses their unique intellectual, academic, psychosocial, and cultural needs without endangering their self-esteem or that of others. It is a compilation of culturally responsive and inclusive empowerment strategies that open opportunities for positive academic and life outcomes previously precluded for some students due to stereotyping, systemic biases, and limited access to resources.

With this definition comes potential barriers students may come up against in their quest to self-advocate. Some of these barriers are specific to 2e students.

For example, symptoms related to various mental health diagnoses may inhibit a student's ability to recognize individual responsibility for initiating change or connecting with other advocates. A central symptom of ASD, for example, is poor social communication skills (American Psychiatric Association 2013), which may make it challenging to network with others who have similar presentations. Students need to develop the psychosocial skills necessary to form connections along their educational journey. A child with ASD may feel isolated and misunderstood and not know how to initiate a conversation about their academic needs. These skills may not come naturally, but they can be taught and practiced over time.

A challenge facing students with ADHD is a tendency to overestimate their academic performance (Manor et al. 2012) or executive functioning skills (Steward et al. 2017), which is known as positive illusory bias. If a child does not have the self-awareness of an academic difficulty in need of advocacy, they are not going to assume responsibility for talking to teachers or professors about educational challenges. Thus, they may flounder, not succeed, and be uncertain of what went wrong along the way.

Another potential barrier for 2e students is accessing options. For example, it is not uncommon for parents to know more about an ADHD diagnosis than their child's teacher does (West et al. 2005), and teachers may have a negative perception of the child and diagnosis (Ohan et al. 2011). Additionally, parents, and later children themselves, are forced to advocate within power structures that are often unequal and in favor of the school (Honkasilta, Vehkakoski, and Vehmas 2015). This can leave a family feeling helpless in getting their child's needs met and the student feeling unable to independently take on the advocacy cause. For example, students may wish to self-advocate for changes in how they are graded, such not being marked down for misspelling words on a chemistry test. If they are not aware of the option to advocate in this situation, their resulting grades may be more of a reflection of their poor spelling than of their excellent chemistry knowledge.

Finally, self-advocacy, like other behaviors, is often taught only through parent modeling. In the Spiers Neumeister and colleagues' study (2013), parents engaged in advocacy before students were able to self-advocate. What happens when 2e children have parents who do not have the knowledge, awareness, resources, or desire to advocate? If children are not taught these skills, the likelihood that they will develop them on their own is low. This becomes a social justice issue, where those with resources are given more opportunities than those without. These barriers perpetuate unequal access to talent development opportunities and accommodations for disabilities among our 2e learners.

Strategies for Educators

Several important strategies exist that aid educational professionals in fostering self-advocacy skills in their students. Here are some to consider:

> **Understand that twice-exceptionality exists (Foley-Nicpon, Assouline, and Colangelo 2013).** Without this fundamental understanding, the families of 2e students are forced to regularly educate others, which is too often a frustrating reality (Besnoy et al. 2015; Speirs Neumeister, Yssel, and Burney 2013). Self-advocacy is much more challenging if the person to whom you are advocating does not know what it is you are advocating for. The education profession still has a long way to go toward identifying and accepting twice-exceptionality among students (Willard-Holt et al. 2013). No two twice-exceptional children are the same, but some characteristics to look for include:

  • frustration over the difference between their knowledge and output

  • challenges relating socially to peers

  • large discrepancies among test scores

  • large discrepancies between test scores and grades

  • differences in a student's behavior and their awareness of the behavior

> **Help twice-exceptional students understand their areas of strength and growth (Dole 2001).** If a student does not have this self-awareness, they will not be able to talk to others about their needs. Of course, this conversation must take a developmental perspective, but high-ability learners can often

understand complex concepts such as twice-exceptionality at a younger age than typically developing students can. Consistently engaging students in these conversations about strengths and limitations, adjusting as they age, is recommended.

> **Assume a strengths-based perspective (Baum, Schader, and Hébert 2014).** Students should be taught that advocating for opportunities in one's talent domains is just as important as advocating for necessary accommodations.

> **Teach students to advocate for their social and emotional needs.** Self-advocacy considerations may not necessarily be for academic domains only. The social and emotional needs of 2e students are often more salient than they are for students with high ability alone (Foley-Nicpon 2015). It is not uncommon for a 2e student to require additional social and emotional supports as they navigate educational and occupational settings.

> **Practice self-advocacy skills with students.** Assertiveness and oral communication training may be beneficial, as well as role-playing how to self-advocate (Speirs Neumeister, Yssel, and Burney 2013). Educators are in ideal situations to help students learn these skills.

> **Support students' self-advocacy efforts.** Educators need to become familiar with their institution's student disability services and should welcome students who want to work with them to implement their identified accommodations.

Conclusion

Because twice-exceptionality is often misunderstood and overlooked in US schools, self-advocacy skills are particularly important for this population of learners. Advocacy efforts should take place in consideration of the various systems in which a 2e student interacts. Learners may need to advocate for more challenge with their math teacher, a lower dosage of stimulant medication with their pediatrician, and more freedom with their parents. Members of these systems may overlook a student's ability and focus too much on their disability, or vice versa—focus so much on their high ability that their disability is unseen and critical support is lacking. The megamodel of talent development reminds us that psychosocial skills are important and may need to be explicitly taught to a 2e learner trying to master self-advocacy skills. Limited existing research about self-advocacy among 2e students purports that advocacy is a developmental effort that, ideally, transfers from parent to child over time and is crucial to educational success. There exist barriers to actualizing these efforts that are specific to the 2e child, such as recognizing their responsibility for initiating change, connecting with advocates, or accessing options. Numerous strategies are suggested for educators, including:

> education about twice-exceptionality

> facilitating understanding of strengths and areas of growth

> assuming a strengths-based perspective

> considering social and emotional needs

> helping students practice self-advocacy

> providing support in higher education environments.

As educators in and out of the gifted field are becoming more aware of twice-exceptionality, self-advocacy efforts will evolve. It is hoped that more stories like David's in which students are able to self-advocate for their needs and change school policy to be friendlier toward twice-exceptionality will be shared. In David's case, he engaged in self-advocacy after a caring teacher inquired about his talent domain and his parents coached him on how to engage in self-advocacy efforts at school. This will happen only if we continue to work across disciplines and systems to increase understanding, support, and service implementation.

Key Concepts

> Twice-exceptional children have a coexisting ability and disability, creating unique issues related to academic performance and identification.

> Examined through the social-ecological model, a student's ability to self-advocate is affected by unique factors in their environments, such as self-awareness of talents or challenges, educators' understanding of twice-exceptionality, and diversity in the educational and psychosocial presentations of twice-exceptionality.

> Examined through the megamodel of talent development, 2e students' self-advocacy depends on having opportunities to develop their talent, which may be inhibited by differences in their psychosocial skills.

> Self-advocacy may not come easily for twice-exceptional learners, particularly for those whose diagnoses are related to social skills deficits, anxiety, and poor executive functioning skills.

> Advocating for opportunities in 2e students' domains of talent is just as important as advocating for accommodations in their domains of disability.

Discussion Questions

1. How do the social-ecological systems theory and megamodel of talent development help us understand issues of self-advocacy for twice-exceptional students?

2. What does the research say about advocacy and self-advocacy among 2e students?

3. What are some barriers to self-advocacy among 2e students?

Recommended Resources

The 2e Resource 2eresource.com

The Belin-Blank Center for Gifted Education and Talent Development Assessment and Counseling Clinic belinblank.education.uiowa.edu/clinic

The Davidson Institute for Talent Development. 2018. "Twice-Exceptionality: A Resource Guide for Parents." dnnlv5ifs.blob.core.windows.net/portals/2/PDFs/Guidebooks/davidson-2e-guidebook. pdf?sr=b&si=DNNFileManagerPolicy&sig=%2BMt9sMbc0q%2FOlDHKRufY58lcqMzLYw8RLolU%2FBkz2ug%3D.

National Association for Gifted Children. 2009. "White Paper on Twice-Exceptionality." nagc.org/sites/default/files /Position%20Statement/twice%20exceptional.pdf.

References

American Psychiatric Association. 2013. *Diagnostic and Statistical Manual of Mental Disorders* (5th ed.). Arlington, VA: Author.

Assouline, Susan G., Megan Foley-Nicpon, and Claire Whiteman. 2010. "Cognitive and Psychosocial Characteristics of Gifted Students with Written Language Disability." *Gifted Child Quarterly* 54 (2): 102–115. doi.org/10.1177/0016986209355974.

Baldwin, Lois, Susan Baum, Daphne Pereles, and Claire Hughes. 2015. "Twice-Exceptional Learners: The Journey Toward a Shared Vision." *Gifted Child Today* 38 (4): 206–214. dx.doi.org/10.1177/1076217515597277.

Barnard-Brak, Lucy, Susan K. Johnsen, Alyssa Pond Hannig, and Tianlan Wei. 2015. "The Incidence of Potentially Gifted Students Within a Special Education Population." *Roeper Review* 37 (2): 74–83. doi.org/10.1080/02783193.2015.1008661.

Baum, Susan M., Robin M. Schader, and Thomas P. Hébert. 2014. "Through a Different Lens: Reflecting on a Strengths-Based, Talent-Focused Approach for Twice-Exceptional Learners." *Gifted Child Quarterly* 58 (4): 311–327. doi.org/10.1177/0016986214547632.

Besnoy, Kevin D., Nicole C. Swoszowski, Jane L. Newman, Amanda Floyd, Parrish Jones, and Caitlin Byrne. 2015. "The Advocacy Experiences of Parents of Elementary Age, Twice-Exceptional Children." *Gifted Child Quarterly* 59 (2): 108–123. doi.org/10.1177/0016986215569275.

Bronfenbrenner, Urie. 1977. "Toward an Experimental Ecology of Human Development." *American Psychologist* 32 (7): 513–531. dx.doi.org/10.1037/0003-066X.32.7.513

Cooper, Eileen E., Maryann Ness, and Mary Smith. 2004. "A Case Study of a Child with Dyslexia and Spatial-Temporal Gifts." *Gifted Child Quarterly* 48 (2): 83–94. doi.org/10.1177/001698620404800202.

Crim, Courtney, Jacqueline Hawkins, Lilia Ruban, and Sharon Johnson. 2008. "Curricular Modifications for Elementary Students with Learning Disabilities in High, Average, and Low-IQ Groups." *Journal of Research in Childhood Education* 22 (3): 233–245. doi.org/10.1080/02568540809594624.

Dole, Sharon. 2000. "The Implications of the Risk and Resilience Literature for Gifted Students with Learning Disabilities." *Roeper Review* 23 (2): 91–96. doi.org/10.1080/02783190009554074.

———. 2001. "Reconciling Contradictions: Identity Formation in Individuals with Giftedness and Learning Disabilities." *Journal for the Education of the Gifted* 25 (2): 103–137. doi.org/10.1177/016235320102500202.

Foley-Nicpon, Megan. 2015. "Voices from the Field: The Higher Education Community." *Gifted Child Today* 38 (4): 249–251. dx.doi.org/10.1177/1076217515597288.

———. 2015. "The Social and Emotional Development of Twice-Exceptional Children." In *The Social and Emotional Development of Gifted Children: What Do We Know?* edited by Maureen Neihart, Steven I. Pfeiffer, and Tracy L. Cross, 103–118. Waco, TX: Prufrock Press.

Foley-Nicpon, Megan, Susan G. Assouline, and Nicholas Colangelo. 2013. "Twice-Exceptional Learners: Who Needs to Know What? *Gifted Child Quarterly* 57 (3): 169–180. doi.org/10.1177/0016986213490021.

Foley-Nicpon, Megan, and Margaret M. Candler. 2018. "Psychological Interventions for Twice-Exceptional Youth." In *APA Handbook of Giftedness and Talent,* edited by Steven I. Pfeiffer, Megan Foley-Nicpon, and Elizabeth Shaunessy-Dedrick, 545–558. Washington, DC: American Psychological Association Press.

Fugate, C. Matthew, Sydney S. Zentall, and Marcia Gentry. 2013. "Creativity and Working Memory in Gifted Students With and Without Characteristics of Attention Deficit Hyperactive Disorder: Lifting the Mask." *Gifted Child Quarterly* 57 (4): 234–246. doi.org/10.1177/0016986213500069.

Honkasilta, Juho, Tanja Vehkakoski, and Simo Vehmas. 2015. "Power Struggle, Submission and Partnership: Agency Constructions of Mothers of Children with ADHD Diagnosis in Their Narrated School Involvement." *Scandinavian Journal of Educational Research* 59 (6): 674–690. doi.org/10.1080/00313831.2014.965794.

Kimball, Ezekiel W., Adam Moore, Annemarie Vaccaro, Peter F. Troiano, and Barbara M. Newman. 2016. "College Students with Disabilities Redefine Activism: Self-Advocacy, Storytelling and Collective Action." *Journal of Diversity in Higher Education* 9 (3): 245–260. dx.doi.org/10.1037/dhe0000031.

Manor, I., N. Vurembrandt, S. Rozen, D. Gevah, A. Weizman, and G. Zalsman. 2012. "Low Self-Awareness of ADHD in Adults using a Self-Report Screening Questionnaire." *European Psychiatry* 27 (5): 314–320. doi.org/ 10.1016 /j.eurpsy.2010.08.013.

McCallum, R. Steve, Sherry Mee Bell, Jeremy Thomas Coles, Kelli Caldwell Miller, Michael B. Hopkins, and Angela Hilton-Prillhart. 2013. "A Model for Screening Twice-Exceptional Students (Gifted with Learning Disabilities) Within a Response to Intervention Paradigm. *Gifted Child Quarterly* 57 (4): 209–222. doi.org/10.1177/0016986213500070.

Ohan, Jeneva L., Troy A.W. Visser, Melanie C. Strain, and Linda Allen. 2011. "Teachers' and Education Students' Perceptions of and Reactions to Children with and Without the Diagnostic Label 'ADHD.'" *Journal of School Psychology* 49 (1): 81–105. doi.org/10.1016/j.jsp.2010.10.001.

Olszewski-Kubilius, Paula, Rena F. Subotnik, and Frank C. Worrell. 2015. "Conceptualizations of Giftedness and the Development of Talent: Implications for Counselors." *Journal of Counseling & Development* 93 (2): 143–152. doi.org/10.1002/j.1556-6676.2015.00190.x.

Reis, Sally M., Susan M. Baum, and Edith Burke. 2014. "An Operational Definition of Twice Exceptional Learners: Implications and Applications." *Gifted Child Quarterly* 58 (3): 217–230. doi.org/10.1177/0016986214534976.

Reis, Sally M., Joan M. McGuire, and Terry W. Neu. 2000. "Compensation Strategies Used by High-Ability Students with Learning Disabilities Who Succeed in College." *Gifted Child Quarterly* 44 (2): 123–134. doi.org/10.1177/001698620004400205.

Schultz, Susan M. 2012. "Twice-Exceptional Students Enrolled in Advanced Placement Classes." *Gifted Child Quarterly* 56 (3): 119–133. doi.org/10.1177/0016986212444605.

Speirs Neumeister, Kristie, Nina Yssel, and Virginia H. Burney. 2013. "The Influence of Primary Caregivers in Fostering Success in Twice-Exceptional Children." *Gifted Child Quarterly* 57 (4): 263–274. doi.org/10.1177/0016986213500068.

Steward, Kayla A., Alexander Tan, Lauren Delgaty, Mitzi M. Gonzales, and Melissa Bunner. 2017. "Self-Awareness of Executive Functioning Deficits in Adolescents with ADHD." *Journal of Attention Disorders* 21 (4): 316–322. doi.org/10.1177/1087054714530782.

Subotnik, Rena F., Paula Olszewski-Kubilius, and Frank C. Worrell. 2011. "Rethinking Giftedness and Gifted Education: A Proposed Direction Forward Based on Psychological Science." *Psychological Science in the Public Interest* 12 (1): 3–54. doi.org/10.1177/1529100611418056.

West, John, Myra Taylor, Stephen Houghton, and Shirlene Hudyma. 2005. "A Comparison of Teachers' and Parents' Knowledge and Beliefs About Attention-Deficit/Hyperactivity Disorder (ADHD)." *School Psychology International* 26 (2): 192–208. doi.org/10.1177/0143034305052913.

Willard-Holt, Colleen, Jessica Weber, Kristen L. Morrison, and Julia Horgan. 2013. "Twice-Exceptional Learners' Perspectives on Effective Learning Strategies." *Gifted Child Quarterly* 57 (4): 246–262. doi.org/10.1177/0016986213501076.

9

Rainbow Dreams: Empowering Gifted LGBTQ+ Students to Self-Advocate

Alena R Treat, Ph.D., and Robert W. Seney, Ed.D.

Introduction

Long considered a nonissue in K–12 education, lesbian, gay, bisexual, transgender, and questioning/queer (LGBTQ+) youth have become visible enough that educators of the gifted must consider the implications of having them in their classrooms (Treat 2017). There is a critical need for intense, personalized social and emotional support for these students, plus additional protections in order to address their unique needs (Whittenburg and Treat 2009; Treat 2017). Historically, however, there has been a trend of discrimination against gifted LGBTQ+ students and a lack of role models in curriculum and educational resources. This will not change without a commitment to long-term, systematic evaluation of curriculum and program improvement (National Association for Gifted Children 2017).

In this chapter, one student's very personal story will shed light on the unique plight of gifted LGBTQ+ students, as well as the importance of supporting their self-advocacy. It is crucial that we teach gifted LGBTQ+ students to speak up and assert their right to an education and a social environment in which they can find security and success.

Six Challenges Faced by Gifted LGBTQ+ Students

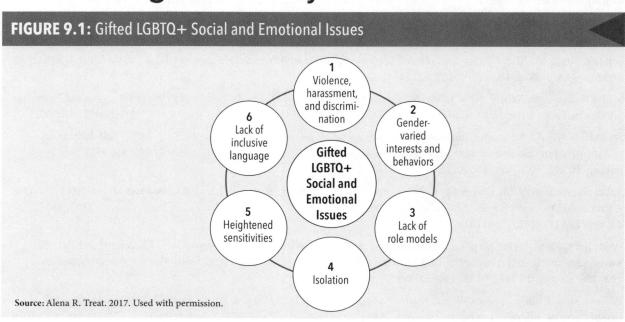

FIGURE 9.1: Gifted LGBTQ+ Social and Emotional Issues

Source: Alena R. Treat. 2017. Used with permission.

1. Violence, Harassment, and Discrimination

LGBTQ+ students are harassed at school, both verbally and physically, twice as often as heterosexual and cisgender students are (Teaching Tolerance 2013). Much of that harassment takes place barely out of the direct sight of teachers.

2. Gender-Varied Interests and Behaviors

Many gifted students exhibit androgynous characteristics and interests, so they do not tend to conform to traditional binary male and female roles. Even though society and gifted education have moved closer to promoting nontraditional roles and domains, such as fostering girls' interests in traditionally male-dominated fields (science, math, and technology), society is not as enthusiastic with regard to boys in nontraditional roles or domains.

3. Lack of Role Models

Typically, neither gifted nor general education curricula identify the sexual orientation or gender identity of eminent individuals. This can result in the unintended consequence of perpetuating depression in LGBTQ+ students due to the implied heterosexual and cisgender assumption and an absence of LGBTQ+ role models.

4. Isolation

Assumed heterosexuality and cisgenderness is one of the leading causes of invisibility and, therefore, isolation for LGBTQ+ students. Gifted LGBTQ+ students, however, may only appear "different" from heterosexual and cisgender students when they resemble LGBTQ+ stereotypes. Many do not fit those stereotypes.

5. Heightened Sensitivities

It is well-known that heightened intellectual, emotional, sensory, imaginational, and psychomotor sensitivities are common among gifted students. However, the bullying, alienation, and isolation many LGBTQ+ students face can intensify these sensitivities.

6. Lack of Inclusive Language

School communications, including both written and verbal, quite often utilize language that assumes heterosexuality, cisgenderness, and traditional family configurations (mother, father, son, daughter). However, this alienates LGBTQ+ students as well as students who have LGBTQ+ family members.

Gavin's Story*

When I was serving as chair of the NAGC Diversity and Equity Committee, our committee was asked to develop Diversity Toolboxes for varied populations (race/culture, English language learners, twice-exceptional, poverty/low socioeconomic status, and LGBTQ+). While working on adding relevant

*As recounted by Alena Treat.

court cases to the *Diversity Toolbox: LGBTQ Students* (National Association for Gifted Children 2017), I read about a remarkable young transgender student (assigned female at birth), Gavin Grimm, attending school in a rural community in Virginia. With the assistance of an American Civil Liberties Union (ACLU) team, Gavin had filed a lawsuit in 2015 against his school district, claiming the school board violated his rights under the US Constitution's equal protection clause as well as under Title IX, the federal law that protects against gender-based discrimination. I needed to learn more.

To contact Gavin, I talked to an ACLU representative who was responsible for his case. Gavin agreed to be interviewed since the topic of self-advocacy by gifted LGBTQ+ students had an "intersectionality that resonated" with him. He told me he had been politically motivated from a young age and felt he had the responsibility to use his voice as a platform because "that's what democracy is all about." At the time of the lawsuit, Gavin's case was one of the few of its kind. There was not a robust body of legal evidence to build on, and Gavin said he "had to lead the fight on this; had to blaze a path." To arrive at that place, Gavin needed to discover himself, find his own voice, and overcome a variety of obstacles. Gavin's story strongly illustrates the social and emotional challenges gifted LGBTQ+ students face as well as the power of self-advocacy.

Gender-Varied Interests and Behaviors

As a child, Gavin had imaginary friends—all male. He rejected female characters and anything associated with femininity. More importantly, his external role models were males, though he didn't turn away from female guidance. Those role models, however, tended to be cartoon characters like Ash Ketchum, one of the Pokémon characters. He was drawn to experiences of boyhood because they were attractive and because he identified with them. Gavin shared that he was probably four or five years old when he realized he was a boy, though it was complicated by the environment in which he lived, a conservative southeastern Virginia town. From his perspective, religion and acceptance were in opposition with each other. This was a source of negativity, pain, and judgment.

It wasn't until Gavin was about twelve or thirteen that he saw a YouTube video, "Transgender Announcement," in which the creator came out as transgender. Gavin's body was going through puberty at the time, and that horrified him. He hadn't heard about the concept of being transgender and felt immediately drawn to that idea while watching the video. He had a dramatic, life-changing "OMG!" moment. He could do that! Gavin decided to come out to his parents as a boy during his freshman year of high school. This was the first step in his self-advocacy.

Heightened Sensitivities

In addition to being a gifted child, Gavin also had a reactive nervous system. He was diagnosed with ADHD and other neurological and mental health disorders in adolescence. His mother's perception of ADHD was exclusively the motor aspect (hyperactivity), but Gavin's type of ADHD was not physical, so it wasn't taken seriously by his teachers. If Gavin wasn't interested in a topic or activity, it was "literally painful" for him. However, when he was thirteen, Gavin and his mother decided to reject his official ADHD diagnosis. As a neurodiverse gifted transgender student, he was "terribly misunderstood." Gavin became bored and disengaged, started acting out, skipped classes, and got behind. His was a "story of failure after failure."

Harassment, Discrimination, and Isolation

During Gavin's years in the public school system, he had been bullied from day one. There was a non-response from adults in the school. Though the adults didn't contribute to the bullying, they would not intervene when Gavin asked for help, for a lifeline. He was told to act differently, that the situation was his fault so there was nothing they could do. He felt like he was being tortured every day. The bullying—as well as the lack of support from adults—felt "evil, targeted." He says that adults and students smirked at him and peered at him. He actually *felt* their hatred. Gavin's test scores fell and, suddenly, he started receiving Fs when he turned in work late. It was clear to him that he was *not* welcome.

In addition, because Gavin was neurodiverse, he was viewed as mentally ill and was a frequent target for harassment. He suffered a lot and often. Gavin "learned to walk with that suffering and not in entirely healthy ways," but he made it through day by day. The constant harassment was a "numbing process." He said, "When you're beat so often, you don't feel anymore." He built up a tolerance for the harassment, but this was not empowering. It was "more like a callus, scar tissue—not as pretty as a suit of armor. It comes at a price. It's damaged tissue. What does it still cost? I'll have to cautiously unlearn it as an adult."

Transitioning

Despite the pain it caused, the bullying Gavin endured taught him to become self-reliant. He stopped going to others for help. He realized no one would understand, so he would have to transition on his own—whether or not he was accepted by his family and peers. Rather than asking permission, he decided, "This is who I am. This is what I need. This is what I'm going to do." It was the beginning of his self-advocacy within the school district.

In the early stages of his transition, Gavin did not feel that transitioning was just a choice. It was something he had to do for his own survival. During the summer following his freshman year, he transitioned and returned to school as a male sophomore in the fall. He did not initially ask to use the boys' restroom. He was afraid he would be attacked in the street or in the parking lot—or his house would be burned down. He used the bathroom in the nurse's office instead. It wasn't perfect, but Gavin kept reiterating that this was nonnegotiable; it was what he needed. He didn't care if others didn't adjust to it. He decided that this was who he was. He wasn't going to make apologies for being trans, and he would make adjustments when necessary. Before, he was depressed and had suicidal ideation, so his demands to live life as a boy actually *enabled* him to live. His story had to be one of trials before triumph. In reading about others' experiences, Gavin had found only two trans individuals who hadn't gone through trauma and were raised with acceptance. He hoped that he didn't have to go through the process of "soul death" in order to survive.

The Bathroom Rights Lawsuit

Using the nurse's office bathroom after transitioning became increasingly humiliating for Gavin. It took too long to get there from his classrooms, and since he was neurodiverse, he needed to be in his seat as much as possible. To get to the nurse's restroom, he had to pass two or three boys' restrooms.

Finally, Gavin approached the school and asked to use the boys' restroom. The principal gave permission, and the superintendent supported the principal's decision. For seven weeks, Gavin used the boys' restrooms. However, once parents and community members found out, they demanded that Gavin be barred from the boys' restrooms. It became popular for people to have their own "Gavin story," and they made up tales about him. The school board had a public vote about the issue. Gavin only found out by chance that the meeting would take place when he saw a post asking people to come to the meeting to "keep that girl out of the boys' bathroom." The meeting included a discussion of Gavin's genitals, and even though they didn't name him, everyone knew who he was. The school board voted six to one that transgender students could use only the restroom that was aligned to their gender assigned at birth. Despite being shown a new, official birth certificate that by court order had been changed from female to male designation, the school board also refused to allow his school records to reflect his male designation.

The school eventually turned a janitorial closet into a unisex restroom, but since it was close to the nurse's office, it only saved two minutes per trip—and it was frequently locked. Neither the nurse's office nor the janitorial closet was available outside of regular school hours, so when Gavin stayed for after-school events, there were no facilities available that he could use. His only solution was to ask a friend or adult to drive him to a local grocery store or to his home. The common act of using a restroom became humiliating. As a result, he developed painful urinary tract infections, which caused him to become distracted and uncomfortable in class. This happened so often that Gavin's mother kept medication in stock at home.

Gavin could not allow this continual denial of restroom rights. "It was wrong, illegal, and not an option for me." He believed the lawsuit was his only route. "It was a no-brainer. The desired outcome was to be able to use the restroom. It was initially made for my own survival."

The Importance of Advocates

In the summer of 2015, Gavin's mother called the ACLU national office, and then she and Gavin filled out an intake form on the ACLU website. At around the same time, a supportive adult in the community reached out to the ACLU of Virginia. The national and state groups began working with Gavin. The sudden activity felt frenzied to him, but he also immediately felt safe. He had acquired a team, a "family who cared about him, the law, and making things right." They gave him a choice every step of the way; his desire and consideration for his safety were always put first. Ultimately Gavin was the one "pulling the strings." With the help of his team, he claimed his full right and his personal responsibility to self-advocate.

The ACLU represented Gavin pro bono. Members of their team came with him to the final school board meeting in 2019. One flew in from New York and several more drove in from Richmond. They were not there out of necessity; they came because their relationship with Gavin was not purely transactional. They were there because they thought the case might be settled that night and, on a personal level, they genuinely wanted to be there together. As Gavin said, "They had an unceasing devotion to civil liberties. It was truly one of the most inspiring things I've ever been witness to."

It took almost five years, but in 2019, two years after he graduated high school, Gavin won his case in the US District Court of the Eastern District of Virginia. According to Harper Jean Tobin, policy director for the National Center for Transgender Equality, "Grimm's case will likely join the 'steady drumbeat' of recent court rulings that have favored transgender students in states including Maryland, Pennsylvania, and Wisconsin" (Finley 2019). And indeed it did when, on August 26, 2020, the Fourth Circuit Court of Appeals also ruled in favor of Gavin, deciding that restroom policies segregating transgender students from their peers and denying transgender students accurate transcripts are unconstitutional and violate Title IX, the federal law prohibiting sex discrimination in education.

TIMELINE OF *G. G. V. GLOUCESTER COUNTY SCHOOL BOARD*

- December 2014: Gloucester County School Board votes six to one that transgender students can only use the restroom that is aligned to their gender assigned at birth.
- June 2015: Gavin and the ACLU sue the school board under Title IX and refer the case to the Department of Justice.
- July 2015: Judge Doumar of the United States District Court for the Eastern District of Virginia dismisses Gavin's Title IX claim and denies his request for an injunction.
- August 2015: Gavin appeals to the Fourth Circuit Court of Appeals.
- April 2016: Three-judge Court of Appeals panel overturns Judge Doumar's decision.
- April 2016: Court of Appeals sends the case back to the District Court for further proceedings.
- May 2016: School board moves for a rehearing, but the Fourth Circuit declines to rehear the case.
- June 2016: Judge Doumar issues a preliminary injunction in Gavin's favor.
- August 2016: The Supreme Court stays the Circuit Court's decision.
- October 2016: The Supreme Court agrees to take up the case.
- March 2017: The Supreme Court reverses its decision to hear the case and vacates the judgment in Gavin's favor, citing the Trump administration's rescinding of protections for transgender students.
- May 2018: Judge Allen of the US District Court of the Eastern District of Virginia denies the Gloucester County School Board's motion to dismiss the case and rules that Gavin has a valid claim of discrimination.
- August 2019: Judge Allen decides in Gavin's favor, granting his request for summary judgment. Gavin is awarded attorney's fees, court expenses, and a nominal $1.00 in damages, and the court issues a permanent injunction requiring the school board to update Gavin's official school records to reflect his gender identity.

Gavin's Goals and Advice to Gifted Trans Teens

Gavin is currently studying at a university to become a middle school English teacher. His future goals include "to be the best educator I can be for the children that I serve and to continue to advocate for the trans community."

When asked about his advice for gifted trans teens, Gavin stated:

"Being neurologically different is almost synonymous with giftedness. So much more is expected of us. We've proven that we're smarter, so that bar is set for us. But many of us who suffer or live with mental illness or neurological difference find that as we age, support tends to go away, so our experiences as gifted kids fall behind. We get less support when we need more support. When grades fall, it gets worse. As you start performing less, you get behind and that bar gets farther away; it becomes a cycle of lack of support. There's not enough of a dialogue about that. That bar exists in a context—in a world that is expecting you to function in one way. That bar, in terms of the public education system, does not serve students—is counterintuitive to the way most people learn. That bar is meant for people who fit very neatly into the system; it is not applicable for many. It is so frustrating to feel as if you're being compared to others, but there will be space to find where your actual bar is. It is not modeled after a society of neurotypical minds. You'll find your niche eventually. It may not be in public school. It may not be in the public eye. If you make your niche your own, it will be optimal for you; it will lead to your greatest happiness. At the core, remember not to try to measure up to the metrics society has set up for us. They do not service anybody. NO child left behind—unless you're neurologically different in any way. So much is determined by what's expected by society. It's the metric we all have to live with, make it through, or live in harmony with. Right now, it affects the lives of every person."

I've no doubt that Gavin will make a huge difference in the lives of middle school students. He is already well on his way to making a difference for transgender students across the nation. Considering Gavin's acute awareness of his own neurological differences and the impact of societal expectations, I have a feeling he will eventually play a major role in adapting the educational system to meet the needs of *all* students, not just those who fit the mold.

In fact, Gavin has already begun to play a major role on the national level. On January 3, 2020, he tweeted: "I am honored to announce that I have been elected to the @ACLU Board of Directors for a one-year term!! I am elated, and I will work hard to do this position justice. Thank you to the ACLU and to everyone who has supported me through my fight." Gavin is not only a talented self-advocate, he is a dedicated advocate for others as well.

Strategies for Educators

As states, districts, and schools work (albeit sometimes slowly) to assure the inclusion of underserved LGBTQ+ learners in gifted education programs, there are some strategies that concerned educators can begin to implement immediately: LBGTQ+-friendly/inclusive curriculum, research-based inquiry, and bibliotherapy.

LGBTQ+-Friendly/Inclusive Curriculum

As we are becoming more aware of the identities of gifted LGBTQ+ students and their social and emotional needs, we are also becoming more aware that to meet their academic needs, we must reflect who they are. The NAGC publication *Needs and Approaches for Educators and Parents of Gifted Gay, Lesbian, Bisexual, and Transgender Students* (NAGC 2017) encourages teachers and schools to create and design a curriculum that is LGBTQ+ friendly or inclusive. An LGBTQ+-friendly or inclusive curriculum exists when study is based on lessons that avoid bias and include positive representations of LGBTQ+ people, history, and events. It is inclusive and affirming of all students. When these curricula are in place, school environments will be safer for all students, resulting in a less hostile school experience and increased feelings of connectedness to the school community. All students will feel empowered to speak up for themselves and seek the educational experience that addresses their wants and needs.

LGBTQ+-friendly curriculum benefits all students by exposing them to more inclusive and accurate accounts of history, presenting the contributions of LGBTQ+ individuals both in historical and contemporary times. It challenges stereotypes and promotes acceptance of all people. It benefits LGBTQ+ students, specifically, by validating their existence and experiences, reinforcing their value and self-worth, and providing space for their voices.

While a full discussion of the principles of design for LGBTQ+-friendly curriculum is beyond the scope of this book, the following goals provided by GLSEN are excellent:

> Incorporate LGBTQ+ history, themes, and people into your regular curriculum.

> Ensure that LGBTQ+ students see themselves reflected in your lessons.

> Create opportunities for all students to gain a more complex and authentic understanding of the world around them.

> Encourage respectful behavior, critical thinking, and social justice.

What is suggested here is that LGBTQ+-sensitive curricula not only inform all students on LGBTQ+ issues, but also create understanding and empathy, allowing gifted LGBTQ+ learners to find a more comfortable stance in the emerging pro-LGBTQ+ world (Friedrichs 2014). As they relate their skills and interests to pertinent, realistic, relevant curricula, gifted LGBTQ+ students discover a better understanding of self and will build greater self-acceptance. They become equipped to take their place in creating a better, more sensitive world (Friedrichs, Manzella, and Seney 2017, 24).

Research-Based Inquiry and Bibliotherapy

Two other strategies suggested in creating an LGBTQ+-friendly curriculum are research-based inquiry and bibliotherapy (Seney 2018).

In this context, research-based inquiry is the in-depth study and research into critical issues surrounding the LGBTQ+ culture: the history of the gay movement in the United States, the role and contribution of LGBTQ+ individuals to historical and modern societies, and the political progress for LGBTQ+ people in basic civil rights, marriage, and military service. For example, recent political attacks in the United States on transgender individuals make this a very timely topic for investigation and research (Friedrich, Manzella, and Seney 2017).

Several studies (Friedrichs 2012; Friedrichs and Etheridge 1995; Peterson and Rischar 2000; Treat 2008; Whittenburg and Treat 2008) show that LGBTQ+ students are interested in reading and learning about successful individuals who are like themselves. This interest provides opportunity and motivation for investigating and researching prominent, successful individuals in the LGBTQ+ community. By focusing on LGBTQ+ people, topics, and issues, students can see themselves reflected in the curriculum, and they can begin to move toward meeting their own needs academically, personally, and emotionally (Seney 2018).

Like research-based inquiry, the strategy of using literature and bibliotherapy readily speaks to a strength and interest of many, if not most, gifted learners: reading. Through their reading, gifted LGBTQ+ students extend their own knowledge bases, respond to their own curiosity, and independently extend their learning into deeper levels (Seney 2018). An excellent resource is the list of books for children and teens provided by the American Library Association's Stonewall Book Awards. These honor "books with exceptional merit relating to the GLBT experience" (ala.org/rt/rrt/award/stonewall/honored). This award is now known as the Mike Morgan & Larry Romans Children's & Young Adult Literature Award.

Bibliotherapy is the term used to describe the technique of having students read about individuals in literature who may have similar experiences to their own (Recob 2008; Seney 2018). It is a counseling technique adapted for classroom use. When reading about a problem or issue, readers realize—with the benefit of some safe distance—that others have the same problems that they do. This is the first, and perhaps most important, step in effectively dealing with their situation. The goals of bibliotherapy are to defuse the problem, create an accepting environment in which the problem can be discussed, create recognition and ownership of the problem, and create a support group that has pledged to tackle the problem together. In bibliotherapy, the reader is moved through the following four phases:

1. **Identification.** The reader recognizes the protagonist's conflict as a real situation.

2. **Catharsis.** The reader recognizes that they have the same problem.

3. **Insight.** The reader identifies possible solutions.

4. **Application.** The reader applies the insights to their own life (Seney 2017).

Two excellent resources to guide teachers, counselors, and parents are *Bibliotherapy: The Interactive Process* by Arleen McCarty Hynes and Mary Hynes-Berry and *Bibliotherapy: When Kids Need Books: A Guide for Those in Need of Reassurance and Their Teachers, Parents, and Friends* by Amy Recob.

Meeting Social and Emotional Needs

To address the six major issues that gifted LGBTQ+ students face, teachers, administrators, and other school staff can implement the following solutions to increase gifted LGBTQ+ students' comfort level and nurture their maximum development (Treat 2017; Sedillo 2017), enhancing their ability to self-advocate.

Strategies to Address Violence, Harassment, and Discrimination

Educators can address these issues in several ways:

> Prominently display a "Safe Space" or "Safe Zone" placard/sticker, rainbow flag, or equality symbol.

> Review nondiscrimination policies with *all* students, especially noting those applicable to LGBTQ+ issues.

> Display contact information for your school's anti-bullying coordinator.

> Publicly praise any individuals who actively encourage or promote an inclusive environment.

> Identify bullying hot spots, such as restrooms and other places out of teachers' sight, and take action to make them safe. One way is to assign students or staff to consistently monitor those locations.

Strategies to Address Gender-Varied Interests and Behaviors

Teachers can assist by ensuring that nontraditional roles are valued in their classrooms.

> Counter stereotypes in textbooks or discussions with examples of people in nontraditional roles.

> Use gender-neutral terms (such as firefighter rather than fireman).

> Avoid stereotyping students (for example, assuming that boys are noisy and loud, while girls are calm and sweet).

> Highlight any gender stereotypical language used by students in the classroom and use it to invite broader discussion.

Strategies to Address Lack of Role Models

Teachers and administrators can include appropriate role models for LGBTQ+ students:

> Include gifted LGBTQ+ individuals in job shadowing and internship opportunities and as guest speakers and mentors.

> Allow students to research the sexual orientations and gender identities of various famous contributors to society and create presentations or curriculum support materials that can be utilized in future classes. A selection of books and other helpful resources is listed in the references and recommended resources at the end of this chapter.

Strategies to Address Isolation

Teachers can help make the invisible visible and ensure LGBTQ+ students do not feel isolated using the following strategies.

> Include LGBTQ+ issues as a natural part of classroom conversations.

> Help develop self-advocacy abilities in gifted LGBTQ+ students and in those who have LGBTQ+ family members.

> Connect LGBTQ+ students with LGBTQ+ advocates. A few organizations that can help you find advocates include the ACLU, GLSEN, GSA Network, G2 Youth Advocate, Safe Schools Coalition, Transforming Families. Contact information for these organizations is listed in the websites section of this chapter.

Strategies to Address Heightened Sensitivities

Strategies to deal with heightened sensitivities include:

> When planning curricula, include information that allows students to reflect on their overexcitabilities and sensitivities and the significance they may have in an educational setting. This will help increase understanding and tolerance.

> Partner with school counselors and other experts to meet the needs of gifted LGBTQ+ students.

Strategies to Address a Lack of Inclusive Language

In most cases, school communications can be improved significantly to be more inclusive. Strategies for making your school communications LGBTQ+ friendly include:

> Use gender-neutral language in both written and verbal communications and on school forms (parent/guardian rather than mother/father).

> Ensure students are addressed by the correct pronouns.

> Provide opportunities (not requirements) for students to communicate their gender identities and sexual orientations.

When we address these unique social and emotional needs of gifted LGBTQ+ learners, they recognize us as advocates who support them and their self-advocacy.

Conclusion

Gifted LGBTQ+ students' social and emotional needs must be addressed through academics by ensuring that your curriculum is inclusive of LGBTQ+ people and issues. This is not only beneficial to LGBTQ+ learners, who urgently need to see themselves reflected in their studies, but to all students by informing them of LGBTQ+ issues and thus creating empathy.

While the great concerns shared by Gavin in his interview were not totally academic, one cannot help but think that if Gavin's school had instituted LGBTQ+-friendly curricula, his journey would have been easier. It definitely would have resulted in heightened awareness on the part of teachers and other educators. As a gifted student, having a more personalized and appropriately challenging curriculum would also have been beneficial in helping Gavin reach his full academic potential.

> It is imperative that schools implement strategies and approaches that address the needs—academic and social and emotional—of *all* students.

Gavin's school environment was hostile; he had only the support of his mother and, later, the ACLU legal team. Having effective social and emotional support, including in the areas of risk-taking, self-advocacy, honoring and making accommodations for his gender identity, and developing as a unique gifted individual, could have mitigated much of the trauma Gavin endured in school and still deals with today.

It is imperative that schools implement strategies and approaches that address the needs—academic and social and emotional—of *all* students. This is perhaps even more crucial with gifted LGBTQ+ individuals to ensure that they fulfill their potential.

Although the adults at Gavin's school did nothing to support his unique academic and social and emotional needs as a neurodiverse gifted transgender teen, Gavin found within himself the ability to self-advocate and he found others who would help him strengthen that ability. As Deb Douglas stated (2018, 7), "While we hope for changes in the system, administration, teachers, budgets, laws, or initiatives that may eventually take place, *today* many gifted kids are starving for an equal opportunity to develop their unique potential. Instead of asking them to wait for the system to change, we must put the power of change-making into their hands." Gavin's leadership in his court case is one such example.

Key Concepts

> There are six major challenges experienced by gifted LGBTQ+ students that will not be mitigated without a commitment to long-term, systematic evaluation of curriculum and program improvement.

> For gifted LGBTQ+ students, self-advocacy requires risk-taking and the support of responsible adults, including teachers, to correct and avoid violence, harassment, and discrimination.

> Avoiding gender stereotypes and accepting nontraditional gender roles is beneficial for all students, including LGBTQ+ students.

> Affirmation and support for gifted LGBTQ+ students must include access to curricula and role models that are LGBTQ+-friendly and LGBTQ+-inclusive.

> There are strategies teachers can implement to help gifted LGBTQ+ students feel included and accepted.

> Teachers can partner with other professionals, such as school counselors, to address gifted LGBTQ+ students' overexcitabilities and sensitivities.

> Schools and teachers can use inclusive language to improve communications and help gifted LGBTQ+ students feel more comfortable in the classroom and at school.

Discussion Questions

1. Discuss the six major challenges gifted LGBTQ+ students face, and ask the LGBTQ+ students at your school which challenges they have encountered. With their assistance and/or after discussing their responses with other decision-makers, formulate your plan for ensuring your school's gifted curriculum and program positively impact your gifted LGBTQ+ students.

2. How could you better support your gifted LGBTQ+ students and encourage their self-advocacy?

3. What changes could teachers and administrators implement in your school to avoid gender stereotypes and include nontraditional gender roles? Please address both gifted and general education arenas.

4. How could you include LGBTQ+-friendly curricula and role models in your gifted program?

5. What strategies would be appropriate in your school to help LGBTQ+ students feel accepted and included?

6. In what ways could you partner with other professionals to address the overexcitabilities and sensitivities of gifted LGBTQ+ students?

7. What inclusive language strategies could you implement to improve communications and help LGBTQ+ students feel more comfortable in the classroom and at school?

Recommended Resources
Websites

American Civil Liberties Union (ACLU) aclu.org
For almost 100 years, the ACLU has worked to defend and preserve the individual rights and liberties guaranteed by the Constitution and laws of the United States.

GLSEN glsen.org
GLSEN's goal is to ensure that each member of every school community is valued and respected regardless of sexual orientation or gender identity/expression.

GSA Network gsanetwork.org
This network connects school-based GSAs to each other and community resources through peer support, leadership development, and training.

G2 Youth Advocate gsquaredyouthadvocate.com
Created by Teresa Manzella, G2 offers multiple resource ideas and links to other sites for gifted LGBTQ young people.

Safe Schools Coalition safeschoolscoalition.org
The site offers resources in support of LGBTQ youth for educators and parents/guardians, including resources for youth and by topics, type, people who use them, and location.

Transforming Family transformingfamily.org/resources
Transforming Family provides multiple resources for all transgender youth and their families. Some states have local groups.

Books, Articles, and Films

Bongiovanni, Archie, and Tristan Jimerson. 2018. *A Quick and Easy Guide to They/Them Pronouns*. Portland, OR: Limerence Press.

Brummel, Bill, director. 2010. *Bullied: A Student, a School, and a Case That Made History*. Southern Law Poverty Center.

Cohn, Sandy. 2003. "The Gay Gifted Learner: Facing the Challenge of Homophobia and Antihomosexual Bias in Schools." In *Special Populations in Gifted Education: Working with Diverse Gifted Learners*, edited by Jaime A. Castellano, 123–134. Boston: Allyn & Bacon.

College Choice. 2020. "Best LGBTQ Schools." collegechoice.net/rankings/best-lgbt-friendly-colleges-and-universities.

Collins, Cory. 2018. "LGBTQ Best Practices Guide." *Teaching Tolerance* 6: 24–29. learningforjustice.org/sites/default/files/2018-09/Teaching-Tolerance-magazine-60_1.pdf.

Cowan, Tom. 2000. *Gay Men and Women Who Enriched the World*. Los Angeles: Alyson Books.

Cross, Tracy L., Karyn Gust-Brey, and P. Bonny Ball. 2002. "A Psychological Autopsy of the Suicide of an Academically Gifted Student: Researchers' and Parents' Perspectives." *Gifted Child Quarterly* 46 (4): 247–264. doi.org/10.1177/001698620204600402.

Dabrowski, Kazimierz. 1967. *Personality-Shaping Through Positive Disintegration*. Boston: Little, Brown.

Funk, Mason. 2019. *The Book of Pride: LGBTQ Heroes Who Changed the World*. New York: HarperOne.

Hughes-Hassell, Sandra, Elizabeth Overberg, and Shannon Harris. 2013. "Lesbian, Gay, Bisexual, Transgender, and Questioning (LGBTQ)–Themed Literature for Teens: Are School Libraries Providing Adequate Collections?" *School Library Research* 16. ala.org/aasl/pubs/slr/vol16.

Katz, Jonathan Ned. 1992. *Gay American History: Lesbians and Gay Men in the USA*. New York: Plume.

Kosciw, Joseph G., Caitlin M. Clark, Nhan L. Truong, and Adrian D. Zongrone. 2020. *The 2019 National School Climate Survey: The Experiences of Lesbian, Gay, Bisexual, Transgender, and Queer Youth in Our Nation's Schools*. New York: GLSEN. glsen.org/research/2019-national-school-climate-survey.

Madrone, Kelly Huegel. 2018. *LGBTQ: The Survival Guide for Lesbian, Gay, Bisexual, Transgender, and Questioning Teens*. Minneapolis: Free Spirit Publishing.

———. 2017. "12 Ways to Make Your Classroom Safe for LGBTQ Students." freespiritpublishingblog. com/2017/08/21/12-ways-to-make-your-classroom-safe-for-lgbtq-students.

Manzella, Teresa Ryan. 2014. "Gifted and GLBTQ: A Parent's Perspective." *2e: Twice Exceptional Newsletter* July. 2enewsletter .com/subscribers_only/arch_2014_07_Manzarella_Gifted%20&%20GLBTQ.html.

———. 2014. "Home for the Holidays: Reducing the Stress for Your Gifted GLBTQ Kid." *Parenting for High Potential* 4 (2): 2–3.

National Association for Gifted Children. 2015. "Supporting Gifted Students with Diverse Sexual Orientations and Gender Identities: Position Statement." Washington, DC. nagc.org/sites/default/files/Position%20Statement/GLBTQ%20 (sept%202015).pdf.

Owens-Reid, Dannielle, and Kristin Russo. 2014. *This Is a Book for Parents of Gay Kids: A Question & Answer Guide to Everyday Life*. San Francisco: Chronicle Books.

Pearson, Jennifer, Chandra Muller, and Lindsey Wilkinson. 2007. "Adolescent Same-Sex Attraction and Academic Outcomes: The Role of School Attachment and Engagement." *Social Problems* 54 (4): 523–542.

Peterson, Jean Sunde, and Heather Rischar. 2000. "Gifted and Gay: A Study of the Adolescent Experience." *Gifted Child Quarterly* 44 (4): 231–246. doi.org/10.1177/001698620004400404.

Pohl, Bernardo E. Jr., Matthew Fugate, and John Kelly. 2017. "A Moral Debate at the Invisible Rainbow: Thoughts about Best Practices in Servicing LGBTQ Students in Special Education." *Journal of Family Strengths* 17 (2): Article 15.

Public Justice. 2017. "Jury Verdicts and Settlements in Bullying Cases." publicjustice.net/wp-content/ uploads/2016/02/2017.06.12-Spring-Edition-Bullying-Verdicts-and-Settlements-Final.pdf.

Riemer, Matthew, and Leighton Brown. 2019. *We Are Everywhere: Protest, Power, and Pride in the History of Queer Liberation*. New York: Ten Speed Press.

Teaching Tolerance. 2017. "Best Practices: Creating an LGBT-Inclusive School Climate: A Teaching Tolerance Guide for School Leaders." learningforjustice.org/sites/default/files/2017-11/Teaching-Tolerance-LGBT-Best-Practices-2017- WEB-Oct2017.pdf.

Treat, Alena R., and Becky Whittenburg. 2006. "Gifted Gay, Lesbian, Bisexual, and Transgender Annotated Bibliography: A Resource for Educators of Gifted Secondary GLBT Students." *Journal of Secondary Gifted Education* 17 (4): 230–243. files.eric.ed.gov/fulltext/EJ750998.pdf.

USC Rossier. N.d. "Students and Gender Identity: A Toolkit for Schools." rossieronline.usc.edu/students-and-gender-identity.

References

Brinckerhoff, Loring C. 1994. "Developing Effective Self-Advocacy Skills in College-Bound Students with Learning Disabilities." *Intervention in School and Clinic* 29 (4): 229–237. doi.org/10.1177/105345129402900407.

Coleman, Alicia. 2019. "The Effect of a Growth Mindset Program on Mathematics Achievement of High School Upperclassmen." http://hdl.handle.net/11603/13827.

Douglas, Deb. 2018. *The Power of Self-Advocacy for Gifted Learners: Teaching the Four Essential Steps to Success (Grades 5–12)*. Minneapolis: Free Spirit Publishing.

Finley, Ben. 2019. "Virginia School's Transgender Bathroom Ban Is Back in Court." Associated Press. newsleader.com /story/news/2019/07/23/virginia-schools-transgender-bathroom-ban-back-court/1806993001.

Friedrichs, Terrance Paul. 2014. "Advice to Parents from Gifted Gay Male Youth." *Parenting for High Potential* 4 (2): 19–20.

——. 2012. "Counseling Gifted GLBT Students Along Paths to Freedom." In *Handbook for Counselors Serving Students with Gifts and Talents: Development, Relationships, School Issues, and Counseling Needs/Interventions*, edited by Tracy L. Cross and Jennifer Riedl Cross. 153–177. Waco, TX: Prufrock Press.

Friedrichs, Terence P., and Regina L. Etheridge. 1995. "Gifted and Gay: Reasons for Educators to Help." Council for Exceptional Children/The Association for Gifted (TAG) Newsletter, 17 (1): 4–5.

Friedrichs, Terence Paul, Teresa Ryan Manzella, and Robert Seney. 2017. *Needs and Approaches for Educators and Parents of Gifted Gay, Lesbian, Bisexual, and Transgender Students.* Washington, DC: National Association for Gifted Children.

Grimm, Gavin. Interview by Alena Treat. Personal interview, June 12, 2019.

Grimm v. Gloucester County School Board, 4:15cv54 U.S.229 (2019).

Hynes, Arleen McCarty, and Mary Hynes-Berry. 2018. *Bibliotherapy: The Interactive Process: A Handbook.* New York: Routledge.

Lhamon, Catherine E., and Vanita Gupta. 2016. "Dear Colleague Letter: Transgender Students." US Department of Justice, Civil Rights Division and US Department of Education, Office for Civil Rights. justice.gov/opa/file/850986/download.

National Association for Gifted Children. n.d. "Diversity Toolbox: Gifted LGBTQ Students." nagc.org/resources-publications/resources/timely-topics/including-diverse-learners-gifted-education-program-1.

Peterson, Jean Sunde, and Heather Rischar. 2000. "Gifted and Gay: A Study of the Adolescent Experience." *Gifted Child Quarterly* 44 (4): 231–246. doi.org/10.1177/001698620004400404.

Recob, Amy. 2008. *Bibliotherapy: When Kids Need Books: A Guide for Those in Need of Reassurance and Their Teachers, Parents, and Friends.* iUniverse.

Sedillo, Paul J. 2017. "A Response to the Six Social-Emotional Issues for G/LGBTQ Students." In *Teaching Gifted Children: Success Strategies for Teaching High-Ability Learners*," edited by Jeff Danielian, C. Matthew Fugate, and Elizabeth Fogarty. Waco, TX: Prufrock Press.

Seney, Robert W. 2018. "Serving and Honoring Gender Diversity in Education." In *The SAGE Handbook of Gifted and Talented Education*, edited by Belle Wallace, Dorothy A. Sisk, and John Senior. 159–168. Thousand Oaks, CA: SAGE Publications.

Stevens, Matt. 2018. "Transgender Student in Bathroom Dispute Wins Court Ruling." *New York Times.* nytimes.com/2018/05/22/us/gavin-grimm-transgender-bathrooms.html.

Tillier, William. 1998. "Intersections Between Dabrowski's Theory of Positive Disintegration and Wilber's Spectral Model of Consciousness." In *3rd International Symposium on Dabrowski's Theory.* Evanston, IL. Retrieved from positivedisintegration.com.

Treat, Alena R. 2008. "Beyond Analysis by Gender: Overexcitability Dimensions of Sexually Diverse Populations and Implications for Gifted Education." Ph.D. dissertation, Indiana University. drive.google.com/file/d/0B9hHy0SqKizYaXRDNUVUR2RUY1Z3ajVWVHIya25LSFVoUEhV/edit.

——. 2017. "Gifted LGBTQ Social-Emotional Issues." In *Teaching Gifted Children: Success Strategies for Teaching High-Ability Learners*," edited by Jeff Danielian, C. Matthew Fugate, and Elizabeth Fogarty. Waco, TX: Prufrock Press.

Tufankjian, Scout. "*Grimm-04.*" February 2017. ACLU Dropbox Collection. Shared July 18, 2019.

——. "*Grimm-16.*" February 2017. ACLU Dropbox Collection. Shared July 18, 2019.

——. "*Grimm-21.*" February 2017. ACLU Dropbox Collection. Shared July 18, 2019.

Whittenburg, Becky, and Alena R. Treat. 2008. "Shared Characteristics of Gifted and Sexually Diverse Youth." *Perspectives in Gifted Education* 4: 140–176.

10

Power Advocates: Families of Diverse Gifted Learners Taking a Seat at the Table

Joy Lawson Davis, Ed.D., Shauna Mayo, Ed.D., Erinn Fears Floyd, Ph.D.

Introduction

Champions of advocacy initiatives have popularized the phrase "a seat at the table" to suggest that all stakeholders interested in or affected by specific issues, policies, and practices should be at the metaphorical "table," working together to have their concerns heard and addressed. In gifted education, families that have not typically been at the table are those raising culturally diverse students and students from low-income backgrounds. These families have not been at the table often enough because their learners are not typically identified as gifted and do not have access to gifted and advanced learner programs (Ford, 2014; Grissom and Redding 2016). Parents of diverse students are in an excellent position to teach their students how to self-advocate. Parents who speak up and ensure that they are heard are students' best models of self-advocacy.

When whole groups of community members, including families of diverse learners (such as Black, Hispanic, American Indian, Alaskan Native, and low-income students), are left out of conversations regarding how school districts identify and provide appropriate services for gifted learners, the services are generally inequitable and disproportionately serve only one or two groups of students—those who are White and/or affluent. This disproportionality creates programs that are unfair, elitist, and discriminatory.

As a local district coordinator and later a state-level administrator of gifted services, one of our coauthors experienced the impact of active parent advocacy on shaping gifted education policy and practice. What became evident throughout her experiences was that when parent advocacy and advisory groups did not exist or did not represent the demographics of the district and state, students who had no representation at the table were tragically underrepresented and underserved by local gifted and advanced learner programs and even by state-sponsored programs. This unacceptable lack of representation impacts how well the academic and social and emotional needs of students from diverse backgrounds are met—or, more likely, not met.

> Parents who speak up and ensure that they are heard are students' best models of self-advocacy.

In our collective work as gifted education professionals, we have experienced the difference it makes in programming and access to services when parents of students from diverse backgrounds are included as advocates, members of advisory councils, and collaborative partners with school districts. In this chapter, we will provide our own views of the importance of parent and family advocacy, tips from parents, and stories from four families who have used specific strategies to ensure that their gifted children receive appropriate services to meet their intellectual, academic, and social and emotional needs.

Why Parent Advocacy?

Canadian researcher and scholar Francois Gagné created a model to describe how students' natural aptitudes or gifts develop into talents (Gagné 1999). Among the environmental catalysts noted in Gagné's Differentiated Model of Giftedness and Talent are parents and family members who play a critical role in the development of talent. This view of talent development supports a holistic view of the gifted child as defined by Davis (2013). **Figure 10.1** shows all the subgroups and catalysts involved in the life of the gifted child. At the center of the holistic configuration is the gifted child. When working with families from diverse backgrounds, it is important to recognize all the players in the configuration, including neighbors, community leaders, parents, and extended family members (Davis 2013). All these subgroups have an impact on the life and development of the gifted learner.

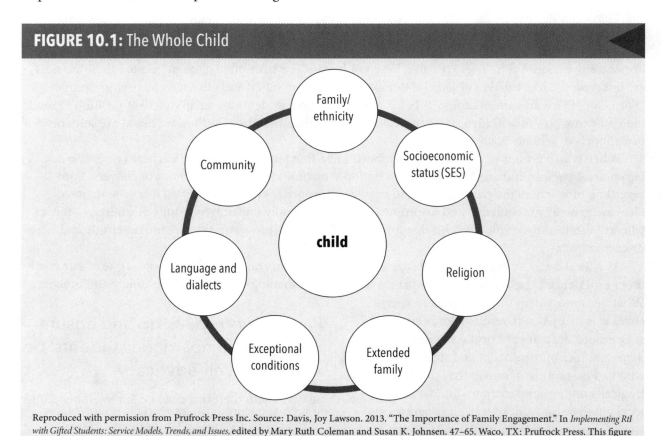

FIGURE 10.1: The Whole Child

Reproduced with permission from Prufrock Press Inc. Source: Davis, Joy Lawson. 2013. "The Importance of Family Engagement." In *Implementing RtI with Gifted Students: Service Models, Trends, and Issues,* edited by Mary Ruth Coleman and Susan K. Johnsen. 47–65. Waco, TX: Prufrock Press. This figure appears on page 52 of the book.

Increasingly, school districts are offering advice and information sessions for parents of gifted learners to help families become better advocates for their students. Too often, though, Black, Hispanic, and AIAN families and families from low-income backgrounds across cultures are not privy to this information or may not be targeted for such sessions. Well-designed sessions have the potential to equip parents with information they can use and share more widely in their own communities. Families who are better informed are more active in their students' education and have greater potential to effect positive change in school programs that serve gifted students. Empowering families also has the potential to strengthen their relationships with school personnel who become collaborators in the development of sustainable advanced learner programs across school districts (Davis 2013).

Parents Know Their Children Best

Parenting research and practice demonstrates that across cultures, regions, and socioeconomic conditions, parents know their children best (National Academies of Science 2016). As the first teachers and lifetime advisors, parents are in the best position to advocate for their offspring's educational and psychosocial needs. In communities with culturally diverse families and those with families living in poverty, research and anecdotal insights help us understand that the extended family—including grandparents, adult siblings, aunts, and fictive kin such as community members and faith leaders—also plays an important role in educational support for children (Davis 2010). For school personnel to actualize this type of support, they need to be aware of the historical role of underrepresented communities in the school achievement of students.

Culturally diverse families originate from a variety of backgrounds. Many have practiced the art of advocacy out of the need to ensure that their gifted children were able to access services for advanced and gifted learners provided through school districts, out-of-school organizations, and university settings. Becoming an advocate is a complex and tedious task. The families featured in this chapter will reveal advocacy strategies they have used and continue to use to ensure their gifted children have fair and equitable access to high-end advanced learner classes and specialized services for gifted children. Some of their stories are disheartening. They represent a stark reality in schools across the nation. The fact that children of color and those from low-income backgrounds are still underrepresented in gifted and advanced learner programs makes the advocacy of diverse families a pressing concern. Their impassioned stories and the unique advocacy strategies offered here will help other families and educators working to end historical injustices in gifted and advanced learner programs in America's schools.

Family Stories
John's Story

John is a twice-exceptional Black student who started reading at an early age. His mother shares her advocacy story.

My son, John, is twice-exceptional. We learned about his learning disability after he began school. He also, however, started reading at age two. Teachers found it hard to believe that he could read at such an early age. I imagined that his being Black had something to do with their disbelief. I can remember telling his preschool teacher that he could already read, and her response was, "What do you mean, read?" A few days later, my son came home and said that his teacher had him read in front of several other teachers and the principal. When I asked the teacher why she had him reading for others in the school, she looked at the floor and no longer made eye contact with me. She stammered and never came up with a reason. I finally walked away. When we later had a meeting about kindergarten readiness she said: "Maybe he can read, but he has no idea what he is reading." I took him out of that school immediately.

I sent him to another school, but I decided at that moment that it was going to be my responsibility to make sure he was always educated at a higher level.

My son is very smart, but at a young age he had problems with coloring, cutting, and handwriting. Instead of seeing the strengths he possessed, a lot of his teachers let his deficits color their opinion of him. They said he was lazy and not trying. He would do outstanding on a standardized multiple-choice test, but in class, teachers would take away full credit for his answers because they could not read his handwriting, and his grades began to suffer. I was begging for help but was told there was nothing wrong, he just needed to "try harder." Finally, a caring teacher suggested we have John tested, and we found out that he had dyspraxia. Once he received his diagnosis, he started taking his iPad to school and typing all his responses. Afterward, his grades and scores skyrocketed, and he has excelled ever since.

For my child to receive the education he deserved, I had to take on that responsibility myself. I went far above and beyond what was being covered in school at home with my son, especially during the elementary years. You could say he was both home schooled and public schooled. He would do above-level online courses in the summer, and I always stayed involved with what was going on at school. I volunteered, I wrote emails, I was room mother. I did everything I could to be as involved as possible. No matter what grade or what school he was in, they knew who I was.

One key piece of advice I would offer is this: before school starts each year, when you find out who your child's teacher is, write the teacher an email introducing yourself and your child. Let the teacher know your child's strengths and weaknesses and make sure to keep the lines of communication open. Ask questions. If something doesn't seem right, ask more questions and don't be afraid to take it as far as you need to become satisfied. Not everyone is going to like you, but they will respect you for it. Don't be scared to speak up. Don't fear retaliation. You will not only be helping your child, but you will make it easier for other children like them that are coming behind. Read and stay current with what is out there, and advocate, advocate, advocate!

Isaiah's Story

Isaiah, the oldest son in his family, is Black and Asian American. His mother discusses her story of advocating on behalf of her son, who is 3E (culturally diverse, gifted, and with other exceptional conditions).

My son Isaiah is a sophomore attending a specialized high school for gifted students in a large urban district in the northeast. My son is bicultural. I am Chinese/Taiwanese and my husband is Haitian. When Isaiah was just two, I noticed his exceptional ability as we traveled by train from Manhattan to the Lower East Side, where I worked. He learned the names of the trains and the color of each line quickly. He had an excellent sense of direction, and by age three he could actually give accurate directions to other family members as they traveled by train. By the time he was four, I noticed that he began adding and subtracting without any prompting. I was not the kind of mother teaching skills every day. I allowed my son to learn in a more natural style.

I noticed early that he was different. He began having some concerns in a regular preschool program, so I worked with his teachers to have him evaluated for the special education program so he could receive services. He was diagnosed as having obsessive compulsive disorder (OCD), and received an Individual Education Program (IEP) under the category of "other health impaired." He had an IEP to address his socialization skills, he was assigned an occupational therapist, and he also had a play therapist. Having to navigate the system on his behalf was easier for me than some parents because I knew the system and understood which agencies and organizations would provide support. As a 3E learner (culturally diverse, gifted, and with other exceptional conditions), he received support on a regular basis until he was in middle school when he was declassified. When he was evaluated for gifted services, he scored 117 on the Stanford-Binet, which was not high enough to allow him to go to one of the specialized programs in New York City. Later he took the Otis-Lennon School Ability Test (OLSAT) and scored in the ninety-ninth percentile. This score qualified him for one of the slots in the city's and gifted and talented programs. I chose to have him attend a school where there were more Black and brown students so he would be more comfortable.

One of the biggest challenges I faced getting the services Isaiah needed was advocating for him as a 3E learner. For so many students who are gifted and have other exceptional conditions, schools are not always as willing to serve them for their disability once they learn that the student scored in the gifted range on a nationally standardized test. I am currently advocating for Isaiah's IEP to be reopened. He was doing better in school when he had the extra support.

As my son continued in school, he often felt discouraged because he believed his teachers were not that dynamic, and often he was not particularly impressed by his teachers' content expertise. He found that some who were strongest were teachers with special education licensure. They understood student strengths and how to provide the support needed.

Some of the advice I would give other parents of diverse gifted students is to be sure to know the right organizations at the state and national levels who provide advocacy information for parents. Look for groups where you can get reduced membership fees. Also understand that there is sometimes a stigma attached to "being gifted," and your child may come in contact with educators and other students who will discourage them because of their ethnicity. My main advice is to nurture your child's gifts without putting too much pressure on them and to avoid the well-meaning but damaging statement, "You have a lot of potential, but you're not doing well enough!" Greatness is not about the best grades. It is about persistence, determination, and drive. Let them find their own way into their gifts!

Breanna and Brooke's Story

Breanna and Brooke are twin Black girls. Their mother shares her story of advocating for her daughters.

My story is about my twin daughters, who attended an international school during their early childhood years. I am an African American gifted woman and an educator of gifted students. I also raised two gifted daughters who are now ages thirty and twenty-six. So, I easily recognized the gifted traits in my twin girls, Breanna and Brooke. The twins' first formal educational experience was at a private, American-curriculum school for girls in the United Arab Emirates (UAE). Our family lived in the UAE when the twins were aged three to eight. Upon our return to the States, my husband and I spent a significant amount of time researching public schools to identify one in an affordable neighborhood with a diverse student body and high academic standards. When we thought we had found the ideal school, we enrolled the girls. At the end of the first day of school, I eagerly went to the twins' third-grade teacher and excitedly asked: "How did they do?" I absolutely expected Mrs. F. to tell me how well the twins got along with the other children, that they asked a great deal of questions, and that they were a joy to have in her class. "Horribly!" Mrs. F responded, without blinking an eye.

The teacher said my daughters talked the entire day, and that was absolutely unacceptable in her class. I have to be honest: Breanna can talk! And talk! And talk!

Even though the teacher had fifteen years of professional experience, I gently explained to her that she could separate the sisters to eliminate the possibility of them disrupting her class with their chatter. A week later, I again asked Mrs. F: "How are the girls doing?" "Horribly!" she again responded. "Your children don't know anything about anything!"

Mrs. F. said our daughters could not focus during her lectures, did not know how to take notes, and frequently interrupted her lectures with comments about how the topic related to life in Dubai. "I don't care about their life in Dubai! No one does," Mrs. F almost screamed. I knew then that Mrs. F did not understand my brilliant children.

I immediately went to the principal and requested that he make arrangements to test Breanna and Brooke for gifted services. He told me that my daughters had missed the timeframe for testing and that I could get them tested privately. My husband I secured the funds from a family member and had the girls privately tested by a psychologist recommended by a mom at the school. Both of the girls reported that the psychologist's evaluation was "very simple." The twins' IQ scores were not high enough for automatic gifted qualification; however, they were high enough for further evaluation under the state's Plan B for students receiving free or reduced lunch. As part of the evaluation process, the girls had to undergo vision and hearing tests. That went fine; however, we went to a private developmental ophthalmologist for further evaluation. That was when we learned that one of the twins has a rare eye tracking disorder called convergence insufficiency that causes her eyes to jumble letters and words when she reads. This created yet another barrier; we had to fight with the school system for the teacher to provide accommodations. Eventually, our daughter with the vision condition qualified for accommodations under the Other Health Services category.

After a stressful year of daily struggle, our family ended up moving to Alabama. My husband landed a position with the Southern Poverty Law Center in Montgomery. For a number of reasons, we didn't even attempt to have the Alabama education department identify the twins as gifted. Instead, we enrolled them in a private college preparatory school. This was a major financial sacrifice for our family.

The best advice I would give other parents of underrepresented groups of gifted learners is to rely on your faith as you advocate for your children; they are depending on you. I would also suggest that you study your school system's and state's gifted education plans and connect with gifted scholars who often freely provide advice and support.

Alan's Story

Alan is a gifted Black student. His mother shares the challenges she faced in having his educational needs met.

My son was three or four years old when I really started seeing his gifts. He is very analytical; therefore, he was not into typical toddler activities. He always gravitated toward the abstract. He started reading early and always liked studying *National Geographic* magazines. He thrives on expressing himself through drawing and creating art projects. He also enjoyed music early. He picked up instruments and just started playing them. Currently, he is in dance class and really enjoys that as a form of expression.

The major barriers or challenges we have faced are teachers who don't understand how to pull out the strengths of Black children (boys in our case) and the lack of concern or sincerity in meeting my son where he is. Representation matters. Even with my son's high IQ (measured at 130), it was difficult to get teachers to pay attention to his strengths and work to develop them accordingly.

I reached out to experts in the field, contacted my local school board, and talked to my son's principal. It wasn't until I threatened to take legal action that I received the proper resources for my son. This should not be the case. Parents of gifted students (or any child) should NOT have to threaten schools with legal action to get the services their child rightfully deserves and needs.

The advice I'd give to parents is to remain vigilant and never stop fighting for what your child deserves, even when it feels like you're hiking uphill with a backpack full of rocks. Your children need to know and see that you have their back. I never regret any of the time that I have spent advocating for my son.

Advocacy Barriers

Research shows that gifted and talented students from marginalized populations are underrepresented in gifted and advanced learner program services (Milner and Ford 2007). As the families tell us in their stories, school district personnel were not willing to acknowledge their children's high abilities and, therefore, did not work with the parents to help their gifted learners receive access to services. Excluding marginalized gifted and talented students from receiving gifted and talented services robs these students of opportunities for rich learning experiences. Parents of these populations of students often encounter a vast array of barriers when attempting to ensure that their children receive services matched to their abilities. In the stories shared, the barriers included teacher bias and unfair identification practices, among others.

> When parents are not aware of services available for their children, it is difficult for them to be effective advocates.

Parents from culturally diverse groups may also experience a lack of information about the gifted and talented programs offered in a school district. School districts do not routinely disseminate information about gifted education throughout all communities. When parents are not aware of services available for their children, it is difficult for them to be effective advocates. Parents should receive information on the district's gifted policy, gifted identification protocols, characteristics of giftedness, and gifted program delivery and service options. Additionally, parents should have access to information about gifted parent advisory and advocacy groups to support their high-ability and gifted children. Most school districts are required by local or state mandate to have parent advisory councils for their gifted programs. Advisory councils with equitable representation are better equipped to address the concerns of all populations of gifted students than those committees that only represent one ethnic or income group.

Another barrier often faced by parents is the fear that their ability to successfully advocate for their children is insufficient. Many factors can create this fear, such as a parent's memories of their own negative school experiences. Negative experiences with former teachers and administrators can make parents hesitant to advocate for their children. These experiences may induce in parents a fear that their child will have similar traumatic experiences in school with educators who do not believe in their potential or who withhold valuable program information.

Lack of time may also be a barrier to a parent's ability to advocate for their gifted child. For gifted students who come from low-income or single-parent homes, this can be a particular concern. In single-parent homes, one parent is responsible for all household needs and may have to work more than one job. In some cases, even with two parents whose income is limited, parents may work multiple jobs just to make ends meet. Time and resource limitations exist that impact parents' availability to meet with administrators and teachers to discuss opportunities for their gifted child. All the families who shared their stories indicated that they spent a great deal of time researching schools, attending meetings, and gathering information to prepare for meetings with school personnel.

A compilation of these barriers to family advocacy and their impact on children's access to services, as well as possible solutions schools can provide, is shown in **table 10.1**.

TABLE 10.1: Barriers to Accessing Gifted Education and Advanced Learner Programs for Culturally Diverse Families

BARRIER	IMPACT	POTENTIAL SOLUTION
Lack of information	Parents are unaware of gifted services and benefits for their children	Wider dissemination of materials throughout all communities served by schools, including in homes and varied community locations such as grocery stores, health facilities, retail stores, churches, barbershops, and beauty salons
Lack of understanding of program availability and criteria for participation	Parents do not clearly understand how districts and schools identify students	Create brochures delineating all criteria and the process for identifying and determining if students have a need for gifted education options Host parent information sessions throughout the community
Teacher bias toward students of color and students from low-income households	Students of color and those from low-income households are overlooked Deficits rather than strengths are noted by teachers Educators have lower expectations for these students	Cultural competency training for all teachers that focuses on implicit bias, microaggressions, social justice, cultural strengths/norms/traditions, and impact of stereotype threat
Limited access to enrichment programs	Inequitable preparation and sustained exposure to high-end learning experiences	Provide enrichment programs at no or low cost Offer scholarships Provide transportation for after-school programs Engage college students as instructors or mentors
Biased identification strategies, including testing	Strengths of students may not be adequately measured Spaces for programs allocated for students whose parents can pay for outside testing	Use universal screening or local norms Ensure that tests selected are free of bias Include interviews, work samples, and family or peer referrals in identification protocols
Stereotyping	Misconceptions about student abilities based on prior experiences with larger group Students are given an "oppressed group" status	Build teachers' knowledge about stereotypes Provide training on strategies to create classroom environments that focus on the strengths of students and deemphasize deficits
No gifted and talented program offerings	Students lack challenging coursework and options tailored to their individual intellectual and academic needs	Advocate for mandated and funded local services for gifted students Provide districtwide gifted education professional learning Design service options that provide rigor and challenge to high-ability and gifted students

Twenty-Five Critical Advocacy Strategies for Families of Diverse Gifted Learners

The following strategies were provided in response to an informal online survey of parents of traditionally underserved gifted students in schools across the nation. We believe these strategies can break down the barriers to parent advocacy, and support parents in empowering and advocating for their gifted students as they seek out and participate in gifted education and advanced learner programs. We recommend that educators share these strategies with families and parents.

1. **Know your child's strengths.** You are your child's best advocate because you know your child's strengths and weaknesses. Don't be afraid to ask for the services your child is entitled to receive. Speak up when things don't seem right and support school personnel as they work with you.

2. **Be informed.** Gather as much information as you can from the school district's gifted and talented department as well as your state's Department of Education about available gifted services. Know the criteria used to make placement determinations. Get to know school personnel so you are able to speak to the appropriate people when necessary.

3. **Document, document, document.** It is important to keep good records of all meetings and other interactions with school district personnel at every level. Document meetings, testing dates, and so on. Everything is important.

4. **Seek and join a gifted advocacy group.** There are several benefits to joining a gifted advocacy group. Broadening your support base is one of the biggest benefits. When there is support, it helps you determine the key next steps and know that you are not alone in your efforts. Additionally, it opens up opportunities to make important connections and network with like-minded people. Another benefit is that an advocacy group helps everyone remain focused on the most important aspects of advocating for children who are not receiving gifted services.

5. **Find champions in the school district who support and understand gifted education.** It is important to understand that there are "champions" in the school district who can support you as you advocate for your child. These champions can help you better understand the operation of the school district and plan your next steps. Support from district staff can help you make difficult decisions so you can ensure your child is receiving the proper educational and support services.

6. **Never give up on your child.** Even if your child does not have a formal gifted identification, it does not mean your child is not gifted. For students of color and low-income students, there are multiple barriers to gifted education program access. Remain vigilant in accessing resources and opportunities to develop and display your child's strengths.

7. **Gather data.** Obtain evaluations from non-school personnel, such as medical professionals, psychometrists, or psychologists, to assist with diagnosis or identification if you are able. These evaluations may require you to pay out-of-pocket fees, but they will provide valuable information regarding your child's strengths and needs.

8. **Follow gifted education diversity and equity scholars on social media.** These scholars have expertise in gifted education, multicultural education, and underrepresentation of marginalized student populations in gifted education. They can share valuable resources and will often discuss your individual needs privately.

9. **Join a network and grow your community.** When you are facing something, chances are you are not alone. When you join a network and grow your community, you make valuable connections to people who may be experiencing or have experienced issues similar to yours. These connections can open you up to new ideas, strategies, and techniques that you can use to advocate for your child. More importantly, a network is a safe space for you as a parent to share your joys, accomplishments, concerns, and fears, knowing that you are sharing with those who understand.

10. **Advocate early and get outside assistance from national organizations.** Connecting with national organizations can help you better understand the dos and don'ts of gifted education on a national level. National organizations work closely with the US Department of Education to ensure that students identified as gifted are receiving fair and equitable opportunities. Seeking assistance from national organizations gives you an opportunity to have access to educators who can share information that may not otherwise be easily available to you.

11. **Don't worry about being a pain to your local school.** The teachers need your input on how to help your child. It may feel awful at first to ask for more or to worry that others will perceive you as thinking you are special. But teachers know that a rising tide raises all boats. Getting your child the help they need benefits the entire class.

12. **Leverage resources provided through your local library.** Your library can often order materials to further engage your child.

13. **Do not rely solely on the school system to challenge and support your child.** Make sure that you, as a parent, expose your child to activities not offered in school communities.

14. **Be persistent!** Don't stop asking for what your child needs. Do your own research on giftedness and try to share bits of knowledge with teachers.

15. **Learn your state's gifted laws.** Every state has laws pertaining to the education of gifted students. However, no two state's laws are identical. Thus, it is important that you become familiar with the laws of the state in which you currently reside and understand that those laws may be significantly different from the laws in any other state.

16. **Know that gifted children are not perfect.** Understand that gifted students will also make mistakes. As parents, make sure you explain to your child that while they are considered gifted, you do not expect them to be perfect. Doing this will certainly relieve some of the pressure that your child may experience. Instead of expecting perfection, teach your child to have a growth mindset. A growth mindset teaches your child that through hard work, good things come and that some things may be a little more difficult than others—but the key is to keep trying.

17. **Pay attention.** Don't allow your child to be labeled negatively. Many gifted students get into trouble due to a lack of challenge and mediocre teaching styles. Mediocre instruction leads to boredom for the student, which often manifests itself through inappropriate behavior. Get to know your child's teacher and their teaching style. Review assignments and make sure that they are challenging for your child. Don't settle for less than quality instruction and ensure your child is always provided with opportunities to do their best.

18. **Tell your children that they are not alone and they should never be afraid to let their beautiful light shine.** Their light is a beacon to other children like them. It is easy for gifted students to want to "dim" their light so they can be accepted by their peers. Teach them to find peers who are like them and who encourage them to be and do their best. As a parent, always encourage your child and let them know there is nothing wrong with being gifted and showing it.

19. **Encourage your child to find what they love most.** Every gifted child has different strengths and interests. It is important that as a parent you encourage your child to pursue their areas of interest. Don't try to make your child be someone else. Instead, know about multiple intelligences and encourage your child to find their niche.

20. **Look for free and affordable activities and events in your community.** Local libraries and community centers often offer activities for students within surrounding communities. Exposure is vital to helping gifted students expand their worldviews and learn about how diverse society is.

21. **Take charge of your child's growth.** Your first priority is to make sure that your child reaches their full potential. This will not happen if you place their education, growth, and development completely in the hands of someone else. Get engaged and remain engaged throughout your child's educational journey. Remember, you are and always will be your child's best advocate.

22. **Try not to compare your child to other people's children.** Every gifted child is unique because *all* children—gifted or not—are unique. Comparing your child to someone else is not beneficial to your child or to you. Comparison will lead to unnecessary and invalid disappointment.

23. **Continuously stay dialed in to your child's behaviors and moods.** Notice any changes, no matter how subtle. Often children do not know how to express themselves verbally when things are bothering them. However, changes in behavior will occur—some significant, and others not as much. Make sure you consistently communicate with your child and let them know that you are there to listen and support them no matter what may be taking place.

24. **Help your child access opportunities.** All children have a capacity for greatness, but they need guidance in learning how to access opportunities. As a parent, find those opportunities that interest or excite your gifted child. Once you find them, make sure they are accessible to your child.

25. **Stay current on educational practices and learn about your child's learning preferences.** Every child has their own learning preference. As a parent, make sure you know whether your child learns better by doing, hearing, listening, or seeing. Once you know this, make sure you also know about the most current research-based practices for each of these learning preferences. Doing this is another way to advocate for your child to receive the best possible education.

Conclusion

It is a major undertaking for parents to advocate for their gifted children, but family advocacy is crucial to ensuring that diverse gifted learners receive all-important services that will help them develop academically. Watching their families advocate for them, especially when the advocacy is received and acknowledged by schools, teaches gifted students important skills such as how to speak up for themselves, ask questions about services, and take a lead in developing appropriate services for other students like them. These skills are all part of strengthening students' self-advocacy.

Family advocacy is also important for these gifted students' psychosocial development. Gifted children, and especially diverse gifted children, are unique and possess an array of traits that make them stand out from other children their age. Parents can be crucial allies in helping schools recognize the unique psychosocial needs of diverse gifted students—to feel a sense of belonging, to fit in, to have cultural and academic peers, and to develop resilience (Davis 2019; Scott 2012). Recognizing the value of family involvement and encouraging family advocacy is one of the most important things educators can do to support diverse gifted students.

Barriers are a part of the educational journey for parents who are advocates for their children. These barriers are discouraging for families and often may appear to be insurmountable; however, it is important for parents to understand that they are their children's best advocates and that there are ways to eliminate or overcome many of the barriers that exist. To ensure that gifted children are able to realize their dreams, a high level of active engagement from children's families is required.

> Parents can be crucial allies in helping schools recognize the unique psychosocial needs of diverse gifted students.

There is no one-size-fits-all model for gifted students. To increase family engagement in the lives of their gifted students and to create more active partnerships between parents and educators, educators are called to be more collaborative with parents for the benefit of all gifted students. Educators must understand that for culturally diverse and low-income students, accessing programming can be particularly challenging. Educators can help bridge these gaps by helping parents understand that the best weapon to fight against inequities is information and that a key component of family advocacy is to gather the best information they can access and use it to get involved and become the strongest advocate possible for their child.

Encourage parents of gifted students (and those yet to be identified) in your community to use their voice, share their knowledge, grow their network, and make those decisions that will lead to the best possible outcomes for their children. Help parents understand that no matter how others may view them, the most important thing is that children know that parents are their champion, fighting daily to ensure that their giftedness is fully developed and they are prepared for the future. Make sure parents remember that no one knows their children better than they do. Encourage them to never relinquish their ability to advocate for their gifted children, because the responsibility for their children's education does not rest solely with others; it starts and ends with the parents. Guide parents to use their power of advocacy to take a seat at the table and maintain it to be a voice for their gifted children and others like them. Doing so will strengthen program services and improve life outcomes for all gifted learners.

Key Concepts

> Parent and family advocacy are critical to increasing diverse students' access to gifted education programs.

> Parental understanding of giftedness and the way it impacts student behavior is very important.

> Schools that build partnerships with diverse families, engage them in programming, and solicit their input strengthen inclusion practices.

> Parents play a critical role as advocates and supporters in developing their students' self-advocacy.

> Diverse families can be change agents by helping schools design equitable programming.

> Diverse community members have the potential to support students.

Discussion Questions

The following questions may be used by families and educators to initiate discussions with school personnel to strengthen advocacy and open doors for more effective collaboration between families and schools.

1. Several barriers are mentioned in this chapter that prevent culturally diverse parents, in particular, from fully understanding the benefits of gifted education. Among the barriers is a lack of information about gifted education identification and services. How can this barrier be overcome in your district or school?

2. Which families and communities are the most engaged in your district's gifted programs?

3. Is your current local advisory committee demographically representative? If not, what can you do to increase representation of underrepresented groups?

4. How do you currently solicit feedback from diverse families about their gifted children's strengths and needs?

5. How can your district become more receptive to parent advocacy and help parents from diverse backgrounds teach their children to self-advocate?

6. How can your district improve its outreach to community organizations and faith leaders that serve culturally diverse communities?

7. How can your district create a series of information sessions that are more appealing to and practical for diverse families?

8. How can you improve teacher training to ensure that teachers of the gifted are more culturally responsive?

Recommended Resources

A Black Education Network aben4ace.org

Council for Exceptional Children exceptionalchildren.org

Davidson Institute davidsongifted.org

Hoagies' Gifted Education Page hoagiesgifted.org

Johns Hopkins Center for Talented Youth: Talent Search cty.jhu.edu/talent

National Association for Gifted Children: Gifted by State nagc.org/information-publications/gifted-state

National Association for Gifted Children: Recursos Para los Padres de Familia nagc.org/resources-publications
/resources-parents/recursos-para-los-padres-de-familia

National Association for Gifted Children: Resources for Parents nagc.org/resources-publications/resources-parents

Supporting Emotional Needs of the Gifted sengifted.org

References

Davis, Joy Lawson. 2010. *Bright, Talented, & Black: A Guide for Families of African American Gifted Learners.* Scottsdale, AZ: Great Potential Press.

———. 2013. "The Importance of Family Engagement." In *Implementing RtI with Gifted Students: Service Models, Trends, and Issues,* edited by Mary Ruth Coleman and Susan K. Johnsen, 47–65. Waco, TX: Prufrock Press.

Davis, Joy Lawson. 2016. "Talent in Every Community: A Glimpse into the World of Parenting Gifted Children of Color" In *Gifted Children of Color Around the World: Diverse Needs, Exemplary Practices and Directions for the Future (volume 3),* edited by Joy Lawson Davis and James L. Moore III, 71–85. Bingley, UK: Emerald Publishing.

———. 2019. "Reframing Professional Learning to Meet the Needs of Teachers Working with Culturally Diverse Gifted Learners." In *Best Practices in Professional Learning and Teacher Preparation: Special Topics for Gifted Professional Development (volume 2),* edited by Angela M. Novak and Christine L. Weber, 51–70. Waco, TX: Prufrock Press.

Davis, Joy Lawson, and Shawn Anthony Robinson. 2018. "Being 3e, A New Look at Culturally Diverse Gifted Learners with Exceptional Conditions: An Examination of the Issues and Solutions for Educators and Families." In *Twice Exceptional: Supporting and Educating Bright, Creative Children with Learning Difficulties,* edited by Scott Barry Kaufman, 278–289. New York: Oxford University Press.

Ford, Donna Y. 2014. "Segregation and the Underrepresentation of Blacks and Hispanics in Gifted Education: Social Inequality and Deficit Paradigms." *Roeper Review* 36 (3): 143–154. doi.org/10.1080/02783193.2014.919563.

Ford, Donna Y., Kenneth T. Dickson, Joy Lawson Davis, Michelle Frazier Trotman Scott, and Tarek C. Grantham. 2018. "A Culturally Responsive Equity-Based Bill of Rights for Gifted Students of Color. *Gifted Child Today* 41 (3): 125–129. doi.org/10.1177/1076217518769698.

Gagné, Francois. 1999. "Gagné's Differentiated Model of Giftedness and Talent (DMGT)." *Journal for the Education of the Gifted* 22 (2): 230–34. doi:10.1177/016235329902200209.

Goudelock, Jessa D. Luckey. 2019. "High-Ability African American Children: Navigating the Two-Edged Sword of Giftedness." *Parenting for High Potential* 8 (2): 2–5, 20–22.

Grantham, Tarek C., Mary M. Frasier, Angie C. Roberts, and Eric M. Bridges. 2005. "Parent Advocacy for Culturally Diverse Gifted Students." *Theory into Practice* 44 (2): 138–147. doi.org/10.1207/s15430421tip4402_8.

Grissom, Jason A., and Christopher Redding. 2016. "Discretion and Disproportionality: Explainingthe Underrepresentation of High-Achieving Students of Color in Gifted Programs." *AERA Open*. doi:10.1177/2332858415622175.

Milner, H. Richard, and Donna Y. Ford. 2007. "Cultural Considerations in the Underrepresentation of Culturally Diverse Elementary Students in Gifted Education." *Roeper Review* 29 (3): 166–173.

Scott, Michelle Trotman. 2012. "Socio-Emotional and Psychological Issues and Needs of Gifted African-American Students: Culture Matters." *Interdisciplinary Journal of Teaching and Learning* 2 (1): 23–33.

Conclusion Deb Douglas, M.S.

As each chapter of this book has made abundantly clear, the challenges facing underrepresented gifted students are significant, but the potential for change and growth is immense, and there are concrete steps we can take to empower underserved gifted learners to take charge of their own education. First, we must do a much better job of recognizing their unique gifts and talents and identifying their intellectual and academic needs. We must find ways to communicate more clearly with them and their families. We must connect them with the programming that best matches their interests. We must support their progress through social and emotional guidance that is designed for their specific needs. And every step of the way, we must be intentional in teaching them the skill of self-advocacy so they are able set their own course—no matter what barriers they may face in the future.

> The challenges facing underrepresented gifted students are significant, but the potential for change and growth is immense.

Components and strategies within each of these key ideas are summarized in the sections that follow, allowing individual educators, professional learning teams, and administrators to assess their district's current status, determine needs, and set goals for improvement.

Ensure That Students' Gifts and Talents Are Recognized

Work to eliminate old stereotypes of giftedness that might keep us from identifying gifts and talents in underrepresented learners.

1. Provide administration and staff with professional learning on the special characteristics and needs of underrepresented gifted learners as well as the means to appropriately challenge and support them. Ensure that everyone understands the complexity of the intersectional status of gifted students from special populations.

2. Consider annual pre-screening of all students within the school or district, ensuring that students from all special populations are included. End-of-year screening by classroom teachers is especially beneficial.

3. Utilize multiple criteria, including non-verbal assessments, when identifying gifted learners. Use strength-based approaches rather than deficit-based approaches.

4. Confirm that the percentage of special population learners identified with gifts and talents is equivalent to the percentage of those students in your school's or district's general population.

Communicate Clearly with Learners and Their Families

Clear and direct communication is key to students' self-advocacy.

1. Be invitational, respectful, and inclusive. Welcome them to this new adventure. Assure students (and their parents or caregivers) that you have identified their special gifts and/or talents that go beyond the norm for their grade level and you want to help them have the educational experience that is right for them.

2. Negate the stereotype of all gifted learners being alike, allowing students to see themselves as gifted with their own great potential and capabilities.

3. Share state laws and statutes related to gifted learners, your district mission/vision statement, and your district plan for gifted learners. Let them know it is your intent to meet their needs, but you want them to partner with you in deciding how to do so.

4. Provide students and families with information regarding the nature of giftedness, meeting individual learner needs, and accelerated and enriched programming options that match those needs.

5. Find staff, community members, or older students within the special population who can serve as culture brokers and mentors for your students.

6. Translate all materials used in gifted identification and programming into the primary languages used by families in your district. For other languages, bring in interpreters.

7. If families are unresponsive to your outreach, try alternative measures. Be sure that program materials are widely distributed in all communities via print, in person, and online. Never assume a family isn't interested in being involved.

Ensure That District Programming Matches Student Needs for Acceleration and Enrichment

Remember that one size does not fit all. Not all programming is appropriate for all gifted learners. Not all gifted learners need all available programming.

1. List options that already exist to address the needs of gifted learners.

2. List opportunities that could exist if they would best address the needs of specific underserved gifted learners.

3. Ensure that teachers are prepared to develop and deliver culturally responsive, high-end curriculum and have access to resources to do so.

4. Ensure that counselors, social workers, school psychologists, and teachers understand the unique social and emotional needs of gifted learners, and specifically those from special populations.

5. Assist students and their advocates in selecting the options and opportunities that are right for them.

Teach Self-Advocacy Skills and Strategies

Directly and with intentionality, give students the information, insights, and strategies needed to comfortably and successfully self-advocate.

1. Remind learners of their right to an appropriately challenging education and social and emotional support.

2. Assure them that they have the right and the responsibility to partner with you in determining their own educational course.

3. Introduce them to the adults and older students who can serve as their advocates.

4. Whenever possible, connect underserved gifted learners with same-ability peers who may have similar interests and needs so they can advocate together.

ACCESSING APPROPRIATE OPTIONS

Are your students able to access the accelerated and enriched opportunities that are right for them? Possible concerns to consider include:

- **Time.** Does the student have time to take on the challenge? School schedules are sometimes inflexible, homework and after-school activities are time consuming, and part-time jobs may interfere.

- **Finances.** Most public school options are provided at no cost, but if there are additional fees for the chosen option (such as an online course, summer program, or residential school), can the student or family afford it? Will the school district pay for it? If not, are grants or scholarships available?

- **Materials.** In the same vein, does the option require additional books, lab equipment, or computer software? Are the materials readily available? Who will pay for them?

- **Technology.** What technology is required? Does it need to be available both in school and at home? And again, who will pay for it?

- **Transportation.** If an option requires traveling to another location near or far, does the student have reliable, consistent, and affordable transportation?

- **Communication skills.** Has the student developed sufficient writing, speaking, and listening skills to effectively communicate their plan to those who must endorse it and advocate for them?

- **Family support.** Is the student's immediate family committed to supporting their efforts, providing assistance when needed, and celebrating their successes? At the very least, will they agree to not get in the student's way?

- **Peer support.** Does the student have friends and classmates who are interested in their work and value their effort? A peer group that doesn't understand and isn't supportive could undermine a student's success.

Source: Douglas, Deb. 2018. *The Power of Self-Advocacy for Gifted Learners: Teaching the 4 Essential Steps to Success.* Minneapolis: Free Spirit Publishing.

Find Ways to Make Self-Advocacy "Portable"

Too often, some gifted students are unidentified and underserved because their lives are quite fluid. They may be in your class or your school this month and gone next month or next year. How can you prepare them to maintain their self-advocacy through these transitions?

1. Consider ways in which the information you've gathered about them and their experiences in your gifted programming can be transferred, wherever they land.

2. Create a student portfolio containing your district contact information, letters of recommendation, a description of identification and programming the student participated in, and a list of recommended future options and opportunities. Ensure that both you and the student (or their family) have copies. Include a definition of self-advocacy and suggestions for supporting the student's self-advocacy.

3. Encourage the student to include a personal statement in the portfolio describing their goals and highlighting their experiences in gifted programming and self-advocating.

4. If possible, communicate directly with advocates at the student's next location.

You've heard a lot of voices in this book. Voices from experts in the field. Voices from the past. Voices from the classroom. Voices from the hearts of some very bright young people. Each voice reminds us that too many dreams have been deferred for too long. Too many gifted learners are still waiting for us to recognize them, support them, and empower them to self-advocate. It is critical that we raise our voices together until all underrepresented gifted students believe that someone is listening, that we are ready to help, and that their dreams can be realized.

About the Contributors

Dina Brulles, Ph.D., is gifted education director at Paradise Valley USD in Arizona, gifted program coordinator at Arizona State University, and governance secretary for the Board of Directors of the National Association for Gifted Children (NAGC). Dr. Brulles's efforts emphasize designing inclusive gifted program models and creating equitable identification processes. She is a recipient of the NAGC's Gifted Coordinator Award (2014), Professional Development Award (2013), and Book-of-the-Year Award (2019). She is the author of many publications, including *Helping All Gifted Children Learn*.

Jaime Castellano, Ed.D., is a nationally recognized educator, author, and researcher. In 2017, he was awarded Supporting the Emotional Needs of the Gifted National Educator of the Year. His work focuses on identifying and serving gifted Hispanic/Latino students, gifted English language learners, and other marginalized gifted students. He is a professor at Florida Atlantic University, Department of Exceptional Student Education, and serves as a mental health case manager with Multilingual Psychotherapy Centers, Inc., in West Palm Beach, Florida. His books include *Reaching New Horizons: Gifted & Talented Education for Culturally and Linguistically Diverse Students.*

Charles D. Cederberg, Ph.D., received his master's in mental health counseling from Boston College and his doctorate in counseling psychology from the Department of Psychological and Quantitative Foundations at the University of Iowa. His areas of professional interest include psychosocial well-being and talent development of high ability and twice-exceptional young people; autism spectrum disorder; pediatric neuropsychology; social class and classism; materialism, greed, and mental health; and personal branding in professional psychology.

Edward C. Fletcher Jr., Ph.D., is a distinguished associate professor of workforce development and education at Ohio State University and faculty fellow in the Center for Education and Training for Employment. His research agenda focuses on the role and impact of career and technical education contexts (for example, career academies) on students' schooling experiences and long-term outcomes related to postsecondary education and in the labor market, particularly for African American and low-income students. Dr. Fletcher currently serves as a principal investigator on the IT College and CAREERS Readiness project funded by the National Science Foundation.

Erinn Fears Floyd, Ph.D., is an award-winning gifted education, diversity, and equity scholar. She is the former director of professional learning for the NAGC and state director of gifted education for the Alabama Department of Education. She currently serves as the director of training and partnership development for the Consortium for Inclusion of Underrepresented Racial Groups in Gifted Education (I-URGGE). Dr. Floyd has conducted training for state organizations, schools, and localities nationally and internationally. She is an inaugural recipient of the Dr. Mary Frasier Teacher Scholarship for Diverse Talent Development.

Megan Foley-Nicpon, Ph.D., is a professor in counseling psychology and Department Executive Officer for Psychological and Quantitative Foundations at the University of Iowa. She also serves as the associate director for research and clinic at the Belin-Blank Center for Gifted Education and Talent Development. Dr. Foley-Nicpon is a licensed psychologist whose research and clinical interests include assessment and intervention with high ability students with disabilities and the social and emotional development of talented and diverse students. She is an associate editor for the *APA Handbook of Giftedness and Talent*, has written more than fifty referred articles and book chapters, and has given more than one hundred presentations at international, national, and state professional meetings in the areas of gifted, counseling psychology, and twice-exceptionality.

Donna Y. Ford, Ph.D., is a distinguished professor of education and human rcology and Kirwan Institute Faculty Affiliate in the Department of Educational Studies, the Special Education Program, at Ohio State University. Her highly recognized work focuses primarily on the recruitment and retention of minoritized students in gifted and talented education, underrepresentation, achievement gap, multicultural education, and educator cultural competence. All of her work is grounded in equity and social justice. She has a dozen books, over 350 publications, and thousands of presentations, and has received numerous awards.

Marcia Gentry, Ph.D., professor, educational studies, directs the Gifted Education Resource Institute at Purdue University where she enjoys working with doctoral students and engaging in research and gifted education professional development. She remains active in the field through service to NAGC and AERA and by writing, reviewing, and presenting research aimed to improve education for children, youth, and teachers. Her work continues to have a special focus on underserved youth, particularly American Indian/Alaska Native, Indigenous, and minoritized youth with gifts and talents.

Tarek C. Grantham, Ph.D., is a professor of educational psychology at the University of Georgia. He serves as coordinator for the Gifted and Creative Education Graduate Program, and he codirects the University-School Partnerships for Achievement, Rigor, and Creativity initiative. Dr. Grantham's research addresses equity for underrepresented groups in advanced programs, gifted Black males, motivation, and creativity policy. He is a Presidential Appointee to the Board of Directors for the NAGC and a recipient of the Dr. Alexinia Baldwin Gifted & Special Populations Award and the Georgia Association for Gifted Children Mary M. Frasier Excellence and Equity Award.

Anne M. Gray, Ph.D., is Bilagáana, married to Táchii'nii, with four Diné daughters. She is a recent graduate from the Gifted Education Research and Resource Institute (GER²I) at Purdue University, where she coordinated the Super Saturday/Super Summer K–8 enrichment programs and conducted research regarding underrepresented populations in gifted education. Prior to graduate school she taught gifted education and middle school science at a Bureau of Indian Education grant school for six years. Her research focuses on American Indian/Alaska Native, Indigenous, and minoritized youth with gifts and talents, and equity in gifted education using a critical race theory lens.

Vinay Konuru is a graduate of Pine View School, where he initiated a task force of students and administrators to call out and work to solve systemic racial inequities in the gifted education process. He began this project as a freshman, and the team officially became known as Diversifying and Integrating Gifted Schools (DIGS) the following year. The team has helped put into place a universal screening program in their county and hosted discussions on the topic with both students and the community. Vinay is studying at Princeton University, but will continue to help future leaders keep DIGS active.

Shauna Mayo, Ed.D., is an assistant professor at Virginia State University. She teaches graduate and undergraduate courses in elementary education, curriculum and instruction, educational leadership, and gifted education. Dr. Mayo has been an elementary teacher, instructional specialist, and school administrator. Dr. Mayo's research and writing interests include improving underrepresentation of minority students in gifted education, diversity issues in education, and issues involving bullying.

James L. Moore III, Ph.D., is vice provost for diversity and inclusion at Ohio State University, and first executive director of the Todd Anthony Bell National Resource Center on the African American Male. He is also the inaugural EHE Distinguished Professor of Urban Education in the College of Education and Human Ecology. Dr. Moore is the author over 130 publications; has obtained over $25 million in grants, contracts, and gifts; and has given over 200 scholarly presentations nationwide and internationally. In 2018 and 2019, he was cited by *Education Week* as one of the 200 most influential scholars and researchers in the United States.

Robert Robertson, Ed.D., is a career educator specializing in second language acquisition, writing development, and STEM education. Throughout his career, Rob has taught students from kindergarten to college. He has worked in both the United States and Europe as a teacher, program coordinator, educational programs director, adjunct professor, and professional development facilitator. He has coauthored articles and book chapters on gifted ELLs, bilingual education, writing development, and classroom teaching strategies. He currently lives in Phoenix, Arizona, and consults in school districts across the state in the areas of English language learners, strategic planning, STEM integration, and instructional strategies for teachers.

Bob W. Seney, Ed.D., professor emeritus, Mississippi University for Women, has worked in gifted education for over forty-five years, serving as classroom instructor, district administrator, head of private schools, and university professor. He is known for his work with gifted readers. At the university he directed the graduate programs in education and was the primary instructor in the Masters of Gifted Studies program. He was the director of the Mississippi Governor's School, a three-week summer residential program for gifted high school students. Upon retirement, he was named professor emeritus for his service to the university and the field of gifted education.

Tamra Stambaugh, Ph.D., is the executive director of Programs for Talented Youth and an associate research professor at Vanderbilt University. Stambaugh's research interests include students living in rural settings, students of poverty, and curriculum and instructional interventions that promote gifted student learning. She is the coauthor/editor of several books, book chapters, articles, and curriculum units. She currently serves as a member of the NAGC Board of Directors. Stambaugh has been recognized for her work by multiple national and local organizations and frequently presents on topics related to gifted education nationally and internationally.

Timothy W. Stambaugh, Ph.D., is a licensed clinical counselor who has worked with academically gifted students for over twenty-five years. He currently serves as a clinician at Vanderbilt University Medical Center, Department of Psychiatry, and is often invited to speak in community settings on the mental health needs and interventions for supporting the social and emotional health of gifted students. He also serves as a counselor educator and adjunct professor in clinical counseling. His research interests focus on understanding the role of gifted students' boredom, belonging, and curriculum fit on feelings of anxiety and depression.

Alena R. Treat, Ph.D., has been an active advocate, researcher, and author on gifted LGBTQ+ issues for over thirty years. She has been an administrator of gifted or intellectually gifted programs, a gifted coordinator, specialist, and teacher. She directed two Javits grants, one of which she authored. As past chair of the NAGC Diversity and Equity Committee, she co-authored the Diversity Toolbox: Gifted LGBTQ Students. She also served on the NAGC GLBT Task Force and NAGC Workgroup on Sexually Diverse Populations. She is currently teaching Administration and Supervision of Gifted Programs online and is a part-time gifted elementary teacher.

Gilman W. Whiting, Ph.D., is an author, a global scholar and presenter, and creator of the Scholar Identity Model™ (SIM). He serves as an associate professor and director of graduate studies in the Department of African American and Diaspora Studies at Vanderbilt University. He directs the Scholar Identity Institute (SII), and the Black male initiative at Vanderbilt. Dr. Whiting is the founding chair of the Achievement Gap Consortium. His areas of research include psychological and social behavior of underperformance in special and gifted education and disparity; sociology of race, sports, and American culture; qualitative research methods; and young fatherhood initiatives.

Brian L. Wright, Ph.D., is an associate professor and program coordinator of early childhood education in the Department of Instruction and Curriculum, the College of Education, and Coordinator of the Middle School Cohort of the African American Male Academy at the University of Memphis. His research examines high-achieving African American boys in urban schools (preK–12); racial-ethnic identity development of boys and young men of color; STEM and Black males; Black men as early childhood teachers; and teacher identity development. Dr. Wright is author of the award-winning (2018 NAME Philip C. Chinn Book Award) *The Brilliance of Black Boys: Cultivating School Success in the Early Grades*.
[about the authors]
About the Editors

Joy Lawson Davis, Ed.D., is an award-winning author, scholar, professional learning trainer (nationally and internationally), and practitioner in gifted education and teacher education. Her areas of expertise are increasing equity in gifted education programs, twice-exceptional learners from diverse backgrounds, and family advocacy. She also served for five years on the Board of Directors of NAGC. Dr. Davis is also an adjunct professor in the School of Education at Johns Hopkins University. She is the author of many publications including two books: *Bright, Talented, & Black: A Guide for Families of African American Gifted Learners* and *Gifted Children of Color Around the World*.

Deb Douglas, M.S. C&I, advocates for gifted children around the world, providing GT Carpe Diem workshops for students, professional development for educators, and support for parents. After coordinating gifted programming for Manitowoc (Wisconsin) Public Schools for over twenty years, she served as president of the Wisconsin Association for Talented and Gifted and as a member of NAGC's Parent Advisory Board. Her publications, including her book *The Power of Self Advocacy for Gifted Learners* (Free Spirit Publishing, 2018), provide parents and educators with the tools needed to encourage and support gifted learners as they create their unique routes to graduation and beyond.

Index

A

Ability grouping, 81
Academic achievement, 45, 46
Academic self-confidence, in Scholar Identity Model™, 37
Accelerated college credit options, 35
Acceleration, 53, *104*
Access, 108–109
ACLU, 130, 132
ADHD, 116, 118, 121, 128
Administrators. *See also* Educators
    support for Hispanic gifted students, 48, 51
    treatment and attitude toward Black students, 33
Advanced Placement (AP) classes
    Black students in, 30–31
    sharing with Black students, 35
Advocacy. *See* Parent advocacy; Self-advocacy
African Americans. *See* Black students
AIAN. *See* American Indian and Alaska Native (AIAN) learners
Alaska, 65
American Association of School Counselors, 102
American Counseling Association, 102
American Indian and Alaska Native (AIAN) learners, 61–75, 142–143
    asset perspective of, 69
    avoiding essentialization among, 61
    barriers to identification, 66–68
    bringing visibility to, 68
    current status in gifted education, 65–66
    deficit perspective and omission of, 61, 64, 67–68
    future outlook for, 70
    invisibility of, 61, 64, 67, 68
    number of Native Nations, 64
    percentage of AIAN in state student population, *65*
    student self-advocacy, 62–64, 69, 71
    student stories of, 62–64, 67–68, 70–71
    teachers educating themselves about culture(s) of, 61
American Indian and Alaska Native (AIAN) professionals, 73–74

Annual pre-screening, 156
AP (Advanced Placement) classes, 30, 31, 32–33, 35, 63, 97
Arizona, 46, 65
Art teachers, 49
Asian children, in low-income households, 93
Assessment of support for self-advocacy, 24, 27–28
Asset perspective, 69
Autism spectrum disorder (ASD), 119, 120
Awareness, as third step for student advocacy, 13–14

B

Baldwin, Alexinia, 31
Band teachers, 49
Barriers
    for ELLs in gifted education, 79–81
    experienced by Hispanic learners, 46–48
    to gifted education by marginalized populations, 147, *148*
    to gifted education for Hispanic learners, 79–81
    for gifted services in ELL communities, 81
    to identification of American Indian and Alaska Native (AIAN) students, 66–68
    to parent and family advocacy, 147, *148*
    to self-advocacy by low-income students, 95–100
    to self-advocacy by twice-exceptional learners, 120–121
Bathroom rights lawsuit, 129
Belonging, feelings of, 105
Bibliotherapy, 34, 133–134
Bilingual education methods, 82
Black brilliance, pedagogy of, 35
Black families, parent advocacy and, 142–143
Black girls, 38, 145–146
Black scholars, 31
Black students
    affirming the gifts and talents of, 32–33
    attitudes and misperceptions about gifted and talented, 31–32
    at Pine View School for the Gifted, 8, 12
    ignoring interests of, 29–30
    intersectionality and, 4
    from low-income households, 92–93

To download the reproducible form on page 27, visit freespirit.com/eugs.

About the Editors

Joy Lawson Davis, Ed.D., is an award-winning author, scholar, professional learning trainer (nationally and internationally), and practitioner in gifted education and teacher education. Her areas of expertise are increasing equity in gifted education programs, twice-exceptional learners from diverse backgrounds, and family advocacy. She also served for five years on the Board of Directors of NAGC. Dr. Davis is also an adjunct professor in the School of Education at Johns Hopkins University. She is the author of many publications including two books: *Bright, Talented, & Black: A Guide for Families of African American Gifted Learners* and *Gifted Children of Color Around the World.*

Deb Douglas, M.S. C&I, advocates for gifted children around the world, providing GT Carpe Diem workshops for students, professional development for educators, and support for parents. After coordinating gifted programming for Manitowoc (Wisconsin) Public Schools for over twenty years, she served as president of the Wisconsin Association for Talented and Gifted and as a member of NAGC's Parent Advisory Board. Her publications, including her book *The Power of Self Advocacy for Gifted Learners* (Free Spirit Publishing, 2018), provide parents and educators with the tools needed to encourage and support gifted learners as they create their unique routes to graduation and beyond.

Other Great Resources from Free Spirit

The Power of Self-Advocacy for Gifted Learners
Teaching the 4 Essential Steps to Success
by Deb Douglas

For teachers of gifted students in grades 5–12, counselors, gifted program coordinators, administrators, parents, and youth leaders.

208 pp.; PB; 8½" x 11"; includes digital content.

Free PLC / Book Study Guide

freespirit.com / PLC

Teaching Gifted Kids in Today's Classroom
Strategies and Techniques Every Teacher Can Use (Updated 4th Edition)
by Susan Winebrenner, M.S., with Dina Brulles, Ph.D.

For teachers and administrators, grades K–12.

256 pp.; PB; 8½" x 11"; includes digital content.

Start Seeing and Serving Underserved Gifted Students
50 Strategies for Equity and Excellence
by Jennifer Ritchotte, Ph.D., Chin-Wen Lee, Ph.D., and Amy Graefe, Ph.D.

For educators and administrators of grades K–8.

192 pp.; PB; 8½" x 11"; includes digital content.

Free PLC / Book Study Guide

freespirit.com / PLC

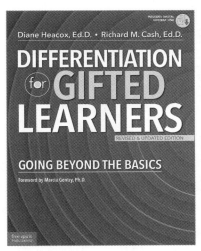

Differentiation for Gifted Learners
Going Beyond the Basics (Revised & Updated Edition)
by Diane Heacox, Ed.D., and Richard M. Cash, Ed.D.

For K–8 teachers, gifted education teachers, program directors, administrators, instructional coaches, and curriculum developers.

264 pp.; PB; 8½" x 11"; includes digital content.

Free PLC / Book Study Guide

freespirit.com / PLC

Inspiring Student Empowerment
Moving Beyond Engagement, Refining Differentiation
by Patti Drapeau
For educators, grades K–12.
208 pp.; PB; 8½" x 11"; includes digital content.
Free PLC / Book Study Guide
freespirit.com / PLC

A Teacher's Guide to Flexible Grouping and Collaborative Learning
Form, Manage, Assess, and Differentiate in Groups
by Dina Brulles, Ph.D., and Karen L. Brown, M.Ed.
For teachers and administrators, grades K–12.
200 pp.; PB; 8½" x 11"; includes digital content.
Free PLC / Book Study Guide
freespirit.com / PLC

Get Gifted Students Talking
76 Ready-to-Use Group Discussions About Identity, Stress, Relationships, and More (Grades 6–12)
by Jean Sunde Peterson, Ph.D.
For advising teachers, counselors, youth workers, parents of teens, grades 6–12.
304 pp.; PB; 8½" x 11".

Self-Regulation in the Classroom
Helping Students Learn How to Learn
by Richard M. Cash, Ed.D.
For K–12 teachers, administrators, and counselors.
184 pp.; PB; 8½" x 11"; includes digital content.
Free PLC / Book Study Guide
freespirit.com / PLC

Interested in purchasing multiple quantities and receiving volume discounts?
Contact edsales@freespirit.com or call 1.800.735.7323 and ask for Education Sales.

Many Free Spirit authors are available for speaking engagements, workshops, and keynotes. Contact speakers@freespirit.com or call 1.800.735.7323.

For pricing information, to place an order, or to request a free catalog, contact:

Free Spirit Publishing Inc. • 6325 Sandburg Road, Suite 100 • Minneapolis, MN 55427-3674
toll-free 800.735.7323 • local 612.338.2068 • fax 612.337.5050
help4kids@freespirit.com • freespirit.com